Single Subject Research
Applications in Educational and Clinical Settings

Stephen B. Richards
Associate Professor
Center for Pedagogy
Winthrop University
Rock Hill, South Carolina

Ronald L. Taylor
Professor
Exceptional Student Education
Florida Atlantic University
Boca Raton, Florida

Rangasamy Ramasamy
Associate Professor
Exceptional Student Education
Florida Atlantic University
Boca Raton, Florida

Rhonda Y. Richards
Assistant Dean
College of Education
Winthrop University
Rock Hill, South Carolina

D0226431

SINGULAR PUBLISHING GROUP, INC.
SAN DIEGO · LONDON

Singular Publishing Group, Inc.
401 West "A" Street, Suite 325
San Diego, California 92101-7904

Singular Publishing Ltd.
19 Compton Terrace
London N1 2UN, UK

Singular Publishing Group, Inc., publishes textbooks, clinical manuals, clinical reference books, journals, videos, and multimedia materials on speech-language pathology, audiology, otorhinolaryngology, special education, early childhood, aging, occupational therapy, physical therapy, rehabilitation, counseling, mental health, and voice. For your convenience, our entire catalog can be accessed on our web-site at **http//www.singpub.com**. Our mission to provide you with materials to meet the daily challenges of the everchanging health care/educational environment will remain on course if we are in touch with you. In that spirit, we welcome your feedback on our products. Please telephone (**1-800-521-8545**), fax (**1-800-774-8398**), or e-mail (**singpub@mail.cerfnet.com**) your comments and requests to us.

© 1999, by Singular Publishing Group, Inc.

Typeset in 10/12 Palatino by So Cal Graphics
Printed in the United States of America by Bang Printing

All rights, including that of translation, reserved. No part of this publication may be reproduced, stored in a retrieval system or transmitted in any form or by any means, electronic, mechanical, recording, or otherwise, without the prior written permission of the publisher.

Library of Congress Cataloging-in-Publication Data

Single subject research : applications in educational and clinical
   settings / by Stephen B. Richards . . . [et al.].
      p.   cm.
   Includes bibliographical references and index.
   ISBN 1-56593-799-6 (pbk. : alk. paper)
    1. Single subject research. 2. Psychology—Research—Methodology.
 3. Education—Research—Methodology. I. Richards, Stephen B.,
1954–
BF76.6.S56S57 1998
150′ .7′2—dc21
DLC
for Library of Congress
                                           98-28028
                                              CIP

Contents

PART 2

Overview and Application of Single Subject Designs
105

PART 3

Analyzing Results from Single Subject Studies

263

Preface

We would like to provide some orientation to this text. Undoubtedly, some people will desire a greater degree of complexity than that with which some issues are addressed. The research literature contains a wealth of examples and discussions that include virtually every aspect of each of the major single subject designs, applied behavior analysis, and analysis of data procedures. Our aim is to provide the reader, who is presumably not yet an expert on single subject research, with the information necessary to understand the literature and develop a single subject research study *in general*. By *in general*, we mean that the reader should acquire the knowledge to understand the process of designing, implementing, and evaluating a single subject research project. Any researcher should review the literature extensively for information relevant to the particular targeted behaviors, individuals, interventions, and environments of her or his study. We believe we have provided sufficient examples and illustrations to understand the variety available, but realistically have not "covered all the bases" of all options that may be available for any potential study.

This book is primarily intended for those working in educational/clinical settings. This of course includes teachers and related services personnel such as speech and language clinicians. We have avoided any significant discussion of the use of single subject designs with industrial applications or adults with addictions and substance abuse problems, although examples of these types of studies are published and may have relevance to a particular reader. Single subject designs are versatile and may be used in many different situations, although our focus is on children, adolescents, and adults with disabilities.

The first four chapters of the book are closely related and deciding on the order of presentation was a point of debate among us. We decided to address historical aspects and basic concepts first, because these are necessary to understanding much of the terminology and underlying assumptions in the remaining chapters. Methods for changing behavior and methods for recording behavior are included in the second and third chapters, as these serve as cornerstones to the use of applied behavior analysis—itself a cornerstone of single subject research with individuals with disabilities. The fourth chapter addresses the many general considerations with which the researcher or reader of research must be familiar. Chapter 4 concludes the background knowledge need-ed to fully understand the designs and studies that are discussed in the remaining chapters.

Chapter 5 begins the discussion of the actual designs and their vari-ations with the basic A-B and withdrawal (sometimes referred to as reversal) designs. Chapter 6 includes examples and discussion of the application of these designs. Chapters 7–12 continue in the same vein, with a chapter devoted to the overview of the design followed by a chapter devoted to applications. The designs discussed include multiple baseline designs, alternating treatment designs, and changing criterion designs.

The final chapter outlines procedures for data analysis. This chap-ter includes visual, quantitative, and qualitative analysis. One chapter cannot address all of the possibilities, particularly for quantitative and qualitative methods. We believe we have provided guidance to the read-er in what types of procedures are available, when they might be applied, and the limitations of their various uses.

Our ultimate goal is to provide readers with options. Today, our experience is that researchers tend to discuss either group/quantitative designs or the use of qualitative methods. Each is useful and provides information necessary to improve services and outcomes for people with disabilities. It is also our experience that many individuals in our field have limited knowledge of or are only vaguely familiar with single subject research designs. This may be because teachers of research design and application consider these designs too simple or specialized to devote extensive time to them in classes. This is unfortunate, and we hope that this text will at least in some small way alleviate this. These designs are well suited to educational and clinical settings and for use by professionals who regularly are charged with addressing the needs of individuals or small groups.

We have striven to make the language of the text consistent with the research literature terminology used, while also making it understand-able to the novice. We sincerely hope we have succeeded in this aim. We also hope your eyes will be opened to the possibility of different re-search options, a body of research literature with which you may not be familiar, and an appreciation for professionals who endeavor to solve problems in the real world through systematic and ethical practices with respect for and ultimate value placed on the individual.

PART 1

Conducting Single
Subject Research:
Issues and Procedures

CHAPTER 1

Historical Concepts and Important Concepts in Single Subject Research

IMPORTANT CONCEPTS TO KNOW

HISTORICAL ASPECTS OF SINGLE SUBJECT RESEARCH

Applied

Behavioral

Analytic

The Individuals With Disabilities Education Act

BASIC CONCEPTS AND DEFINITIONS OF TERMS

Independent, Dependent, and Extraneous Variables

Baseline, Intervention, and Follow-Up Phases

NOTATIONS

THE X-Y OR LINE GRAPH

The Dependent Variable

The X-Axis

The Independent Variable and Phase Change Lines

Data Paths

The Legend

HISTORICAL ASPECTS OF SINGLE SUBJECT RESEARCH

In the early 20th century, J. B. Watson argued that psychologists should focus efforts on observable behavior. Watson declared that the theoretical goal of behaviorists was the prediction and control of behavior (Watson, 1913). Watson stressed the need for obtaining data that were of scientific merit and not dependent on interpretations based on consciousness or other mental processes (Cooper, Heron, & Heward, 1987). Although applied behavior analysts today do not ignore the importance of such mental processes, Watson outlined tenets that are part and parcel of single subject research. Watson argued that behaviorists should focus on the relationships between stimuli in the environment and the subsequent responses of individuals (the stimulus-response paradigm for human behavior). By the 1930s, B. F. Skinner had published *The Behavior of Organisms*, a landmark book, which extended the knowledge and prevailing views of behaviorism. Skinner distinguished between respondent (reflexive) behavior and operant (or voluntary) behavior. Skinner asserted that operant behavior was largely influenced by events that succeeded, rather than just those that preceded, the behavior. Skinner and colleagues conducted many experiments over subsequent decades outlining the principles that have become important in applied behavior analysis (e.g., reinforcement and punishment paradigms). Initially, Skinner's work focused pirmarily on animal research, but he later focused attention on the potential impact of applying behavioral principles in human endeavors including education (e.g., see *Walden Two* and *Science and Human Behavior*). Skinner acknowledged the importance of events that go unseen (cognitive and emotional processes) that influence human beings, but also stressed that the responses to those events may still be observable and well within the domain of behavior analysts.

By the 1950s and 1960s, behavior analysts were publishing studies that examined the effects of the application of behavioral principles to both normally developing and atypically developing individuals. By 1968, the *Journal of Applied Behavior Analysis* (JABA) had begun publication. Therein, many single subject studies were (and continue to be) reviewed and published. New designs and variations on existing designs were investigated. In the initial issue of JABA, Baer, Wolf, and Risley (1968) discussed major dimensions of applied behavior analysis.

Baer et al. (1968) noted that research that focuses on socially important behaviors may be **applied**, **behavioral**, and **analytic**. We summarize their elaboration on these concepts in the following passages. **Applied** refers to the interest displayed by society in the problems being studied. In applied research, there is typically a close relationship between the stimuli and behavior being studied, and the individual whose behavior is changing. Society and the individual have a vested interest in the behavior change and recognize the potential change as a valid endeavor. **Behavioral** refers to the pragmatic nature of the study. First, emphasis is placed on what a person can do rather than what she or he can say (except when the behavior under study is some verbal response). Second, reliable quantification of behavior must be achieved and that measurement often involves systematic observation by other people. Third, it is equally important to question not only what behavior was changed during a study, but also whose behavior has changed. Therefore, the explicit measurement of the observations for reliability (as we discuss in Chapter 3) is necessary. The **analytic** aspect of applied behavioral research refers to a believable demonstration that events controlled by the researcher account for the presence or absence of the behavior in question. Baer et al. (1968) noted that two single subject designs, the reversal and multiple baseline designs, were viable methods for generating a favorable judgment that the analytic goal has been met. Further, applied behavior analysts seek to encourage "valuable" behavior. That is, behaviors are targeted that will be reinforced extra-experimentally, thereby maintaining changes when the experimental conditions are withdrawn. Good technical descriptions of procedures are also necessary for the analytic goal to be met. This refers to the complete identification and description of any techniques applied to encourage behavior change. This bears directly on the need for **replication**, a process required not only to meet the analytic goal, but also to generalize results and demonstrate the robustness of any behavior change procedures. Considerable detail must be given in applied research reports to ensure the reader could reasonably replicate the events described. Baer et al. (1968) also stressed that applied behavior analysts must describe their procedures within a conceptual system that allows understanding and expansion of technologies. For example, describing the exact method by which a child is taught to discriminate letters of the alphabet is good; describing the process in terms of fading antecedent stimuli and differential reinforcement is better. The latter allows professionals to discuss procedures in a more universal sense and to recognize commonalities and differences among various experimental methods. Another area of concern for these authors included the effectiveness of the techniques used. Baer et al. noted that if behavior changes did not produce practical value, then the study has failed. Similarly, behavior changes ideally should be maintained over time, be generalized to new settings and new situations, and result in the emission of new but related behaviors. In summary, Baer et al. stated that an *applied* behavior analysis will make obvious the importance of the behavior changed, its quantitative characteristics, the experimental manipulations which analyze with clarity what was responsible for the change, the technologically exact description of all procedures contributing to that change, the effectiveness of those procedures in making sufficient change for value, and the generality of that change. (p. 97).

Since Baer et al.'s landmark piece, many developments have occurred in the field of applied behavior analysis and single subject research. New designs have emerged along with variations of existing ones. New techniques for measuring, changing, and analyzing behavior have been developed. The field continues to expand, at least in part because of the ever growing number of researchers and practitioners who have used this approach and maintained the conceptual system that Baer et al. advocated. The field of special education and delivery of related services is one in which researchers and practitioners have demonstrated an increased interest in single subject research.

In 1975, the passage of Public Law 94-142, the Education for All Handicapped Children Act, later referred to as the Individuals With Disabilities Education Act (1991, 1997), heralded a new era in education and related fields. Provision of services to persons with challenges (and strengths as well) became common rather than extraordinary in our public schools. The focus of education for these students was individualization of goals and objectives with measurable outcomes. Progress through academic content was and is important, but educators and therapists also aim at assisting individuals in improving speech and language, behavioral and emotional adjustment, vocational skills, physical functioning, social skills, and myriad other areas. The scope of educational interventions has been greatly broadened and, consequently, methods for determining the effectiveness of those interventions are needed. The mandate to focus on the education of the individual makes the use of single subject research designs a natural in settings where people with special needs are served.

The remainder of this chapter is devoted to basic concepts in single subject research. These concepts are important to understand the more fundamental aspects of the designs and methodologies used by applied behavior analysts.

BASIC CONCEPTS AND DEFINITIONS OF TERMS

Certain conventions used in single subject research are similar to those used in other research designs. These include the concepts of independent, dependent, and extraneous (or confounding) variables. Other concepts are more unique to single subject designs. These include the concepts of baseline, intervention, and follow-up phases; the notations used; the basic x-y graph and the use of each axis in relation to the independent and dependent variables; the plotting of data collected; and the legend for a figure that includes an x-y graph. Some of these concepts receive additional attention (e.g., extraneous variables) in other chapters, particularly Chapter 4, "Issues in Single Subject Research." However, this discussion should provide the reader with a developing understanding that will better enable her or him to comprehend immediately succeeding chapters.

Independent, Dependent, and Extraneous Variables

As in other types of research, the terms *independent* and *dependent variables* are used to describe the elements in a study that are related to the demonstration of a functional relationship. The independent variable is the intervention(s) used to encourage change in human behavior in single subject research. In essence, the independent variable is the treatment or intervention that the researcher controls in order to influence changes in the dependent variable. It is worth noting that only the individual participant may change his or her behavior. The educator or therapist may create conditions (e.g., through the manipulation of antecedents and consequences) that encourage change, but clearly one cannot change another person's behavior. For the sake of convenience, however, we will refer to changing the behavior of individual subjects with this understanding.

The dependent variable is used to measure changes (or the lack thereof) that demonstrate that the desired outcomes of the study are or are not being achieved. The term **dependent** is useful, because if a functional relationship exists in the study, the dependent variable should change in accordance with (or dependent on) the presence or absence or changes in the independent variable. For our purposes, we will equate the dependent variable with the term **target behavior** (see later discussion). Changes in the target behavior are used to determine whether the treatment or intervention is having the desired effect. For example, if positive reinforcement is being applied for progressively better accuracy in solving mathematics problems, the systematic application of positive reinforcement should have a direct influence on the dependent variable or target behavior (the accuracy in solving math problems).

We acknowledge that some experts may assert that "technically" the target behavior and dependent variable are not always the same. For example, the target behavior could be speaking louder. The dependent variable could be the decibel measurement of the actual loudness of the individual's voice. Again, to avoid confusion (or perhaps the tedium associated with repeatedly making this possible distinction) we will interchangeably use **target behavior** and **dependent variable**.

Extraneous (or confounding) variables are any elements of a study that may confuse or obscure the believability that the independent variable and dependent variable share a functional relationship. Examples could include who is delivering the intervention, where the intervention is being delivered, the emotional or physical maturation of the individual subject, the influence of concerned parents or significant others, and so on. The possibilities are, unfortunately, endless. Extraneous variables are discussed at greater length in Chapter 4.

Baseline, Intervention, and Follow-Up Phases

In most single subject research designs, the baseline phase is the first stage. Baseline data in an applied study are data collected when the independent variable is not being implemented. This does not mean, however, that during the baseline phase the individuals in the study setting do nothing. The status quo is maintained unless clearly harmful to the individual or others. For example, the researcher begins collecting data on accuracy in solving math problems. The environment currently includes the grading of papers as the consequence of the target behavior performance. Rather than alter the current conditions, the researcher would collect data concerning the target behavior under these conditions. The purpose of the baseline measure is at least twofold. First, the researcher should gain a standard of current performance on the dependent variable by which future changes may be compared. Second, the baseline provides additional opportunity to glean information that may reveal important aspects about the dependent variable performance and the environment. For example, the researcher may begin collecting data and soon discover that performance is very uneven. That is, the dependent variable measure seems to fluctuate from one measurement to the next. This should tip off the researcher that some variables that may not have been identified as yet are influencing performance. The baseline phase should end when there is stability in performance on the dependent variable (stability and the procedures to determine stability are further defined in Chapters 4 and 13). It is not unusual for individuals to suggest that baseline should represent three measurements or some similar figure, although there is no specific number of observations that the researcher should use. In some instances, the baseline may be shortened or skipped altogether when ethical treatment demands so. For example, if an individual is harmful to himself or others, to prolong a baseline phase (or even to implement a baseline phase) to gain acceptable stability could be dangerous. In other situations, the dependent variable is unlikely to change until the independent variable is introduced. An individual who is acquiring new communication skills may be very unlikely to acquire those skills unless there is some direct intervention designed to improve those skills. In such situations, the baseline may be extremely abbreviated (i.e., a sufficient number of measures to demonstrate the skills are currently not in the individual's repertoire). Once stability or an acceptable number of measurements is obtained based on ethical treatment considerations, the intervention phase(s) should be implemented (although, as the reader will discover in the chapters devoted to the specific designs, there are variations to this procedure).

The intervention phase(s) is implemented following the baseline phase or, when justified, immediately and without a baseline phase. We will refer to the intervention phase in the singular, but the reader should be aware that there may be multiple intervention phases. The researcher systematically implements the independent variable during the intervention phase. Typically, some level of performance (criterion) on the dependent variable is identified a priori to determine when the desired outcome has been achieved. The researcher continues to measure the dependent variable to determine the effectiveness of the independent variable. Should progress not be achieved, the researcher may alter the independent variable or even identify a new one altogether. When this contingency arises, there may be a need to introduce another baseline phase to once again establish stability in the dependent variable. Also, reintroducing the baseline may serve to avoid multiple treatment interference of having one intervention immediately following another (see Chapter 4). Once the desired outcomes have been achieved during the intervention phase, a follow-up phase is advisable although not always implemented in research studies. In some designs, there may even be a return to a baseline phase following intervention phase (e.g., in withdrawal designs). Again, the reader should understand the basic concept of baseline phase followed by intervention phase, which is typical and is most useful at this point.

The follow-up phase is intended to measure the effects of the independent variable on the dependent variable over time. This phase is implemented after the successful intervention phase. The status of the independent variable may be that it is no longer in effect, or it may be at a reduced level of intensity, or it may be maintained at a previously successful level. Generally, the overall goal during follow-up is to remove the independent variable, particularly if it requires a rather intrusive effort, to demonstrate that its effects will continue long after its withdrawal. In other words, the researcher wishes to demonstrate that the changes in the dependent variable are relatively permanent and will be maintained even in the absence of the independent variable. In teaching or clinical practice, this would be comparable to maintenance, independent practice, or possibly generalization of the target behavior. Independent variables that are clearly an enhancement to the environment (e.g., verbal praise) may be maintained by those who work with the individual even if the independent variable is officially withdrawn. Perhaps the most important point to remember in this discussion is that a follow-up phase strengthens a study by demonstrating the effectiveness of the intervention over time and thereby strengthens the social and ecological validities of the study.

NOTATIONS

In single subject designs, letters are used to denote certain phases or aspects of a design. In most (but not all) instances, the first phase of a single subject design is the baseline phase. It is denoted by the letter **A**. Each subsequent letter (**B–Z**) is used to denote a particular independent variable (or intervention phase). Occasionally, a combination of letters (e.g., **BC**) is used to denote that a combination of treatments or independent variables is being simultaneously applied to the dependent variable or target behavior. If a phase is repeated during a study (e.g., see Chapters 5 and 6 for withdrawal designs), the same letter is used to denote the phase. For example, a researcher implements a baseline phase (A), followed by an intervention phase (B), followed by a return to a baseline phase (A), followed by the implementation of a new independent variable (C). This study would be denoted as an A-B-A-C design. See Figure 1–1 for a sample depiction of this notation. The researcher is telling others that both A phases involved the same conditions and that the B and C phases differed significantly from the A phases and from each other. A hyphen typically is inserted between the letters to denote the separate phases. Some researchers prefer to assign a number as well when phases are repeated (e.g., A1-B1-A2-B2). Occasionally, a package intervention is used that combines more than one independent variable (e.g., positive reinforcement along with response cost). When this occurs, the phase is denoted by the multiple letters BC (with B representing positive reinforcement and C representing response cost). Thus, a notation might be A-BC-A-B. The notation in this example would reveal that during a final intervention phase, only positive reinforcement was used as an intervention. The combinations

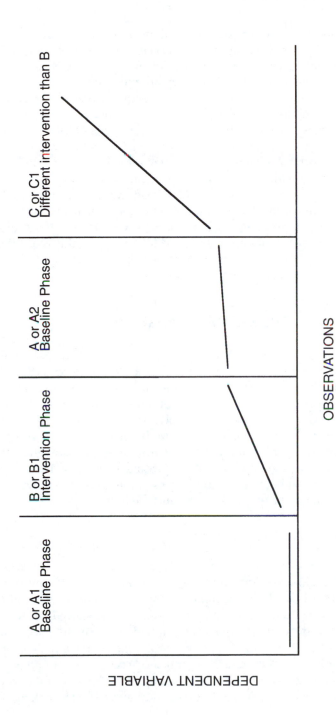

Figure 1–1. Example of notation system used in single subject research.

of letters denoting phases are virtually infinite. However, the researcher should be aware that when multiple interventions are implemented in single or multiple phases (e.g., BC-D-E-BE phases), the effects of one independent variable may begin to have an effect (multiple treatment interference) on either simultaneous or subsequent ones. That is, the researcher's ability to determine which was the effective independent variable may be seriously diminished. In our example of the combined use of positive reinforcement and response cost, it may be impossible to tell if either was the more effective or if they must be used in combination to be effective. Although the desired outcome (the change in the target behavior) may be achieved in such a case, which is fortunate, the researcher may have trouble explaining why it was achieved. When a follow-up phase is implemented, it may be noted with the words "Follow-Up" or some notation that is used to make clear this is a different phase. We would not recommend it be denoted with a letter that suggests it is an intervention phase.

THE X-Y OR LINE GRAPH

The x-y graph, or line graph, is the typical but by no means only manner in which the results of a study are depicted. We will discuss the line graph because of its widespread use. The reader may wish to examine other possibilities (e.g., bar graphs, histograms, contingency tables) if the data and various components of a study are more easily understood by using some other method. The line graph has a number of components that are commonly found in research reports. These include the dependent variable, the depiction of the passage of time or the various measures of data, the data path and breaks in that path, the independent variable and its phase change lines, and the legend.

The Dependent Variable

In Chapter 3, you will read a more detailed discussion concerning recording of target behaviors and the manners in which different types of data may be reported. For example, one may record how frequently a targeted behavior occurs, how long it occurs, or even how intense the behavior is. The dependent variable is graphed along the y-(or vertical) axis (see Figure 1–2). Tick marks, or lines that indicate the units of measure (e.g., number of occurrences, number of seconds or minutes, or degrees of intensity), are evenly spaced along that axis (with the exception of logarithmic data that are discussed in Chapter 13). The tick marks

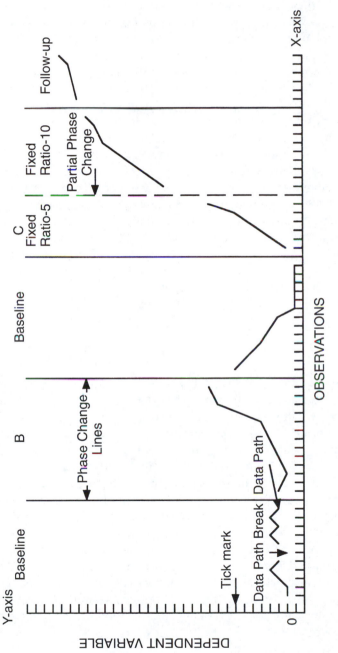

Figure 1–2. Example of an x-y graph used in single subject research.

should be displayed so that the visual picture created when changes occur in the dependent variable does not mislead or confuse the viewer. The spaces between and the number of marks should serve to accurately display changes in the dependent variable. For example, a researcher is measuring the rate of an individual's behavior and that rate is expressed in terms of how many responses are made per minute (e.g., 1.00 response or 0.50 response per minute). Changes in the dependent variable may be quite small from measurement to measurement, perhaps changing by tenths of a response per minute. If the researcher chose to allow each tick mark to represent 0.10 response per minute and to space those marks more widely, then even a small change might result in a visual picture that suggested a rather marked change. In some cases, where relatively small changes in the dependent variable represent significant change (e.g., changes in self-abusive behavior) based on social and ecological standards of validity, such a practice may be warranted. However, in most instances the y-axis should be scaled in such a way that small changes appear small when plotted and big changes appear significant. The researcher is in the best position to determine how data may be depicted through the scaling of the y-axis and should be careful to not create literally a false picture for the viewer.

The X-Axis

The x-axis is used to display the various measurements made of the dependent variable. Usually, the x-axis depicts the passage of time. As with the y-axis, the researcher includes tick marks, or lines appropriately scaled. Each tick mark represents an observation and measurement of the dependent variable (see Figure 1–2). A tick mark might represent an observation across 5 min, across 1 hr, a morning, or a whole day or longer (though usually not more than 1 day). The length of the observation may in fact vary from tick mark to tick mark (see Chapter 3 for an explanation of varying observation periods), but the results of the observation are always expressed in the same terms (e.g., frequency or duration or rate or intensity of a behavior) as determined by the dependent variable graphed along the y-axis. The tick marks along the x-axis serve to create a visual picture of how the dependent variable has changed as the number of observations increases and, more importantly, in conjunction with changes in the baseline, intervention, and follow-up phases of a study.

The Independent Variable and Phase Change Lines

As these various phases are implemented, solid vertical lines drawn parallel to the y-axis and perpendicular to the x-axis are used to depict each phase change (see Figure 1–2). The phase itself typically is written at the top of the graph and may be expressed by the letter notations discussed earlier or by wording that describes the phase (e.g., Baseline 1, Positive Reinforcement, Baseline 2, Response Cost, or A1-B-A2-C). Occasionally, a dotted or broken line may be drawn similar to the phase change line to depict a change within a phase but not a complete change in the independent variable (see Figure 1–2). For example, positive reinforcement is being delivered to a student on a ratio of one reinforcer to 5 correct responses (called a fixed-ratio schedule, discussed in Chapter 2). The researcher moves from this fixed ratio to a ratio of one reinforcer for every 10 correct responses. Such a change is not a complete change from the use of the independent variable of positive reinforcement, but may represent a change worth noting to the viewer. A broken line with appropriate headings (e.g., Fixed Ratio-5, Fixed Ratio-10) would help to explain the change that occurred.

Data Paths

Data paths are lines that connect each data point plotted along the x-y axes. Individual data points are plotted. For example, following a researcher's first observation of the dependent variable, the researcher would track vertically up from the x-axis from the tick mark denoting the first observation. The researcher would continue to track horizontally from the appropriate tick mark on the y-axis that corresponds with the data obtained on the first observation. Where the two tracks intersect a point would be plotted. This process is repeated for the data gathered from each observation session (remembering a session could vary considerably in length of time and could include a number of individual observations that are summarized and compiled across the overall session). As they are plotted, the points are usually connected by a solid line. This solid line is not typically drawn across phase change lines. Also, the zero level of the dependent variable on the y-axis may be marked just above the intersection with the x-axis to avoid cluttering the x-axis should zero level responding occur. Should the collection of data be interrupted due to unforeseen circumstances (e.g., the individual becomes sick and is unable to be observed), the data path is also interrupted and there should be some indication where the actual break in data collection occurred (see Figure 1–2). The x-axis should also be amended as needed to reflect this break in data collection and a special notation to the viewer may be included along the x-axis or at the break in the data path. Generally, if the individual participant is a student and no data are collected on weekends, it is unnecessary to treat such natural weekend breaks as breaks in the data path. To include such breaks would not be wrong; we merely wish to point out that this type of break has been omitted when reporting data from school environments.

There are circumstances in which more than one data path is plotted on the same line graph (e.g., performance by two or more individuals in the same study, the performance of the same individual under different conditions). In this case, a different path is assigned for each dependent variable path (e.g., a solid line for one, a dotted line for another) and often the actual data points making up each path may be assigned different shapes (e.g., solid circles, squares, triangles). Color coding may also assist in this process. The key to plotting multiple data paths is to use a graph sufficiently large and clear that the viewer can easily discern each path and the differences in performance for each dependent variable (see Chapters 9 and 10 on alternating treatments designs). Also, within this text, we have presented variations of x-y graphs.

The Legend

The more complicated a line graph becomes (e.g., multiple data paths, use of several independent variables depicted), the more important the legend becomes. A graph can become very cluttered and confusing, if not unreadable, if a researcher includes too much in it. The legend allows the researcher to abbreviate and to use alphabetic notations instead of whole words, which can be explained in the legend.

In this chapter, we have provided a brief historical perspective on single subject research and applied behavior analysis and a discussion of basic concepts. This chapter, particularly the basic concepts portion, sets the stage for the following discussions. It is not until Chapter 5 that we discuss any specific designs; the next two chapters provide the reader with a more detailed background in applied behavior analysis and Chapter 4 provides a thorough examination of principles and procedures found in virtually all single subject research designs.

Summary Checklist

In applied behavior analysis:
Applied—Refers to the interest of society in the problem being studied.
Behavioral—Refers to the pragmatic nature of the study; emphasis is on what the person can do rather than what she or he can say.

Analytic—Refers to a believable demonstration that events controlled by the researcher account for the presence or absence of the behavior in question.

Individuals With Disabilities Education Act—The recently amended (1997) federal legislation originally signed into law in 1975, which mandates a free, appropriate education to all children with disabilities.

Independent variable—The intervention(s) or treatment(s) used to encourage (or maintain) change in behavior; the independent and dependent variables should share a functional relationship.

Dependent variable—The target behavior that is measured to determine the effects of the independent variable; changes in the target behavior should be dependent on changes in the independent variable (a functional relationship).

Extraneous variable (or confounding variables)—Almost any element in the study that confuses or obscures the functional relationship.

Baseline phase—Generally, the first phase in a study, during which initial performance on the target behavior is measured before implementation of the intervention (independent variable).

Intervention phase—A phase when the intervention has been introduced and data are collected to determine effects on the target behavior (dependent variable).

Follow-up phase—Typically, a final phase of a study when the researcher continues to measure performance on the target behavior although the independent variable may have been withdrawn following successful intervention.

Notations—The system of letters used to identify the type of design used; A refers to a baseline phase; B and all subsequent letters to intervention phases. Each letter (e.g., B, C) refers to a different intervention; combinations (e.g., BC) refer to package, or combinations of, interventions; numbers may be attached (e.g., A1, B1) to denote a first baseline phase or a first intervention phase when there are subsequent baseline or intervention phases (e.g., A2, B2).

x-y line graph—The typical line graph used to graphically depict the quantitative data collected in single subject research; data are plotted at the appropriate intersects along the x- and y-axes.

Dependent variable on x-y graph—The target behavior performance is plotted along the y-axis; the y-axis must be calibrated (with tick marks used to denote units of measurement) so that changes in the dependent variable are appropriately depicted.

X-axis—The x-axis is used to depict observations across time (using tick marks to denote which observation is being plotted along the y-axis).

Independent variable and phase change lines—Implementation of and changes in the independent variable are depicted through lines drawn parallel to the y-axis; broken vertical lines indicate a change in the independent variable but not a complete phase change (e.g., from a fixed to a variable ratio reinforcement schedule).

Data path—Each data point that is plotted on the graph is connected by a line; the data path line is not typically drawn across phase change lines; breaks in the data path indicate an interruption in the observation or measurement of the dependent variable; multiple data paths are sometimes required (e.g., for alternating treatments designs).

Legend—A guide to the x-y graph that allows the researcher to abbreviate on the graph and clarify (e.g., FR-5 on the graph could be further explained as a fixed ratio-5 response schedule of reinforcement in the legend).

References

Baer, D. M., Wolf, M. W., & Risley, T. R. (1968). Some current dimensions of applied behavior analysis. *Journal of Applied Behavior Analysis, 1,* 91–97.

Cooper, J. O., Heron, T. E., & Heward, W. L. (1987). *Applied behavior analysis.* Columbus, OH: Merrill.

Watson, J.B. (1913). Psychology as the behaviorist views it. *Psychological Review, 20,* 158–177.

CHAPTER 2

Methods for Changing Target Behaviors

Extinction
Differential Reinforcement
Other Methods to Decrease Behavior
  Response Interruption
  Overcorrection

As noted previously, the independent variable may be thought of rough-
ly as the intervention used in the study. More specifically, it is that variable (or those variables) manipulated by the practitioner or researcher
that are intended to encourage a change in or maintenance of the level
of the dependent variable or target behavior. Within the context of applied behavior analysis, a variety of interventions are available for use
as independent variables. These include methods for increasing or
maintaining behavior and methods for decreasing or eliminating behavior. The methods discussed are not mutually exclusive. That is, the
interventions may be used alone or in combination and may be used in
combination with other independent variables not discussed in this
chapter. In fact, when a practitioner wishes to encourage a decrease in a
maladaptive target behavior, it is important ethically to encourage a corresponding increase in an adaptive response. Currently, many advocates
for individuals with disabilities (particularly those with severe disabilities) stress that methods for decreasing behavior that focus on punishment are to be discouraged if not ruled out altogether as treatment options. Certainly, the use of more aversive techniques (e.g., electric shock,
foul-smelling or foul-tasting substances) to decrease a maladaptive target behavior has come under scrutiny for a number of reasons. These include the efforts of advocacy groups, review by professional and human
subjects boards, and a reluctance to employ pain-inducing or other potentially unpleasant or unusual procedures (see Chapter 4 for a discussion of ethics in single subject research). Still, it is necessary in a text such
as this to discuss available intervention options; therefore, punishment
techniques will be presented. The use of any intervention should be justified through the ethical considerations and done on an individual basis with informed consent.

As noted previously, we will use the term **intervention** as synonymous with **independent variable**, and **behavior** or **response** as synonymous with **dependent variable**. It should be stressed that these are
convenient terms related to applied behavior analysis and that the concepts of independent and dependent variables may encompass a very

broad spectrum of actual applications (e.g., medication/other medical interventions and responses on a behavior-rating scale or to interview questions, respectively). Also, it is a convenience to refer to changing another person's behavior through intervention. It is worth noting, however, that only the individual participant may actually change his or her behavior. One of the goals of single-subject research is to demonstrate a functional relationship between the intervention and behavior change (independent and dependent variables). The researcher or practitioner may create conditions (e.g., through the manipulation of antecedents and consequences) that encourage change, but clearly one cannot change another person's behavior.

METHODS TO INCREASE OR MAINTAIN BEHAVIOR

It is necessary to discuss first the basic principles of operant conditioning. The essential paradigm for operant behavior includes an antecedent (or antecedents) that occurs before the behavior and may potentially influence the occurrence of the target behavior, followed by the behavior itself, which in turn is followed by a consequence (or consequences) that may potentially affect the future occurrence of the behavior under the same or similar circumstances (antecedent conditions; see Figure 2–1).

It is the consistent pairing of antecedent with behavior, behavior with consequence, and consequence with antecedent that encourages a change in or maintenance of the target behavior. This allows the practitioner or researcher to predict the impact of the independent variable on the target behavior. Generally, experts suggest that consequences (whether they are reinforcing or punishing consequences) be delivered immediately after the target behavior to increase the likelihood that the pairing of the two is noted by the individual.

When referring to interventions that may be used to increase or maintain behavior, we are referring to **positive** and **negative reinforcement**. Reinforcement occurs when the probability that a behavior will occur in the future under the same or similar antecedent conditions is increased (or maintained) by the delivery of a consequence following the behavior. There are several critical issues to understand about reinforcement. First, reinforcement should not be perceived as meaning "good." It is a phenomenon, an occurrence, not a quality. It is perfectly possible for desirable responses (e.g., wiping one's mouth with a napkin or correctly sounding "th") as well as undesirable responses (e.g., throwing food or dysfluent speech) to be reinforced. Second, the notion that we are affecting the future probability of behavior is important. The behavior that is reinforced (i.e., to which the consequence is applied) has al-

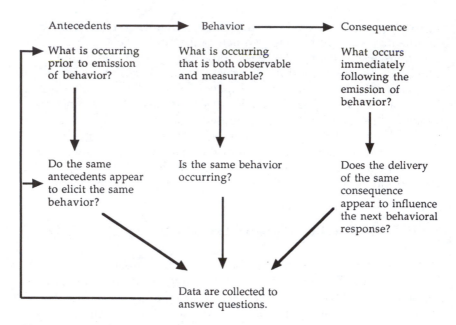

Figure 2–1. Paradigm for operant conditioning.

ready occurred. That particular response cannot be altered because it has already happened (at least accepting our current concepts of time and space continuua). The manner in which behavior is influenced in the future (e.g., more frequent, with greater intensity) determines whether or not reinforcement has actually occurred. Therefore, collection of data to verify this finding is necessary to ensure reinforcement has occurred. Third, although we would like for reinforcement to be systematic, it need not be so. Of course, the aim in this text is to provide examples of systematic reinforcement. Still, it should be noted that reinforcement may occur accidentally (e.g., a child's aggression may be reinforced through attention). Fourth, the individual being reinforced determines whether a consequence is actually reinforcing or not. That is, the practitioner or researcher may believe a consequence has a reinforcing quality, but it is the individual's future behavioral responses that reveal whether reinforcement has occurred. Every individual has his or her own unique history of reinforcement that will influence the degree to which a consequence serves as a reinforcer. What the researcher may believe is a reinforcer may hold no such quality to the individual participant. Finally, the antecedents and reinforcing consequences of behavior are not always observable. Because human beings are complicated organisms living in an equally complicated world, the variables affecting behavior can be numerous, and intrinsic to the individual as well as extrinsic. Therefore, the antecedents and consequences that influence the occurrence of any particular behavior are not always easily identifiable. For example, a researcher may be working with an individual to eliminate aggressive responses. The researcher has been quite successful in identifying antecedents and consequences that appear to influence the occurrence of aggression in the study setting. Yet, the target behavior remains largely unchanged. The individual has developed cognitive processes through which he justifies his aggression toward others because he believes they are out to get him. The individual has an older brother who served as a high-status model for the individual and is currently on the run because of aggressive criminal acts. This modeling affects the individual's perceptions about the appropriateness of aggression. Each of these influences has an effect on the occurrence of aggressive acts and may not have been identified by the researcher. In single subject research, we are, however, concerned with verifiable relationships, so we tend to focus on those aspects that are both observable and measurable.

Positive Reinforcement

Perhaps one of the more misunderstood notions related to applied behavior analysis is that positive reinforcement means that something good is happening. In fact, **positive** here refers to the type of consequence delivered, not to the quality of the reinforcing event. Table 2–1 illustrates the relationship between type of consequence delivered and the different types of reinforcement and punishment. As depicted, when positive reinforcement occurs, a consequence is delivered that involves adding to the environment. Examples might be the delivery of praise, the awarding of a token, or allowing a student to engage in a preferred activity. In each example, the goal is to increase the probability that the target behavior will occur again in the same or similar conditions. Giving attention for inappropriate remarks made in class or therapy might also increase the probability of remarks being made in the future when in the same class or therapy session. This is not necessarily a "positive" event in terms of desirable outcomes, but it does represent positive reinforcement. The key to determining if reinforcement has occurred is in evaluating whether behavior has strengthened or increased. This key concept holds true also for negative reinforcement.

Bribery

It is important to distinguish between **bribery** and positive reinforcement, as the two may be inappropriately assumed to be synonymous.

Table 2–1. Characteristics of Reinforcements and Punishments.

	Antecedent	Behavior	Consequence
Positive reinforcement	No specific requirement	Future probability strengthens/ increases under same/similar antecedent conditions	Something is introduced/added to individual's world
Negative reinforcement	Must be aversive to the individual	Future probability strengthens/ increases under same/similar antecedent conditions	Aversive antecedent is removed from individual's world
Positive punishment	No specific requirement	Future probability weakens/ decreases under same/similar antecedent conditions	Something is introduced/added to individual's world
Negative punishment	Preferred stimulus available	Future probability weakens/ decreases under same/similar antecedent conditions	Stimulus is removed from individual's world

As noted previously, when operant conditioning occurs, there are antecedents to behavior, a behavior, and consequences. In operant conditioning, the consequences of behavior are paramount in encouraging the individual to make desirable changes in his or her life. When bribery occurs, a "reward" is delivered as the antecedent to the desired behavior. This is a very important difference. In bribery, the stimulus that is intended to reinforce behavior is given before the behavior in hopes that the desired behavior will occur afterwards. In reinforcement, reinforcers are delivered contingent on the occurrence of the desired response.

The following serves as an example. A student is observing some game being played when the teacher calls on him or her to complete some academic work. The student says, "I want to play the game, not do my work." The teacher remarks, "Okay, but as soon as you are finished with the game you must come do your work." Bribery has occurred. The teacher could have withheld the opportunity to play the game and made it contingent on satisfactorily completing work. This would more likely result in positive reinforcement. In the former scenario, the teacher has delivered the stimulus intended to serve as reinforcer as an antecedent to the desired behavior in hopes that the work will be performed later. That is, of course, not a hope we would consider well founded.

Negative Reinforcement

When negative reinforcement occurs, behavior also is increased. That defines the occurrence of reinforcement in the most fundamental sense. Negative reinforcement appears to be a frequently misunderstood concept in our experiences with university students and practitioners alike. We have witnessed students using the term synonymously with punishment. We have also seen it used to refer to a situation when an undesirable behavior is reinforced (i.e., a "negative" outcome from the practitioner's perspective). Both of these are wrong. The term **negative** does not connote either a desirable or undesirable outcome, but rather the particular use of consequences to increase or strengthen behavior. Recall the **positive** in **positive reinforcement** refers to *adding* something to the environment as a consequence of a behavior. The **negative** in **negative reinforcement** refers to the *removal* of a stimulus as a consequence of emission of a behavior (see Table 2–1). The result is an increase in the probability of the response occurring once again. Negative reinforcement also involves the presentation of a special antecedent stimulus as well. That antecedent is aversive to the individual; its removal as a consequence of the emission of the target behavior is what reinforces that response. The red lights and buzzers that are activated when a person starts a car are intended to be aversive antecedents that in turn are shut off or removed when the seatbelt is buckled. The likelihood that you will buckle your seatbelt when being exposed to these same stimuli should increase if negative reinforcement has occurred. In other words, you will buckle up before the car is started or shortly afterwards to avoid or escape the buzzers and lights. Negative reinforcement relies on the desire of people to *avoid or escape* undesirable stimuli. The seatbelt situation serves as an example of a desirable response being negatively reinforced.

As with positive reinforcement, undesirable responses may also be negatively reinforced. When a practitioner notices that a student is escaping or avoiding some situation (or person or environment), this should be a clue that negative reinforcement may be occurring. For example, a student who repeatedly disrupts a class only to be removed from the class may be receiving negative reinforcement (even though the practitioner may believe punishment is occurring!). If the class includes some stimulus that is aversive to the student, and disruptive behavior results in removal from the presence of that aversive stimulus, it may lead to an increase in disruptive behavior. This represents an example of an undesirable behavior being negatively reinforced.

There are several other key concepts and terms associated with reinforcement. These include the Premack principle; reinforcer menus; satiation; primary, secondary, and generalized reinforcers; quality of reinforcers; and reinforcement schedules.

Premack Principle

The Premack Principle (Premack, 1959) is applied liberally in both educational and home environments. It refers to engaging in a highly preferred activity as a consequence for performing a less preferred activity. Determination of a highly preferred activity should be based on the individual's actual behavior, not assumptions made by the researcher or practitioner. Some individuals might choose to play video games in their free time, whereas others might watch television or read. When the identified high preference activity is presented contingently, the likelihood that the less preferred activity will be performed in the future is increased. Sometimes referred to as "grandma's rule," this operant conditioning strategy is as old as parenting and teaching. Common situations that exemplify the Premack Principle are "finish your homework and then you may watch television," "complete your voice exercises and then you may listen to a CD," and "finish your math work and then you may choose a game to play with your friend." The Premack Principle is frequently used because the reinforcing consequence (activity) often is available in home, school, and clinical settings. It is important to remember that access to that reinforcing activity must be controllable as well. If the individual can gain access to that highly preferred activity noncontingently, then attempted use of the Premack Principle with that activity may be futile.

Shaping

Shaping refers to providing positive reinforcement for responses of the target behavior that are closer and closer to the performance criterion.

By **criterion**, we mean the expected level of performance of the target behavior that is deemed necessary for the behavior to be functional and performed successfully. For example, signing one's name should be accomplished so that it is legible (one criterion) and within a reasonable period of time (another criterion). One could sign one's name but it could be unreadable or take so long to accomplish the task that it is not functional. In shaping, the individual is reinforced each time she or he emits a response that is closer to or meets the performance criterion. One potential difficulty in shaping is how the closer approximation to the performance criterion is being determined. For example, in learning musical instruments, the judgment of the teacher is usually the determinant of whether the individual has improved her or his musical performance. The less subjective the determination, the better. Generally, shaping is used when the topography of the behavior is being progressively changed (see Chapter 3 for a discussion of topography as a dependent variable).

Reinforcer Menus

As we stated previously, each individual has his or her own history of reinforcement (and punishment). What is reinforcing to one individual may or may not be reinforcing to another. We may make assumptions about potentially reinforcing stimuli or consequences based on a variety of variables (e.g., individuals of the same age, ethnicity, and socioeconomic background may share some similar reinforcers), but we may not be certain without careful examination on an individual basis. For example, we may assume that candy has a reinforcing quality for children in general, but it may not for any particular child. Teacher attention in the form of lavish praise may be considered potentially reinforcing for younger children, but may be less so for adolescents. It may be necessary before conducting a study with one or more individuals to develop a reinforcer menu if positive reinforcement is to serve as an independent variable. A reinforcer menu is a compilation of various stimuli (e.g., activities, things to eat, types of praise or statements, objects) that possess a reinforcing quality for the the individual. There are a variety of strategies for determining the reinforcer menu for an individual. Hall and Hall (1980) outlined nine steps to assist in selecting reinforcers: (1) consider the age, interests, and appetites of the individual; (2) consider the behavior to be reinforced and the degree and quality of reinforcement that would be comparable to the behavioral effort (see the "Quality of Reinforcers" section in this chapter); (3) list potential reinforcers based on this information; (4) identify reinforcing activities that may be applied using the Premack Principle; (5) interview or ask the person about what he or she likes and dislikes; also ask others what they observe about the individual's preferences; (6) consider using consequences that will be new to the individual; (7) use reinforcers that are readily available and occur naturally in the environment; (8) select the reinforcers that you will make available based on the previous steps; and (9) record data to ensure the applied consequences are actually producing a reinforcing effect. Additional means for identifying reinforcers may include observing the student in natural settings to determine preferences and exposing the individual to activities/stimuli noncontingently to determine preferences and possible new reinforcers. The researcher is attempting to obtain as large a variety of potentially reinforcing stimuli as possible. By varying the actual reinforcing consequence regularly, the researcher may avoid the occurrence of satiation. And, in the case of alternating treatments designs (see Chapters 9 and 10), the determination of which consequence has the greatest reinforcing quality may be critical to the study itself.

Satiation

Satiation occurs when a previously reinforcing stimulus no longer possesses its reinforcing quality. Generally, the individual has been overexposed to the stimulus so that it is no longer effective. In short, the individual may no longer choose to emit the target behavior in order to obtain the consequent stimulus. This occurs frequently when food or drink is used as a reinforcer, but may occur with objects, tokens, and activities as well. For a consequent stimulus to possess a reinforcing quality, a state of deprivation should exist. By **deprivation**, we do not mean a state of neglect or abuse, but rather that access to the stimulus should be controlled. Subsequently, obtaining it is important to the individual. In other words, the consequent stimulus has sufficient value for the individual to merit the behavioral effort required to obtain it. The use of various reinforcers (reinforcer menu) may assist in providing a number of quality or valued consequent stimuli. However, the researcher must also be wary about varying the type of reinforcer because it may also confound the results of an experiment. For example, a student may perform a target behavior exceedingly well on days when the opportunity to play a card game is available, and perform less well when only a choice of reading materials is available. Thus, the researcher may also need to control what type of reinforcer is delivered. This can be a key element in an alternating treatments design. In addition to considering satiation by varying reinforcers, the practitioner or researcher must also consider the type of reinforcer delivered.

Primary, Secondary, and Generalized Reinforcers

Reinforcing stimuli may be categorized into three groups: primary, secondary, and generalized reinforcers. Primary reinforcers are those stimuli with which an individual requires no prior experience in order for the stimuli to possess reinforcing qualities (Kazdin, 1975). Food, beverages, and affection are examples of primary reinforcers. Generally, we can think of these as being life sustainers, although some take exception (e.g., some might argue that affection is a primary reinforcer that is clearly not necessary to sustain life but also requires no prior experience). As a rule, primary reinforcers are used exclusively only when other types of reinforcers cannot be identified. Secondary reinforcers require some experience and derive their reinforcing properties from being paired with primary reinforcers (Kazdin, 1975) or existing secondary reinforcers. For example, the use of praise or a pat on the back that has been paired with affection generally begins to acquire a reinforcing property all its own. Generalized reinforcers are a special type of secondary reinforcer. A generalized reinforcer is one that may be exchanged for any one of a variety of primary or secondary reinforcers (backup reinforcers), and through that pairing the generalized reinforcer obtains its quality or value (Kazdin, 1975). Money is the most obvious example of a generalized reinforcer. Tokens and point systems are more commonly used in school and clinical settings.

Generalized reinforcers have a number of advantages in that they may be delivered easily, be saved, and provide for individualization of the backup reinforcers; and at times they may be taken away to punish inappropriate behaviors. Secondary reinforcers, when they involve attention and praise, are also generally easily delivered and have the advantage of being immediate and readily available. Primary reinforcers are not easily delivered, may interfere with diet restrictions, and may be subject to rapid satiation. Whenever primary reinforcers are used, they should be paired with secondary or generalized reinforcers with an aim toward using the latter two.

Quality of Reinforcers

The quality of reinforcers is yet another consideration for the researcher as she or he examines independent variable options. The type, degree, number, and so forth of reinforcer delivered should be reasonably commensurate with the achievement of the target behavior (or its reduction). For example, awarding a student $10 for completing a single seat assignment might be viewed by most educators and clinicians as rather excessive. Awarding $10 for achieving a 90% mastery level on a 9-week math test or for delivering a public address may be more commensurate. It should be noted that the history of the individual participant and the magnitude of the changes sought in the research project will greatly influence this decision. Generally, the more difficult it is to emit the target behavior, the greater might be the quality or quantity of the reinforcement.

Reinforcement Schedules

When reinforcers are delivered systematically as in a research project, a schedule is typically predetermined. Schedules may be categorized as either ratio, interval (Ferster & Skinner, 1957; Skinner, 1953), or duration (Alberto & Troutman, 1999).

Ratio Schedules

Ratio schedules are employed in projects when the target behavior (dependent variable) is easily observed each time it occurs. For example, the number of times or frequency of speaking complete sentences can be counted. Ratio schedules may be further categorized into continuous, fixed, and variable ratio schedules.

Continuous Schedules. In **continuous schedules**, every correct response is reinforced. Continuous schedules are used typically when the target behavior is being newly acquired. Despite what might be a commonsense notion that this schedule would result in great strength (the continued emission of the target behavior without delivery of a reinforcing consequence), the opposite is actually true. For example, inserting coins in a vending machine is very close to a continuous schedule of reinforcement. You insert your money and receive your selection. However, if the machine malfunctions and fails to deliver any selection (or your money back), you are not likely to continue inserting money in the anticipation that reinforcement will be forthcoming. For that reason, continuous schedules are used to establish correct responding and then are typically leaned or thinned toward intermittent schedules that require more than one correct response to regularly obtain reinforcement (Skinner, 1953). Continuous schedules of reinforcement may be abbreviated as CR or CRF schedules in the research literature.

Fixed Ratio Schedules. These schedules require that the individual perform a set number of responses of the target behavior before the delivery of reinforcement. For example, a student may have to utter 4 complete sentences before a reinforcer is delivered. The number of responses required may be gradually increased as responding improves (e.g., from 4 to 6 to 10 responses required to receive reinforcement). Fixed ratio schedules may be abbreviated as FR schedules (e.g., FR-4 would mean a fixed ratio of 4 correct responses required before the delivery of reinforcement). Fixed ratio schedules help to build resistance to extinction because the target behavior must occur without reinforcement being available, making it difficult or impossible to anticipate when reinforcement will be delivered.

Variable Ratio Schedules. These schedules require the individual to emit an average number of correct responses to obtain reinforcement. Variable ratio schedules may be abbreviated as VR schedules (e.g., a VR-10 schedule would require an average of 10 correct responses to obtain reinforcement). The average is achieved by varying the number of correct responses required so that when all correct responses are divided by the number of reinforcers delivered that average number is obtained. By using a VR schedule, the individual is less likely to anticipate accurately when reinforcement will be delivered and should emit the target behavior in a more consistent or steady manner.

A word of caution is necessary. If the ratio of correct responses is increased too quickly or becomes too high in number, **ratio strain** may occur (Cooper, Heron, & Heward, 1987). Ratio strain occurs when the demands placed on the individual become too great or the individual perceives that reinforcement is not coming and decreases or ceases responding. When ratio strain occurs, the practitioner or researcher should return to a previously successful schedule and then slow down the thinning process.

Interval Schedules

Interval schedules are used when the target behavior occurs so frequently that measuring each occurrence would be problematic. When using interval schedules (not to be confused with an interval recording system as described in Chapter 3, "Methods for Recording Behavior"), the first correct response following the elapse of a predetermined time period is reinforced. For example, if the target behavior is uttering complete sentences, the first correct response following a 1-min (or 30-s, or 10-min, etc.) interval would be reinforced. Like ratio schedules, interval schedules may be fixed or variable. That is, reinforcement may be delivered for the first correct response after a **fixed interval** of time (e.g., after 1 min following the last delivery of reinforcement) or after an average or variable interval of time (after an average of 10 s or 10 min). Interval schedules may be thinned just as ratio schedules and may be abbreviated as FI (fixed interval) or VI (variable interval) schedules.

Individuals may begin to anticipate when reinforcement is likely to be delivered, particularly with a fixed interval schedule. Also, the individual may slow responding following reinforcement due to an understanding that reinforcement will not be delivered again for some period of time. As with variable ratio schedules, variable interval schedules help to reduce these problems. The researcher may use a limited hold contingency as well. A limited hold involves specifying a period of time in which reinforcement is available following the elapse of the interval, which encourages a steadier or faster pace of responding (Alberto & Troutman, 1999). It is important to remember that even though reinforcement is being governed to some extent by the passage of time, interval schedules of reinforcement are used with target behaviors that are counted rather than time based. When we are concerned primarily with how long a behavior is emitted, we use response duration schedules of reinforcement.

Response Duration Schedules

Response duration schedules may be either fixed or variable (Alberto & Troutman, 1999). The same thinning procedures as those discussed with other intermittent schedules may be applied. In duration schedules, the researcher is delivering reinforcement based on how long a behavior is continuously emitted. With a **fixed response duration** schedule, the researcher reinforces the individual after the target behavior has been continuously emitted for a fixed period of time (e.g., after every 2 min). With a **variable response duration** schedule, the individual is reinforced following an average length of continuous emission of the target behavior (e.g., VD-5 min). The averaging is achieved in the same manner as with variable ratio schedules, substituting time periods for the number of responses required. With fixed response duration schedules, after being reinforced the individual may stop emitting the target behavior following reinforcement as he or she gains understanding that reinforcement will not be delivered for some period of time or because the time required to earn reinforcement is too great (Alberto & Troutman, 1999). Variable schedules help to reduce this problem.

Reinforcement and its delivery are much more complicated and sophisticated than the often misunderstood and proverbial birdseed delivered to the pigeon for pecking the correct button. In fact, in our experience the concepts discussed in this chapter are frequently misunderstood and misapplied by practitioners. Methods to decrease behavior require perhaps even more skill and knowledge because they often may evoke undesirable side effects as well as changes in the target behavior.

METHODS TO DECREASE BEHAVIOR

As noted previously, there is debate as to whether certain methods to decrease behavior should ever be employed. Corporal punishment is an obvious example. Less obvious examples (use of foul-smelling odors, water sprays to the face) have also been debated. Our position is that the methods to decrease behavior should be discussed, as they are available and potentially useful. Clearly, the use of any method with potentially adverse side effects must be rigorously reviewed. Although punishment is certainly a method that may be used to decrease behavior, other methods are available that are generally perceived to be less restrictive.

Arguments against the use of punishment include the following: (a) the individual learns what not to do, not what to do; (b) it may create a model of aggression and physical control to be emulated by the individual; (c) it may inflict pain or hardship on the individual; (d) at times, it is used with individuals who are unable to express an unwillingness to participate in such measures (e.g., a nonverbal individual with profound disabilities); (e) it merely suppresses behavior and may not eliminate the undesired response, particularly in other settings or situations; and (f) individuals may avoid or escape from environments where punishment is employed. This list is by no means exhaustive.

Although most professionals could hardly be characterized as proponents of punishment, arguments may be made in favor of its use in special circumstances. One such circumstance might be when an individual exhibits a behavior that is clearly dangerous to oneself or to others and must be immediately suppressed (e.g., attempting to stab others with a knife, running into traffic, or arson). When aversive stimuli are presented to suppress (i.e., punish) behavior, Wolery, Bailey, and Sugai (1988) outlined the following considerations: (a) aversiveness must be individually determined; (b) it may be necessary to use more intense levels of aversive stimuli to achieve a desired reduction in behavior; (c) side effects should be expected; (d) the maintenance of the behavior reduction may be variable; (e) the aversive stimuli should be delivered consistently and immediately; and (f) the use of aversives should be restricted and carefully monitored. Each individual researcher or practitioner along with an educational team must consider many variables when designing a single subject study. However, the use of punishment may require more rigorous examination by other appropriate boards (human treatment or human subjects review boards) before approval of use. The side effects are numerous. The use of severe or unusual forms of punishment is generally to be avoided for the sake of one and all. We will discuss punishment methods followed by a discussion of less aversive techniques advocated by opponents to punishment.

Positive Punishment

As with positive reinforcement, this term should not be construed to mean that punishment is a good thing. The *positive* here refers to the consequence for behavior rather than a quality of the phenomenon. Again, an antecedent occurs, the behavior occurs, and the consequence of the behavior is an addition to the environment (e.g., a verbal reprimand), and the result is that the probability of future occurrence under the same or similar circumstances is decreased. The future reduction or weakening of behavior essentially defines punishment (Cooper et al., 1987). As with positive reinforcement, it is important to remember that either desirable or undesirable behavior may be punished. For example, an adolescent who is given lavish praise for an oral response in class becomes less inclined to volunteer answers in the future. Although the practitioner may have thought she was positively reinforcing the student, the consequence was that the student became less likely to emit the behavior under similar antecedent conditions. Thus, she actually was using positive punishment. Intentional positive punishment in the schools and clinical environments is probably most often in the form of verbal reprimands, although there are many other possibilities.

Each student has an **individual history of punishment**, just as for reinforcement. Therefore, what is punishing to one individual may not be to another. The individual's response to the consequence is what determines whether or not punishment has occurred. Additionally, punishing consequences may be primary or secondary. Schedules of punishment are not generally discussed in the literature, as typically the researcher or practitioner would wish to address each and every instance of the targeted behavior. Negative punishment may also be used, although, unlike with negative reinforcement, an aversive antecedent is not necessary.

Negative Punishment

Negative punishment also results in a decrease in the probability of the occurrence of the target behavior. In negative punishment, an an-

tecedent occurs, the behavior is emitted, and the consequence is the removal of something from the environment. The result is that the probability that the behavior will occur again under the same or similar antecedent conditions is reduced. For example, a practitioner asks a group
of students a question, one blurts out an answer, the practitioner takes
away one point from the student's accrued total, and the student does
not blurt out answers during the remainder of the session. Removal of
privileges for misbehavior is another example of negative punishment.
Negative punishment does require the presence of some desired or preferred stimuli that can be removed as a consequence of the target behavior. It is important to remember that removing something from an
individual's world is not always easily accomplished and may lead to
undesirable reactions and side effects.

Response cost is a form of negative punishment. In response cost
the practitioner or researcher assigns a fine for one or more specified target behaviors. When the target behavior occurs, the fine is levied.
Generally, response cost is used in conjunction with token economies or
point systems that focus more on what to do to earn reinforcement than
what not to do (i.e., there are behaviors targeted for reinforcement as
well).

Extinction

Although not typically defined as punishment, extinction bears a re-
semblance to negative punishment. With extinction, the reinforcer(s) of
a behavior is identified and removed or withheld when the behavior occurs (Cooper et al., 1987). Extinction relies on the premise that once reinforcement is withheld, the behavior eventually will decrease or be
eliminated. As an example, an individual may use gestures to communicate when speech is more appropriate and within the individual's
repertoire. The practitioner or researcher could withhold any reinforcement that occurs as a result of gesturing (e.g., responding to a communicative request). In time, the gesturing should decrease if no reinforcer
is available to maintain its strength.

A few words of caution should be given regarding the use of extinction. First, when it is implemented, the targeted behavior may actually "get worse" before a reduction begins to occur (Cooper et al., 1987).
In the example given, the individual may gesture more and may seek
others' attention to look at his gestures before he realizes that reinforcement is not available. This realization can take a period of seconds or
weeks. Generally, one may assume that the longer a behavior has been
reinforced the more resistant it will be to extinction. That is, it will take
a longer period for extinction to occur. It is not always easy or even pos-

sible to hold out and not reinforce during the burst of increased responses that sometimes accompanies the implementation of an extinction intervention. For example, if the behavior to be extinguished is calling out by a student during class discussions, the increase in the
behavior may be so disruptive that it cannot be ignored. Ironically, if the
teacher does respond and teacher attention serves as a positive reinforcer, the calling-out behavior may be strengthened beyond the level
that existed before extinction was introduced (because the teacher has
accidentally used a variable ratio schedule of reinforcement). For this
reason, the nature of the target behavior must be carefully considered.
Second, it is not easy and sometimes is impossible to identify or control
the reinforcer for a given response. Reinforcement may be available in
so many environments and from so many sources that withholding it is
impractical. Reinforcement may have been internalized and therefore
the reinforcing consequence is not observable and not controllable by
the researcher. Third, the withholding of reinforcement may result in intense reactions from the individual. Finally, some behaviors simply
should not be treated through extinction. For example, a child may run
away for the reinforcement of being chased. However, one cannot simply allow children to run away and forget about them. It is important to
note that **spontaneous recovery** also may occur. Spontaneous recovery
refers to circumstances when, for no apparent reason, an individual
emits a behavior that had been extinguished (Cooper et al., 1987).
Generally, the intervention may be reinstituted and the behavior eliminated once again and in less time than the original procedure. Extinction
may be best employed when practitioner attention is reinforcing a relatively mild maladaptive response that has not been subjected to powerful and extensive reinforcement (e.g., ignoring conversational interrupt-
ing). This may reduce the strength of the extinction burst if it does occur
and may lead to a quick and complete extinction of the response.
Extinction probably also is best used in conjunction with differential reinforcement so that the individual may learn new behaviors for which
reinforcement is available.

We will discuss less aversive methods of reducing behavior
through the use of differential reinforcement. Response interruption, response satiation, and overcorrection are methods that also may be used
to weaken target behaviors.

Differential Reinforcement

Differential reinforcement may be the preferred method for decreasing
behavior because it incorporates behavior change strategies that assist in

avoiding some of the more common adverse effects of punishment. With differential reinforcement, the target behavior to be weakened or eliminated is identified. More desirable behaviors are identified that may replace the target behavior (Dietz & Repp, 1983). These desired behaviors are reinforced while the target behavior is also being weakened. The strategies are varied for reducing the target behavior (e.g., positive or negative punishment, extinction, and response interruption). Differential reinforcement has distinct advantages over programs designed only to decrease behaviors in that (a) the individual is also learning what to do as well as what not to do; (b) the individual's overall level of reinforcement is less likely to be reduced; (c) the individual and her or his significant others (as well as human subjects review teams) may find such a program preferable to one that focuses on punishment; (d) the individual observes a model for encouraging behavior change that also stresses reinforcement; and (e) the individual may be less likely to wish to escape or avoid the environment if reinforcement is available.

Differential reinforcement takes several forms. These include differential reinforcement of other (or omitted, or zero rates of) behavior (DRO), differential reinforcement of incompatible behavior (DRI), differential reinforcement of alternative behavior (DRA), and differential reinforcement of low rates of behavior (DRL).

DRO

DRO involves the rewarding of the absence of the targeted behavior for a specified period of time. Although it is not absolutely necessary that the individual understand the absence of the targeted behavior, DRO may be more effective when this is the circumstance. That is, the individual may be more likely to change his or her behavior in the desired direction if he or she understands not to perform the target behavior. The individual is reinforced if the target behavior is not emitted during the specified time period. For example, a student may agree that she emits highly undesirable verbal comments (e.g., cursing, verbal threats, or uncomplimentary remarks to peers). The researcher or practitioner then rewards the student for not emitting the verbal comments for a period of time (e.g., 10 min). Theoretically, the student should be rewarded for behaviors other than the target behavior. In practice, researchers may find it necessary as well to target other undesirable behaviors as well (e.g., other rule violations such as hitting, throwing things, or disrupting the class in some other fashion; see multiple baseline designs in Chapters 7 and 8). The researcher must also develop a contingency if the target behavior is emitted. Generally, the timer is reset and the student is informed as to what was done. Other measures may include response interruption (see later discussion) or response cost. The time required to not emit the behavior is initially set at a realistically achievable level (e.g., one half the average time between emissions during baseline). The student must be able to achieve the reinforcement in order to expect him or her to change behavior. As progress is achieved, the length of time required to obtain reinforcement may be lengthened.

DRI/DRA

Differential reinforcement of incompatible behavior (DRI) and differential reinforcement of alternative behavior (DRA) are similar to one another and somewhat different from DRO. With DRI/DRA, specific adaptive responses are identified to replace the maladaptive responses. With DRI, the targeted adaptive response is one that is physically incompatible with the targeted maladaptive response (e.g., if a child is in her seat, she cannot be out of her seat at the same time). With DRA, the individual is rewarded for a more desirable response but one that is not physically incompatible with the target behavior (e.g., one may give compliments rather than insulting others). With DRI/DRA, the individual is reinforced for the desired response. There must also be a contingency plan for when the targeted undesirable response is emitted as well.

DRL

Differential reinforcement of low rates of behavior is used when the targeted behavior is an appropriate response that occurs at an inappropriate level or is a behavior in need of elimination. In the first instance, going to the bathroom clearly is appropriate behavior, but going several times a class period is not (assuming no physical reasons for this need). In the second instance, smoking cigarettes serves as a common example. With DRL, the researcher systematically rewards the student for emitting fewer and fewer responses until the behavior is occurring at acceptable levels or has ceased altogether (see changing criterion designs discussed in Chapters 11 and 12).

Other Methods to Decrease Behavior

Other methods are available for decreasing behavior, including response interruption and overcorrection. These methods are not typically considered punishment procedures, but may nevertheless elicit some of the same side effects as they may involve physical contact with students and removal of reinforcers. In each of these procedures, the teaching of alternative behaviors that may be reinforced is very desirable as an element of a study.

Response Interruption

Response interruption is exactly as it sounds; the practitioner or researcher literally interrupts the emission of the target behavior (which is to be reduced or eliminated in strength). This may involve a verbal or physical interruption. For example, if a student has had some inappropriate speech targeted for reduction, the practitioner may verbally interrupt the student to stop the targeted behavior. Typically at this point, the individual would be provided with an opportunity to emit more appropriate speech and be reinforced for that. For another example, out of seat behavior may have been targeted for reduction. The intervention may involve physically guiding the student back to her seat whenever she gets up. As before, the student typically would also be reinforced for being in her seat. Response interruption may be used in conjunction with differential reinforcement.

Overcorrection

Overcorrection is a procedure that is intended to teach the individual an alternative or desirable behavior that corrects the effects of the behavior targeted for reduction (Azrin & Foxx, 1971). The corrective response is repeated over and over to enhance the likelihood that that response will be learned, or an exaggerated form of an adaptive behavior is performed (Foxx & Azrin, 1973), hence, the use of the term **overcorrection**. Overcorrection includes two basic intervention procedures: restitutional and positive practice overcorrection.

Simple restitution occurs frequently in clinics, classrooms, homes, and workplaces throughout each day. Simple restitution (which is not overcorrection) involves restoring an environment to its previous condition. For example, a student spills some paint during an art activity and is required to clean up the mess. In everyday life, this typically serves the desired purpose to reduce the likelihood that the undesired response will occur in the same or similar circumstances. The cleanup also provides learning in what must be done when spilling occurs.

Restitutional overcorrection involves restoring the environment to a better than previous condition. When the behavior targeted for reduction occurs, the individual is required to perform exaggerated responses that not only correct the consequences of the target behavior, but actually improve the environment. For example, an individual has vandalized a school setting by writing on walls. As an overcorrection procedure, the student is required to restore not only the areas of walls on which he wrote, but other areas of the wall as well.

Positive practice overcorrection involves the repeated practicing of an alternative to the target behavior. For example, if an individual slams doors each time he leaves or enters a room, the individual could be required to repeatedly practice closing a door quietly each time he slams a door. Positive practice involves teaching the individual a more adaptive behavior than the target behavior.

Overcorrection may involve physically manipulating an individual to perform the correction procedures. Also, the procedure may require individual supervision and be time consuming as well. Overcorrection may not be easily implemented in natural environments and may lead to undesirable reactions if physical contact is needed.

The procedures we have discussed may involve various combinations and variations as reported in the research literature. This is by no means an exhaustive discussion, and the reader is encouraged to more thoroughly examine literature related to applied behavior analysis and other intervention procedures before selecting an independent variable for any particular project. This discussion should provide general guidelines and knowledge for reflection on options available and some of the considerations needed in selecting an independent variable or in understanding procedures often found in the research literature.

Summary Checklist

Positive reinforcement—A consequence is delivered following the emission of a behavior, and the probability that the behavior will occur again under the same or similar circumstances (antecedent conditions) is increased or strengthened; **positive** refers to the consequence being the addition of something to the individual's environment, not a quality such as good.

Bribery—The delivery of a potential reward before a behavior in the hope that the behavior will be performed; frequently confused with positive reinforcement.

Negative reinforcement—An aversive antecedent stimulus is introduced, a behavior occurs, and the consequence is that the aversive stimulus is removed; probability of the behavior occurring again under the same or similar circumstances is increased; **negative** refers to the removal of something from the individual's environment as a consequence, not a quality such as bad; when behavior results in escape or avoidance of some unpleasant situation or event, negative reinforcement may be occurring.

Premack principle—The use of a highly preferred activity as a reinforcing consequence for performing a lower preference activity (target behavior); access to the high-preference activity must be controlled; commonly used in homes, schools, and clinics.

Shaping—Reinforcement of closer and closer approximations to a criterion level of performance of the target behavior; used to teach new behaviors.

Reinforcer menus—Individually determined lists of known or possible reinforcing consequences.

Satiation—Occurs when repeated exposure to a reinforcing consequence results in loss of the reinforcing quality (e.g., too much candy as a reinforcer results in little effort to obtain more candy).

Primary reinforcers—Reinforcers that require no previous exposure to possess reinforcing qualities; often thought of as life sustaining or fundamental to existence (e.g., food, water, warmth).

Secondary reinforcers—Reinforcers that have obtained their reinforcing quality through pairing with primary reinforcers or existing secondary reinforcers (e.g. praise, good grades); generally preferred for use over primary reinforcers.

Generalized reinforcers—Reinforcers (e.g., tokens, points, money) that are delivered in lieu of either of the previous two but can be exchanged later for other reinforcers.

Quality of reinforcers—The type, number, and degree of reinforcement should be reasonably commensurate with the target behavior.

Reinforcement schedules—Reinforcement may be delivered through a variety of schedules; typically, reinforcement should be moved from more frequent and predictable to less frequent and less predictable.

Continuous schedule—Every correct response of the target behavior is reinforced; used to establish new behaviors; not resistant to extinction (i.e., continuance of the behavior is unlikely in the absence of reinforcement).

Fixed ratio and variable ratio—Delivery of reinforcement after a specific number of correct responses or a variable number, respectively; variable ratio schedule should result in more consistent or steadier responding.

Fixed interval and variable interval—Reinforcement is delivered for the first correct response following a specified or variable period of time; variable interval schedule should result in more consistent responding; not to be confused with interval recording of target behavior discussed in Chapter 3.

Fixed response duration and variable response duration—Reinforcement is delivered for the continuous occurrence of a target behavior for a specified or variable length of time (duration); variable duration schedule should result in more consistent responding.

Positive punishment—Following a behavior, something is added to the individual's environment, and the probability of occurrence of the behavior under the same or similar conditions (antecedents) is decreased or weakened; each person has an individual history that determines which consequences will possess a punishing quality; punishment is to be avoided due to its many side effects.

Negative punishment—Following a behavior, something is removed from the individual's environment, and the probability of occurrence of the behavior under the same or similar conditions (antecedents) is decreased.

Response cost—Typically a fine is levied for occurrence of a target behavior (negative punishment); frequently used with token, point, or monetary systems.

Extinction—The withdrawal or withholding of reinforcement following a response; behavior may actually increase before it begins to decrease.

Spontaneous recovery—The unexpected occurrence of a target behavior that had been previously extinguished.

Differential reinforcement—Use of methods of reinforcement to decrease behavior; often preferred because these methods are less intrusive than punishment.

Differential reinforcement of other behavior (DRO)—The individual is reinforced for not emitting the target behavior for a period of time.

Differential reinforcement of incompatible/alternative behavior (DRI/DRA)—The individual is reinforced for an adaptive response that is intended to replace the maladaptive target behavior.

Differential reinforcement of low rates of behavior (DRL)—The individual may be reinforced for reducing the level of responding of a behavior to an appropriate level (e.g., number of times going to the bathroom), or the reinforcement of a target behavior until a zero level of responding is achieved (e.g., smoking cigarettes).

Response interruption—The individual is interrupted when the target behavior is emitted; typically, the individual is redirected toward emitting a more adaptive response.

Overcorrection—Having an individual repeatedly perform a more adaptive behavior or performing an exaggerated adaptive response when the target behavior occurs; overcorrection is intended to teach the individual what to do, not just what not to do; may involve physical contact and often requires one-on-one attention to implement.

Simple restitution—This is not true overcorrection; refers to restoring an environment to its original condition (e.g., mopping the floor after throwing a liquid on it).

Restitutional overcorrection—Restoring the environment to a better than previous condition (in the above example, mopping several floors in addition to the one where liquid was spilled).

Positive practice overcorrection—Repeatedly practicing an adaptive response (e.g., repeatedly practicing quietly closing a door following slamming a door).

References

Alberto, P. A., & Troutman, A. C. (1999). *Applied behavior analysis for teachers* (5th ed.). Englewood Cliffs, NJ: Prentice-Hall.

Azrin, N. H., & Foxx, R. M. (1971). A rapid method of toilet training the institutionalized retarded. *Journal of Applied Behavior Analysis, 4*, 89–99.

Cooper, J. O., Heron, T. E., & Heward, W. L. (1987). *Applied behavior analysis.* Columbus, OH: Merrill.

Dietz, D. E. D., & Repp, A. C. (1983). Reducing behavior through reinforcement. *Exceptional Education Quarterly, 3*, 34–46.

Ferster, C. B., & Skinner, B. F. (1957). *Schedules of reinforcement.* Englewood Cliffs, NJ: Prentice-Hall.

Foxx, R. M., & Azrin, N. H. (1973). The elimination of autistic self-stimulatory behavior by overcorrection. *Journal of Applied Behavior Analysis, 6*, 1–14.

Hall, R. V., & Hall, M. C. (1980). *How to select reinforcers.* Lawrence, KS: H & H Enterprises.

Kazdin, A. E. (1975). *Behavior modification in applied settings.* Homewood, IL: The Dorsey Press.

Premack, D. (1959). Toward empirical behavior laws: I. Positive reinforcement. *Psychological Bulletin, 66*, 219–233.

Skinner, B. F. (1953). *Science and human behavior.* New York: Macmillan.

Wolery, M., Bailey, D. B., Jr., & Sugai, G. M. (1988). *Effective teaching principles and procedures of applied behavior analysis with exceptional students.* Needham, MA: Allyn & Bacon.

CHAPTER 3

Methods for Recording Behavior

TIME-BASED METHODS FOR RECORDING AND REPORTING BEHAVIOR

Duration Recording

Latency Recording

A FEW WORDS ABOUT THESE METHODS

As with independent variables, there is virtually an infinite variety of dependent variables that may be used in single subject research. When we refer to recording dependent variables, we are discussing the methods used to determine the effectiveness of the independent (i.e., treatment or intervention) variables. The focus of researchers has been on dependent variables that are observable and measurable. That is, the occurrence of the target behaviors can be viewed by at least two individuals and measured independently by those individuals, and reasonable agreement can be reached concerning to what extent (e.g., how often or how long) the dependent variable occurred. In this chapter, we will discuss methods for recording target behaviors that frequently serve as dependent variables in single subject research. For example, one could measure how many times a child got out of her seat during a class period. An intervention could be implemented and the effects of that independent variable measured by changes in the frequency of out-of-seat behavior. At times, the general behavior of concern may be much more difficult or even impossible to actually observe. The behavior may be related to some internal cognitive process, which of course cannot be directly observed. Then, the dependent variable or target behavior must be some outcome that reflects the occurrence of the more general behavior. For example, one's overall *goal* may be for the individual to reflect on possible actions to be taken before actually taking action in a stressful situation (i.e., the behavior of concern is reflecting on one's possible actions). But, reflection cannot be directly observed. In this case, the time that elapses between the onset of the stressful situation (waiting is the target behavior) and the beginning of the action may be measured as the dependent variable. Also, the researcher might measure the accuracy of the individual's ability to recite a series of internal steps to follow that are aimed at teaching reflection. The researcher may also measure the outcomes actually occurring. In each of these cases, the researcher identifies a *target behavior* that is observable and is indicative that the overall goal is being achieved. Direct measurement of the target behavior is necessary. These direct quantitative measurement techniques are employed by applied behavior analysts. The general definitions and use of these techniques will be discussed.

The above example illuminates issues related to research and educational or clinical interventions that deserve attention. Except for physiologic measurements, behaviors that occur within the mind and heart are not directly observable. Certainly, we all agree that these responses are important and often critical in determining the actions individuals take. Also, everyone involved in a study may not agree as to whether the behavior changes that occur are truly meaningful, or may differ in their perceptions of the outcomes of a study. Researchers have begun to use other methods of assessment that are less direct than those typically employed in applied behavior analysis, but assist in offering insights that elaborate the outcomes of a study. These include what we will refer to as qualitative measures. We have elected to include our discussion of qualitative measures in Chapter 13. In this chapter, we will discuss how quantitative measures may be used to assist in determining the social and ecological validities and outcomes of single subject research. First, we will discuss target behaviors and methods for recording changes in target behaviors. Second, we will address how interobserver reliability may be determined for each method for recording behavior. Third, we will provide sample data recording sheets that may be useful in constructing the reader's own (these are included in the Appendix at the end of the chapter). Although there are options available to the researcher (e.g., bar graphs), we assume quantitative data typically will be reported using an x-y line graph that was discussed more thoroughly in Chapter 1. We must stress that the possible dependent variable options available to the researcher are not limited to those discussed here, but these do represent some of the more commonly used recording procedures in single subject research.

Quantitative dependent variables may be generally categorized into two groups: (a) those that measure events and are primarily designed to measure the frequency, accuracy, or intensity of a target behavior (event-based); and (b) those that are more time-based and used to measure how long a behavior occurs or how long it takes the behavior to begin. It is important to remember that, because these dependent variables should be observable and measurable and agreement reached in each of these respects, some effort and time is often devoted to specifying the target behavior and the most appropriate procedure. Anecdotal recording often is useful in this process.

ANECDOTAL RECORDS

Anecdotal recording, or ABC recording, involves the measurement of the **antecedents** to a behavior, the **behavior**, and the **consequences** that individuals encounter and/or emit (Bijou, Peterson, & Ault, 1968). Additionally, the time of day and the setting are often recorded as well as who is emitting the behavior. The anecdotal record may take at least two forms. First, it may serve as a kind of running or continuous record of what is going on in a setting over a period of time. The record may focus on any number of individuals in an environment, but one person is frequently the focus. Clearly, to accomplish this type of recording you must devote all your attention to the observation. This is time consuming and is easier said than done. Trying to record all interactions between antecedents, behaviors, and consequences can be challenging indeed. A second method used in anecdotal recording that overcomes some of these challenges is to record the ABCs following an instance of the behavior. For example, a practitioner is concerned with an individual's dysfluent speech and his or her reaction to the dysfluency. The practitioner could record the ABCs in the individual's environment across a period of time or record the ABCs immediately following a dysfluent speech event. The former yields a greater wealth of information, but the latter is less time consuming and interferes less with instruction. A sample recording sheet for anecdotal recording is included as Figure 3–1 in the Appendix. This recording sheet could be used for either of the types of anecdotal records discussed.

The observer should involve others in the environment in reviewing the data to determine if they agree with the accuracy of the record (we will discuss interobserver reliability later). Although two independent observers are generally desirable, at this phase of a study, this may not be possible or clearly necessary. Next, the researcher should analyze the data to determine exactly what is the target behavior and how to record it. Typically, possible independent variables or interventions are discussed as well. When this phase of a study is completed, the researcher must clearly define a target behavior and how to record it and how to determine the accuracy of that measurement. For example, there may be a general concern that an individual is too aggressive. However, aggression may take many forms and involve several behaviors (e.g., hitting, making threatening gestures, making threatening remarks). Anecdotal recording may be used to more clearly define (operationally define) what is aggression for the individual. Barlow and Hersen (1984) stressed that operational definitions should

> refer only to observable characteristics of the target behavior; they avoid references to intent, internal states, and other private events. Clear definitions are unambiguous, easily understood, and readily paraphrased. A complete definition includes the boundaries of the behavior, so that an observer can discriminate it from other, related behaviors. (p. 111)

Thus, it may become clearer how aggression may be recorded (e.g., frequency) and who should record the target behavior and how interobserver reliability may be determined. The study of the antecedents and consequences of aggressive actions may yield insight into how changes in aggressive behavior may be effected (e.g., differential reinforcement of other behavior). Zirpoli and Melloy (1993) noted that anecdotal records may assist in identifying events that maintain inappropriate behavior, appropriate behaviors that are not being reinforced, social skills that need to be learned, and environmental conditions that need modification. Anecdotal recording should be systematic, but may be less rigorous in the sense that interobserver reliability may not be required for the anecdotal record itself. However, agreement about the information gleaned is highly desirable. One manner by which researchers may accomplish this is videotaping (or audiotaping as appropriate) the events of concern. Although the presence of a video camera may also cause reactivity, the tape is a permanent product that may be analyzed more conveniently and with virtually unlimited frequency and by unlimited numbers of individuals. This may help to ensure accuracy.

EVENT-BASED METHODS FOR RECORDING AND REPORTING BEHAVIOR

As noted previously, there are two general groups of measurement procedures. The first group noted (typically concerned with the frequency, accuracy, or intensity of the target behavior) can be categorized as event methods for recording behavior. The second group may be categorized as time-based methods for recording behavior. We begin our discussion of these specific methods with those that are generally considered event methods.

Permanent Products

As just suggested, permanent product data may be gathered through the use of videotapes and audiotapes. There are other forms of permanent products that are used to record target behaviors. Permanent products in the form of paper-pencil (or typed or word processed) products are frequently used in school environments to determine whether an instructional intervention has yielded the desired outcomes. Permanent products can be analyzed for frequency (how often a behavior occurs), cumulative responses (total number of responses), rate (number of responses within a given period of time), trials to criterion (number of responses needed until a performance criterion on the target behavior is reached), topography (correctness of appearance of the behavior), magnitude (intensity of the behavior), and percent correct. Permanent products offer the advantage of allowing later analysis and usually repeated review of that analysis (Alberto & Troutman, 1999). A disadvantage may be that the individual is not observed actually performing the target behavior. For example, an individual may be working on solving word problems. The researcher may decide to record the percent of correct responses. If the individual's performance is recorded based on paper-pencil products that are analyzed ex post facto, the researcher may not actually see what the individual is doing (e.g., what mistakes were made, what distractions occurred). Of course, a researcher or practitioner may also directly observe the individual completing the permanent product. Percent correct, which is frequently used with paper-pencil permanent products, may be one of the more frequently used measures in school settings. Each of the other possibilities will be discussed later.

Percent Correct

Percent correct is determined by deciding what constitutes a correct and incorrect response. The observers then determine which of the responses fall into each category and their ratings are compared to ensure adequate agreement. The overall percent correct of the individual's responses could be calculated by

$$\frac{\text{Number of Correct Responses}}{\text{Number of Correct Responses} + \text{Number of Incorrect Responses}} \times 100\%$$

Technically, we are discussing a method of reporting behavior rather than a specific recording procedure. The researcher may also wish to simply report how many responses were correct and/or incorrect. This method may be used when the number of opportunities to perform the target behavior is unchanging (e.g., the individual always has 20 word problems to solve). That is, the researcher could record 15 correct responses on Monday, 17 on Tuesday, and 18 on Wednesday. Because there are always 20 opportunities, we can easily compare the individual's performance across the 3 days. If the number of opportunities varies, percent correct must be used so we may compare performance across days when there are 20, 25, or 30 opportunities. Otherwise, comparing the number correct across these days might be misleading (e.g., 19 correct out of 20 might actually appear as a poorer performance than

25 out of 30 correct because 25 is more than 19 in total number of correct responses).

As a guideline, we would suggest that the percent method of calculating and reporting accuracy be used when there are a minimum of 10 and preferably 20 opportunities in a given observation session (Wolery, Bailey, & Sugai, 1988). Fewer than 10 responses tends to create too large a fluctuation in the percent calculated if incorrect responses have occurred. For example, a student who makes 4 out of 5 correct responses gets 80% accuracy. He can only achieve 100% or reduce his accuracy by 20 percentage points per incorrect response with only 5 opportunities available. Percent correct should be used when the number of opportunities varies from session to session. See Figures 3–2 and 3–3 in the Appendix for depictions of recording sheets for accuracy and the simpler number of correct responses methods. Wolery et al. (1988) also stressed that percent correct does not provide insight into the absolute number of events, the total number of opportunities, or the total length of time within which events were observed. Additionally, one may improve in terms of speed or fluency, but 100% accuracy remains as good as the performance can be reported (Wolery et al., 1988).

We have discussed permanent products primarily in terms of written responses. However, as noted, videotapes and audiotapes are also permanent products which may be analyzed as well. For example, a speech and language clinician might wish to analyze the percentage of words read correctly from a passage. She might record the child's speech and determine the percentage of words read correctly. Finally, the reader should be aware that use of percent correct for reporting performance is not restricted to permanent product data.

Interobserver Reliability

For convenience, we have elected to include our discussion of how observers are trained in Chapter 4, "Issues in Single Subject Research." Here, we will focus on the mechanics of calculating interobserver reliability.

To calculate interobserver reliability, one must have two observers recording the percent of correct responses (or number of correct responses when opportunities are held constant). The recordings of the two observers are then compared to determine the percent of agreement. This should be accomplished by examining each occurrence of the target behavior and comparing how each observer recorded the response (i.e., as correct or incorrect). Here, we will use a plus (+) to indicate a correct response and a minus (−) to indicate an incorrect response or nonoccurrence. Comparing each occurrence is important. In the example that follows, if we merely compared how many correct responses versus incorrect responses each observer recorded, we would find that each recorded 8 correct and 2 incorrect responses. Theoretically, the researcher might arrive at a 100% interobserver reliability figure. However, if we examine the observers' recordings more carefully, we find this is not the case. Really, the observers disagreed about Opportunities 3, 7, 9, and 10, creating four disagreements. They agreed about the correctness/incorrectness of the individual's responses in Opportunities 1, 2, 4, 5, 6, and 8. As a general rule, interobserver reliability of 90% or higher is considered desirable, 70–89% is considered adequate, and less than 70% raises doubt as to whether the procedures were consistent, fair, and rigorous (Zirpoli & Melloy, 1993).

Opportunity	1	2	3	4	5	6	7	8	9	10
Observer 1:	+	+	−	+	+	+	−	+	+	+
Observer 2:	+	+	+	+	+	+	+	+	−	−

$$\text{Interobserver Agreement} = \frac{\text{No. of Agreements}}{\text{No. of Agreements} + \text{No. of Disagreements}} \times 100\%$$

$$\frac{6}{6+4} \times 100\% = \frac{6}{10} \times 100\% = 60\%$$

A number of the following methods for recording events can be applied to permanent products as well, although they may be used independently.

Frequency

Frequency involves recording the number of responses that occur during an observation session. The length of the observation sessions needs to remain constant. For example, if an individual were to emit four responses in a 30-minute observation session, this should not be compared to four responses in a 1-hour session. See Figure 3–4 in the Appendix for a depiction of a recording sheet for measuring frequency. Frequency is often used in single subject research and is a relatively simple recording procedure. However, as guidelines, frequency should be used when the target behavior is relatively short in duration (i.e., is not exhibited for several minutes per response), can be easily observed and counted (does not occur so often that many responses would be missed or counting them would prove very difficult), yet occurs often enough that significant changes are detectable (occurs more than once a day or once a week for example; Alberto & Troutman, 1995; Zirpoli & Melloy, 1993). This last guideline may be waived when behavior is so severe that any occurrence is inappropriate (e.g., serious physical injury to self or others), but in such cases the goal of the project should be to achieve a zero or extremely low rate of responding. Also, opportunities to emit the target behavior should not be restricted or controlled (i.e., the individual may emit the behavior at any point during the observation rather than having only a specific number of opportunities to produce the target behavior). Interobserver reliability for frequency recording is determined by having two observers each record the number of occurrences and comparing these figures. Typically, one should compare each response as in percent correct, although this may not always occur. It would be worthwhile for observers to compare recordings and discuss when and what they recorded. If the time of occurrence for each response is recorded, then an occurrence-by-occurrence comparison is possible. Otherwise, if significantly different frequencies are recorded, the observers may then attempt to determine why each recorded what she or he did, which was the correct recording, and how to avoid such disagreements in the future. Interobserver reliability for frequency is determined as follows:

Observer 1:   9 responses recorded
Observer 2:   10 responses recorded

$$\frac{\text{Smaller Number of Responses}}{\text{Larger Number of Responses}} \times 100\% =$$

$$\frac{9 \text{ Responses}}{10 \text{ Responses}} \times 100\% = 90\%$$

If disagreements about when responses occurred are known, the researcher may use the more conservative approach by comparing the observers' recordings occurrence by occurrence. In this case, the researcher may use the following formula:

$$\frac{\text{Number of Agreements}}{\text{Number of Disagreements} + \text{Number of Agreements}} \times 100\% =$$

Rate

Rate is a measure of frequency that is directly linked to the length of observation periods. When observation sessions vary in length, rate must be used rather than frequency. Rate is determined by dividing the number of responses observed by the length of the observation (length is generally expressed in terms of behaviors or responses per minute or second but could include hours or even longer periods).

Observer 1:   10 responses recorded
Length of Observation: 20 minutes

$$\text{Rate} = \frac{\text{Number of Responses}}{\text{Length of Observation}} = \frac{10 \text{ Responses}}{20 \text{ min}} = .50 \text{ responses/min}$$

See Figure 3–5 in the Appendix for a recording sheet depicting rate recording. Rate is sometimes used for higher frequency behaviors that would be difficult to accurately count for frequency over an extended period of time. For example, an individual's tic may be the behavior of concern. However, to count the number of responses over a class period may be quite difficult if the frequency would reach a large number of responses or if the length of observation sessions varied. In this situation, the researcher may record the number of responses within a shorter observation period and determine the rate during that period (e.g., during 10 min of the class). It would be necessary to vary when such abbreviated observations occurred to ensure that the number of responses occurring was not at least partially a function of when the individual was observed. When so used, rate becomes an *estimate* of frequency rather than a measure of actual frequency in relation to time observed. This has the advantage of being less time consuming, but may also less accurately depict the actual frequency of the target behavior (e.g., 4 responses might occur during the 5-min observation session followed by 10 responses in the next 5 min when the student is not being observed). The researcher must be careful to ensure that, when rate is used to estimate frequency, that it reflects honestly the overall rate of behavior. Interobserver reliability for rate is determined just as frequency is determined. Both observers would, of course, be recording the responses during the same observation period so time does not figure into the calculation. Still, the researcher should be aware if substantially abbreviated observation sessions yield better interobserver reliability than lengthier ones. In such a case, it would indicate some change may be needed in the recording procedures or in the operational definition of the target behavior.

Trials to Criterion

Trials to criterion refers to measuring the number of responses needed by the individual to achieve some preset level of acceptable performance (criterion). Trials to criterion does not require that the same number of opportunities be available during each session. That number may vary, as the individual may achieve the criterion sooner in some sessions than others. For example, a teacher may be working with an individual on building skills and the target behavior is hammering nails into wood.

The teacher may record how many efforts at swinging the hammer are required before the student successfully completes the task. See Figure 3–6 in the Appendix for a recording sheet for trials to criterion. Generally, trials to criterion is used to obtain an idea of how quickly the individual acquires a skill. When fewer trials are needed, the assumption is that learning is occurring more rapidly or knowledge is being recalled more quickly (Cooper, Heron, & Heward, 1987). Cooper et al. also noted that this method may be useful in determining which type of instruction effected the criterion performance in the fewest number of trials. The researcher reports how many opportunities were given and what criterion was achieved by the individual. The criterion could be an ultimate criterion (e.g., a four-sentence paragraph free of errors) or a criterion set for each session (e.g., utter a preset number of words with an initial *s* sound). Interobserver reliability for trials to criterion is determined in the same manner that frequency is determined except that the researcher divides the smaller number of trials recorded by the larger number of trials recorded rather than by the number of responses. If there is disagreement as to whether or not criterion is ever achieved (e.g., one observer believes it was achieved and the other records it was not achieved at all), then the researcher must compare the smaller recorded criterion (e.g., 80% correct or 8 of 10 steps completed correctly) by the larger recorded criterion (e.g., 100% correct or 10 of 10 steps completed correctly). When there is disagreement as to the criterion level the individual actually obtained, the researcher should immediately address this problem by ensuring all recorders understand the standards for determining the criterion. Otherwise, subsequent data become suspect in their use for judging performance.

Cumulative Recording

Cumulative recording is similar to the "ultimate" tasks to criterion recording. In cumulative recording, you are recording and reporting the total number of responses that occur across each observation session toward some final level of achievement. That is, the number of occurrences observed in a given observation are graphed after being added to the total number of occurrences for all observations to that point (Alberto & Troutman, 1995). For example, an individual is working on selling candy items toward funding a school trip. It would be necessary to keep a record of the total items sold across the length of the project. A sample recording sheet for cumulative recording is included as Figure 3–7 in the Appendix. One might well use a bar graph or an x-y line graph that shows the cumulative total as it changes with each observation to report findings. Interobserver reliability is determined in the same way as frequency. That is, the smaller number of responses recorded for an observation period is divided by the larger number recorded.

Interval Recording

Occasionally, the dependent variable or target behavior may occur with such a high degree of frequency that measurement is virtually impossible across an extended length of time (e.g., self-stimulatory behavior that occurs very rapidly) even using a rate measurement. In this situation, the researcher may elect to use interval recording. Interval recording involves *estimating the frequency* of the response and, accordingly, must be used in a fashion that will ensure the most accurate estimate. In interval recording, the occurrence or nonoccurrence of the behavior is recorded within very short periods of time (or intervals) across a longer observation session. The researcher then reports the number of intervals where occurrences of the target behavior were recorded. Either partial or whole interval recording, or momentary time sampling may be used.

Whole Interval Recording

In whole interval recording, the observer divides the observation period into an equal number of intervals (e.g., a 10-min observation session is divided into 60 ten-s intervals). The observer then records if the target behavior occurs during the entire interval. For example, the researcher may be concerned with rocking self-stimulatory behavior. When an interval begins, the observer records an occurrence if the rocking continues for the entire interval. If the rocking is not occurring at the beginning of the interval or discontinues at any point during the interval, a nonoccurrence is scored. Clearly, the possibility exists that rocking may occur but may not be recorded using this system, hence, the estimate of frequency. Whole interval recording is selected when the target behavior has a degree of duration (or occurs for a long enough period of time) that such instances should be minimized. Also, the target behavior should be one for which the researcher is primarily concerned with events (or episodes) of at least the length of the interval. Suppose the aforementioned rocking behavior generally occurs for a number of seconds and sometimes for entire minutes if not interrupted by someone. Also, there are occasions when the individual may rock only briefly and does not appear to interfere with other activities. The researcher may select whole interval recording as the preferable method that ignores the unimportant events of extremely short duration but acknowledges those that do interfere with normal daily activities. The researcher should ensure that each observation period is of the same length of time. Should the period of time for which there is concern about the target behavior exceed the typical observation period (e.g., observation period is 10 min in length but the period of concern when the target behavior is being emitted is 1 hr), then the researcher should vary the time of day in which the observation period occurs. Ideally, the same length of time is used each day for the entire period of target behavior concern, although this is not always practical.

Whole interval recording *may* provide an estimate of duration as well (see "Duration Recording"). The number of consecutive intervals in which occurrences are scored estimates how long the behavior was occurring (e.g., occurrences scored in five consecutive 10-s intervals would indicate the target behavior was emitted continuously for at least 50 s, but still does not exactly measure the actual duration). In whole interval recording, the researcher must ensure that the recording method does not artificially underestimate the actual frequency as a result of the length of the observation intervals. That is, if the interval lengths are longer than most emissions of the target behavior, many nonoccurrences may be scored when the target behavior is actually being emitted. See Figure 3–8 in the Appendix for a depiction of a recording sheet using interval recording. Whole interval recording is more likely to underestimate actual frequency compared to partial interval recording (Alberto & Troutman, 1990).

Interobserver reliability in whole interval recording is based on an interval-by-interval appraisal of agreement. That is, each observer's recording of occurrence or nonoccurrence should be compared for each interval. Subsequently, total agreements are divided by total number of agreements plus disagreements. Following is an example where a + would indicate an occurrence of the target behavior and a − would indicate a nonoccurrence.

Interval	1	2	3	4	5	6	7	8	9	10
Observer 1:	+	+	+	−	−	−	+	+	-	+
Observer 2:	+	+	+	−	−	−	+	+	+	−

$$\frac{\text{Number of Agreements}}{\text{Number of Agreements} + \text{Number of Disagreements}} \times 100\% =$$

$$\frac{8}{8 + 2} \times 100\% = 80\%$$

Note that the observers each scored a total of six occurrences of the target behavior. A false impression would be given if the researcher were to report that each observer scored six occurrences and four nonoccurrences, although technically this would be true. This might give the impression that 100% interobserver reliability was obtained. In fact, agreement was achieved only in Intervals 1, 2, 3, 4, 5, 6, 7, and 8. Disagreements occurred in Intervals 9 and 10. Therefore, a lower interobserver reliability of 80% was actually obtained. For this reason, the interval-by-interval method of comparison must be made for whole interval, partial interval, and momentary time sampling procedures for recording.

Partial Interval Recording

Partial interval recording is very similar to whole interval with one notable exception (the sample data sheet for whole interval recording could be used for partial interval recording as well). Occurrences are scored if the target behavior is exhibited at any point during the interval. For example, the student may begin a 10-s interval not rocking. After 3 s, he rocks for 5 s, and concludes the final 2 s by not rocking. An occurrence would be scored because the target behavior did occur during the interval (whole interval recording would have resulted in a nonoccurrence because the target behavior did not occur for the duration of the interval). Because occurrences are more likely to be scored using partial interval versus whole interval recording, researchers may prefer this method as a better estimate of frequency. However, partial interval recording may also suggest that the duration of the behavior is greater than it actually is, particularly if the target behavior occurs only briefly during the interval. The researcher must be aware of this distinction to avoid misunderstanding his or her data. Partial interval recording *does not* estimate duration. In fact, an individual may be emitting the target behavior during a tiny percentage of the actual observation period but still be scored in 100% of the interval observations. For example, the extremely brief rocking events alluded to earlier would be scored in a partial interval system. The result could be many consecutive intervals scored when the target behavior occurred (e.g., 1 s of every 10-s interval), although the individual could have actually spent only a relatively small fraction of time observed rocking. Therefore, the partial interval system is preferable for obtaining the higher estimate of frequency. In other words, partial interval recording should be selected when any instance of the behavior during an interval should be scored by the observer. Whole interval recording should be used when the researcher wishes to score primarily those responses that occur for the length of the interval or longer. Also, whole interval recording is typically easier in that observers are not likely to miss an occurrence that must occur for the entire interval length. In partial interval recording, a distraction could cause an observer to not see a response of very short duration. To use our example of the rocking behavior, we would use partial interval recording if we wished to get the best estimate of how often rocking occurred. However, if we wished to estimate the rocking that occurred for a selected number of seconds (e.g., 10 s or longer), we would select whole interval recording. Interobserver reliability for partial interval recording is calculated in the same manner as whole interval recording.

Momentary Time Sampling

Momentary time sampling is a third method of using an interval-based system for estimating the frequency of a target behavior. In this system, the observer looks at (or listens to) the student at the end of an interval and records whether or not the behavior is occurring at that moment. Momentary time sampling is probably the easiest of the interval-based recording systems to implement but may yield the grossest estimate if the intervals are long and relatively infrequent. As with the other two methods, the observation period is divided into intervals but should be short enough to ensure that responses of the target behavior are not frequently missed. Target behaviors that occur for some duration rather than quickly occurring ones are more appropriate for recording using momentary time sampling. For example, a researcher might operationally define a target behavior of appropriate play. During 20-min periods when the individual is to be engaged in play activities, the researcher may divide the observation period into 20 one-min intervals. At the end of each minute, the researcher records occurrence or nonoccurrence of appropriate play at that moment. If appropriate play occurred before or after the momentary observation but not at that moment, a nonoccurrence would be scored. Conversely, if the individual had not engaged in appropriate play for most of the elapsed interval but was doing so at the momentary observation, an occurrence would be scored. A sample recording sheet for momentary time sampling is included as Figure 3–9 in the Appendix. If the number of observations are sufficient and the target behavior is one that typically occurs for at least the length of the intervals and longer, this system can produce a reliable estimate of frequency of behavior (but not an estimate of duration). The observer should be eminently aware if the intervals are too long or the nature of the target behavior is such that the system is significantly underestimating the frequency. Interobserver reliability is calculated in the same manner as with whole interval recording.

An advantage of momentary time sampling is that data may be collected on more than one individual at the same time. For example, one individual could be observed after 30 s, 90 s, 150 s, and so on, while a second individual could be observed at 60 s, 120 s, 180 s, and so on.

We would add a final note to our discussion of interval recording systems. These should not be confused with interval or duration reinforcement systems. The systems could be used simultaneously, but this is not a requirement. The observation interval systems bear no direct relationship to reinforcement systems that rely on intervals or duration of time.

Magnitude

Magnitude is the strength, force, or intensity of a behavior (Cooper et al., 1987). For example, a speech and language clinician may be concerned with the loudness of an individual's voice and need to measure the volume. With magnitude recording, the researcher must decide how degrees of intensity or magnitude of the behavior will be measured. Variables that can be measured mechanically (e.g., decibels) clearly are less subjective than human judgment, and would not require interobserver reliability assuming the measurement instruments were in proper working order and accurately calibrated. Still, human observation may be reliably used, although such applications may be limited (Cooper et al., 1987). For example, an individual may be learning physical education skills. One could observe to determine reliably whether a ball was struck hard enough with a bat to leave the infield of a baseball diamond. In the example of voice volume, one might reliably measure the target behavior by noting whether the person's voice was audible from a distance of 5 ft by someone with normal hearing. Some experts may consider this type of measurement as a permanent product system when a physical object is used to determine the level of the dependent variable. For example, the intensity in using a screwdriver could be measured by examining the assembled object to determine if the screws hold. There is no typically employed data sheet for magnitude recording. The researcher may wish to judge whether or not the required degree of magnitude was achieved. A data sheet very much like one used to record percent of opportunities correct or like one for trials to criterion could be employed. Interobserver reliability would be determined in the same manner as well.

Topography

Topography is the correctness of how a behavior is performed or how it looks. Cooper et al. (1987) referred to the topography of response as the form or shape of the behavior. Again, the researcher must carefully define what represents examples and nonexamples of the performance of the target behavior. Topography may be paired as a dependent variable with shaping as an independent variable (see Chapter 2). As with magnitude, the real challenge in using topography as a dependent variable is determining what represent examples and nonexamples of the target behavior. If permanent products (e.g., paper-pencil, videotapes) are used, this process may be somewhat simplified. Two or more observers may then examine the product independently of one another to gain agreement in this respect. For example, if the purpose of the study is to determine the effectiveness of an intervention to improve handwriting skills, the paper products could be used for measuring the topography of the handwriting. If an individual is working on fine oral motor movements in order to learn certain phonetic utterances, then a videotape and/or audiotape may assist in determining if the correct movements are being made. Athletic skill development is another area with clear implications for using topography. In other situations, safety and/or efficiency may be developed by assisting an individual to change the topography of his or her behavior (e.g., in lifting heavy objects). As with magnitude, the determination of whether the topography of the behavior was correct or incorrect may be linked to the delivery (or nondelivery) of positive reinforcement. Cooper et al. (1987) suggested that topography may be reported as a frequency, rate, percentage, or duration of response. As with magnitude, no typical data sheet is used but a researcher may wish to construct one where the number of opportunities where correct topography is observed and recorded and compared to the total number of opportunities (as in percent of opportunities correct). Interobserver reliability would be determined in the same manner as with other reporting methods. Trials to criterion and the same procedures for interobserver reliability could also be used to determine how many opportunities were needed before the correct topography was recorded.

Levels of Assistance Recording

Levels of assistance refer to the degree of help required by the individual to complete a task or some portion of a task. Wolery et al. (1988) stressed that some individuals would exhibit no correct responses without some level of assistance being provided. This type of recording is frequently paired with task analysis (the process of breaking a skill down into component steps that may be learned more easily). One difference between this type of recording and others is that, in a sense, the observer is recording his or her own (or an interventionist's) behavior as the dependent variable as opposed to directly recording the individual's responses. For example, an individual is learning the skills to dress himself with each step in the process carefully defined (the task analysis). The dependent variable is the degree of help offered by the teacher (e.g., physical prompting, verbal prompting). As less help is required, the assumption is the individual is moving toward independent dressing. For this reason, level of assistance observation and recording requires that the researcher doggedly guard against any deviation in the system of assistance used to ensure that the level delivered is consistent (i.e., faded or increased appropriately). Interobserver agreement would be calculated similarly to percent correct. That is, the researcher would divide the number of agreements on the level of assistance given by the number of agreements plus disagreements and multiply by 100%.

Task Analysis Recording

Task analysis recording is somewhat related to level of assistance recording in that the behaviors to be learned are outlined in a series of clearly defined steps. In task analysis recording, trials to criterion may be used, as the researcher wishes to record how many opportunities or trials are needed for the targeted step to be accomplished. For example, an individual is learning to speak in complete sentences. The researcher wishes to assist the individual in speaking progressively longer and more complex sentences (the steps for which have been clearly defined). The observer may then record how many opportunities it takes the individual to achieve each step or may choose to record the degree of assistance required. Also, the researcher may be concerned with the topography or magnitude of the behavior defined in each step. If so, these types of recording may be used. Figure 3–10 in the Appendix provides an example of recording levels of assistance within a task-analyzed target behavior, as this is a common method with a task analysis. Wolery et al.

(1988) also noted that the number of correct responses or pecent of correct responses may be recorded based on the number of opportunities to perform each step. Interobserver reliability would be calculated as with level of assistance recording, trials to criterion, topography, and so on.

TIME-BASED METHODS FOR RECORDING AND REPORTING BEHAVIOR

Although many experts may include interval recording systems as time-based, we have chosen to include them under event recording. We elected this option because we believe the overall purpose of interval systems is to estimate frequency (with the previously noted rough estimate of duration in whole interval recording). In the following recording systems, the concern is with the length of time the behavior occurs or with how long it takes for a target behavior to begin. Therefore, the measurement of time itself is of concern. In interval recording systems, time is used to determine when and how observations are scored, but the time itself is not recorded as a variable for measuring the target behavior.

Duration Recording

Duration recording involves measuring the length of time from when a behavior begins to its termination. Generally, duration recording is used when the length of time (either longer or shorter) the behavior occurs is the primary concern rather than how often the behavior occurs, although frequency can also be determined within duration recording. For example, the behavior of concern may be carefully defined tantrum behavior. The observer records how long each tantrum lasts. Therefore, both the duration and the frequency are available. This method allows the researcher to determine the total duration (total time engaged in tantrum behavior), the duration per occurrence (the amount of time spent engaged in the target behavior for each episode or event), or the average duration per occurrence (total time spent engaged in the target behavior divided by the number of occurrences). Also, the researcher may report the percent of time observed engaged in the target behavior (total duration divided by total time observed). If the frequency of the behavior is of no concern, the observer may simply record duration, keeping a record of total duration only (e.g., time spent engaged in carefully defined quiet study). The observer may start with a timer as soon as the behavior begins and stop the timer when the behavior terminates.

When the behavior begins again the timer is once again started (but not reset to zero) and the process is repeated. At the conclusion of the observation period, the total time on the timer represents the total duration. This method yields fewer data than the duration-per-occurrence method (i.e., no frequency, duration per occurrence, or average duration) but is probably easier to implement. An example of the use of this method might be to record total time spent studying during each day of the week. If total duration data alone are collected, one can determine how much time was spent studying, but not how much time was spent studying per occurrence of studying. See Figure 3–11 in the Appendix for a depiction of a form for recording duration. Two students could each spend 4 hs studying. One could accomplish this duration in one session. The other might take eight sessions. One point worth noting is related to independent variable implementation. The researcher must be wary that duration is not artificially altered because the target behavior is not allowed to occur (in a reduction of duration program) or is the only option available to the individual (in the case of an increase in duration program). For example, when out-of-seat behavior replaces in-seat behavior, the researcher is likely to have a contingency to deal with this event. Therefore, the time spent out-of-seat is diminished by the intervention (i.e., is not allowed to continue). Therefore, the researcher may wish to record frequency of an alternative and/or target behavior in some instances rather than duration. Interobserver reliability for duration recording is calculated as follows (observers' recordings equal duration in minutes):

Occurrences:	1	2	3	4	5	6	7	8	9	10
Observer 1:	7	3	4	6	4	8	2	7	3	6
Observer 2:	7	3	4	6	4	8	3	7	4	6

$$\frac{\text{Shorter Time Recorded}}{\text{Longer Time Recorded}} \times 100\%$$

In the above example, interobserver reliability could actually be determined in two ways. In the more conservative (and more acceptable method), the interobserver reliability for each occurrence would be determined. This would be 100% for all occurrences except numbers 7 and 9. The seventh occurrence would yield a reliability of 66.66% (2 divided by 3 × 100%) and the ninth a reliability of 75%. In this case, the researcher should report the agreement findings for each observation. She or he could also include the agreement for total duration as well. The first observer would have obtained a total duration of 50 min. The second observer would have recorded 52 min of duration. Interobserver reliability for total duration would have been 96%. This would suggest very good interobserver reliability, but would also be somewhat misleading because the actual agreement had been substantially less than this figure for 20% of the occurrences.

Latency Recording

Latency recording involves measuring the length of time from the delivery of an antecedent stimulus that should elicit the target behavior, to the actual beginning of the target behavior. For example, a teacher might wish to decrease the time it takes for a student to begin work (which is operationally defined). The concern is the student wastes instructional time. The teacher says, "Begin work" (the antecedent stimulus), and records how long it takes for the student to actually begin work. The latency is the period of time from the antecedent delivery to the beginning of work. In this case, a reduction in the latency would be the desired outcome. In other cases, an increase in latency might be desired. For example, if the overall objective is to reduce impulsive behavior, the target behavior might be to wait before acting in a particular situation. In this case, the desired outcome is to increase the length of time between the delivery of the antecedent and the onset of the target behavior (e.g., time between the delivery of an insult to action taken by the insulted individual). See Figure 3–12 in the Appendix for an example of a latency recording sheet. As with duration, latency may be recorded by occurrence or by total latency. Interobserver reliability is calculated using the same method as with duration recording.

A FEW WORDS ABOUT THESE METHODS

Up to this point, we have focused on the quantitative measures used in applied behavior analysis and single subject research. The researcher may also wish to consider other measures that may further enhance her or his ability to explain and understand the complex outcomes of a single subject research design. To that end, we have included a discussion of qualitative measures in Chapter 13.

Methods for recording behavior are not limited to those we have discussed, although these measures and variations are found frequently in the literature. The researcher should investigate studies in which similar measures to those being contemplated have been used. As with the designs themselves, "pure" examples in the literature are not always easily identified, as researchers must adapt procedures to the individual, setting, and goals of the study.

Researchers must also be concerned with how the recording procedures dovetail with the intervention used. For example, a researcher may be working with an individual to alter her dysfluent speech. A particular treatment has been identified and agreed to by all concerned. The researcher must now decide how the treatment and recording procedures will be balanced. The researcher may use event based methods for recording target behaviors in the following manners.

The researcher may use anecdotal recording initially to get important information that may help identify many variables at work in the production of dysfluent speech. This information also may help in operationally defining dysfluent speech and what type of treatment may be preferred. Once these are accomplished, the researcher may decide which recording procedure to use.

If the researcher is interested in obtaining a record of and analyzing the individual's dysfluent speech, she may then use a videotape or audiotape as a permanent product. Percent correct would probably not be used in this case, but if, for example, the individual was given a number of opportunities at speech during each observation, then percent of episodes of dysfluent speech could be recorded. The intervention would be intended to decrease percent of episodes in which dysfluent speech occurred.

If the researcher was observing the individual throughout a day or specific period of time, she would likely use frequency recording. However, if the observation period varied (and the number of opportunities was uncontrolled), then she could elect to use rate. The researcher would design an intervention intended to reduce the number or rate of dysfluent episodes.

If the researcher was aiming toward assisting the individual in achieving fluent speech (e.g., giving a public address) for a particular event (or ultimately with no dysfluency whatsoever), she might elect to record trials to criterion. The researcher would measure how many opportunities were required before the performance criterion was achieved. Cumulative recording is difficult to envision in this sample scenario.

If the individual's dysfluency occurred at a relatively high frequency or was difficult to measure in terms of a specific number of responses (i.e., dysfluent speech was frequently intermingled with fluent speech), then the researcher might elect to use interval recording. Whether she used whole or partial interval, or momentary time sampling, her overall goal would be to reduce the number of intervals in which dysfluent speech occurred. This also provides an example of observational procedures not necessarily equating with visual recording, but could include auditory aspects.

Magnitude probably would not be used in such a study, but if the volume of the individual's speech was also altered during dysfluent episodes, then magnitude might be used. In this case, the researcher would likely wish to help the individual either increase or decrease the volume or pitch of the voice.

Topography might be used if the dysfluent speech resulted in exaggerated physical movements or facial gestures. The researcher might measure the topography of these responses with an aim toward reinforcing topographies that were more typical physical or facial gestures.

Level of assistance or task analysis recording methods could be used if, for example, the individual was to take specific steps during each occurrence of dysfluency. The researcher could measure how much assistance was needed to accomplish each step. In this case, the overall goal would likely be to have the individual perform those steps with little or no assistance.

The researcher may also use time-based procedures for recording target behaviors. Duration per occurrence recording could be used to measure how often dysfluent speech occurred, what was the total time spent being dysfluent, and what was the average duration of each episode. The total time alone spent engaged in dysfluent speech could be recorded. In this case, the overall aim of intervention would be to reduce the length of time spent engaged in dysfluent speech (as measured per episode or by total duration).

Let's suppose the individual blocked when required to speak certain sounds or words, thus causing dysfluency. The researcher could measure the latency between when speech ceased (at the occurrence of the antecedent sound or word) and when speech resumed. In this case, the overall goal of intervention would be to reduce the time spent not speaking.

These examples are intended to show the reader how different procedures might be used with the same target behavior and different intervention goals. Knowledge of these methods for recording behavior is important, but the researcher must be able to adapt and adjust these methods, be able to use them in combination with other possible measures (e.g., qualitative measures), and ensure they accurately reflect what is actually happening to the individual. This last point is perhaps the most important. The ultimate aim in data collection is gathering of information that can later be analyzed to tell the story of what happened to the individual(s) involved. Quantitative methods should lend objectivity to that storytelling. That is the strength of using these quantitative measures. That objectivity is hollow, however, if the researcher fails to measure what is really important about the changes the individual is undergoing. Reliability is essential, but the researcher must not select methods primarily because they are easier to conduct and reliability is more certain, if other methods may be more meaningful for measuring actual outcomes. For example, a momentary time sampling method may be very reliable, but may not actually reveal the true nature of changes in the target behavior.

In our next chapter, we address many of the issues that the researcher must consider in designing a study and ensuring ethical behavior and treatment. The methods for recording the target behavior are an integral part of that process, but cannot be separated from decisions concerning the treatments involved as well as many other variables. In Chapter 4, we discuss issues related to single subject research.

Summary Checklist

Anecdotal records—Refers to recording the antecedents, behaviors, and consequences occurring in an environment and involving the individual subject; often used to identify and define a target behavior and interventions.

Event-based Methods for Recording and Reporting Behavior

Permanent products—These are permanent data forms that may be reviewed repeatedly (e.g., paper-pencil products, videotapes or audiotapes).

Percent correct—Used when the number of opportunities to perform the target behavior may vary from observation to observation.

Interobserver reliability—Two or more observers record the target behavior independently and simultaneously; later, results are compared to determine if the target behavior is being measured reliably; reliability is calculated differently depending on the method used for recording behavior.

Frequency—Used when behavior can be easily counted and the length of observation is constant; opportunities to perform the behavior should not be a controlled number.

Rate—Used as frequency recording except that length of observations vary; the number of responses per unit of time is calculated and reported (e.g. one response per minute).

Trials to criterion—Used to measure events (occurrence of target behavior) when the researcher wishes to determine how many occurrences are required to achieve a criterion level of performance.

Cumulative recording—Used when the aggregate number of emissions is of primary importance.

Interval recording—Method of estimating the frequency of the target behavior using a period that has been divided into equal intervals of time for individual observations; not to be confused with interval schedules of reinforcement.

Whole interval—Provides a smaller estimate of frequency; behavior is recorded only if it occurs throughout the interval.

Partial interval—Provides the greater estimate of frequency; behavior is recorded if emitted at any point during the interval.

Momentary time sampling—Provides the roughest estimate of frequency; behavior is recorded if occurring at a specific moment at the conclusion of an interval; may be used to record behavior of more than one individual simultaneously.

Magnitude—Measure of intensity or strength of the target behavior.

Topography—Measure of the appropriate appearance or correctness of the target behavior.

Level of assistance—Measure of the degree of assistance or help required to emit the target behavior.

Task analysis recording—Often paired with level of assistance recording when the target behavior has been broken down into smaller, more teachable units or steps.

Time-based Methods of Recording and Reporting Behavior

Duration—Used when how long the behavior is emitted is the primary concern; the researcher may record and report duration per occurrence, average duration, or total duration.

Latency—How long it takes for the behavior to occur following the antecedent; the researcher may record and report latency per occurrence, average latency, or total latency.

References

Alberto, P. A., & Troutman, A. C. (1995). *Applied behavior analysis for teachers* (4th ed.). New York: Merrill.

Alberto, P. A., & Troutman, A. C. (1999). *Applied behavior analysis for teachers* (5th ed.). New York: Merrill.

Barlow, D. H., & Hersen, M. (1984). *Single case experimental designs: Strategies for studying behavior change* (2nd ed.). New York: Pergamon Press.

Bijou, S. W., Peterson, R. F., & Ault, M. H. (1968). A method to integrate descriptive and experimental field studies at the level of data and empirical concepts. *Journal of Applied Behavior Analysis, 1*, 175–191.

Cooper, J. O., Heron, T. E., & Heward, W. L. (1987). *Applied behavior analysis.* Columbus, OH: Merrill.

Wolery, M., Bailey, D. B., Jr., & Sugai, G. M. (1988). *Effective teaching principles and procedures of applied behavior analysis with exceptional students.* Needham, MA: Allyn & Bacon.

Zirpoli, T. J., & Melloy, K. J. (1993). *Behavior management applications for teachers and parents.* New York: Merrill.

APPENDIX

Sample Recording Sheets

Name of Person(s) being observed: Date:

Name of Observer: Location:

Time	Antecedents	Behaviors	Consequences

Figure 3–1. Anecdotal recording sheet.

Name of person being observed: Location:

Name of observer:

Time/Date	Number of Opportunities	Number Correct	% Correct

Figure 3–2. Recording sheet for accuracy.

Name of person being observed: Location:

Name of observer:

Time/Date	Number of Correct Responses (opportunities are constant)

Figure 3–3. Recording sheet for correct responses.

Name of person being observed: Location:

Name of observer:

Date/Time   Number of Events/Episodes (length of observation remains constant)

Figure 3–4. Recording sheet for frequency.

Name of person being observed: Location:

Name of observer:

Time/Date Length of Observation	Number of Episodes/ Events	Rate of Responding (Events/Time)

Figure 3–5. Recording sheet for rate.

Name of person being observed: Location:

Name of observer:

Time/Date   Criterion Level   Number of Trials Required to Meet Criterion

Figure 3–6. Recording sheet for trials to criterion.

Name of person being observed: Location:

Name of observer:

Time/Date	Number of Responses	Cumulative Responses (Total responses + this observation)

Figure 3–7. Recording sheet for cumulative responses.

Name of person being observed: Location:

Name of observer: Time/Date:

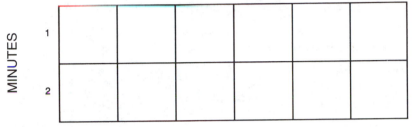

10-Second Intervals

MINUTES   1

2

+ = Occurrence of the target behavior
0 = Nonoccurrence of the target behavior

Figure 3–8. Recording sheet for interval data.

Name of person being observed: Location:

Name of observer: Time/Date:

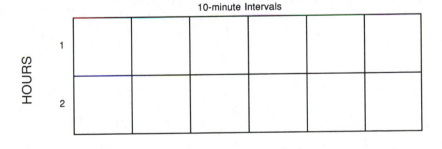

10-minute Intervals

HOURS   1

2

+ = Occurrence of the target behavior at end of interval
0 = Nonoccurrence of the target behavior at end of interval

Figure 3–9. Recording sheet for momentary time sampling.

Name of person being observed: Location:

Name of observer: Levels of Assistance:
                                                                I = independent
                                                                V= verbal prompt
                                                                G= gesture
                                                                M= modeling
                                                                PP= partial physical prompt
                                                                FP= full physical prompt

Steps in Task Analysis

Time/Date	Level of Assistance	1 I	2 M	3 FP	4	5	6	7	Comments

Figure 3–10. Recording sheet for level of assistance.

Name of person being observed: Location:

Name of observer:

Date	Time Behavior Started	Time Behavior Ended	Duration

Figure 3–11. Recording sheet for duration.

Name of person being observed: Location:

Name of observer:

Date	Time of Delivery of Antecedent	Time Behavior Started	Latency

Figure 3–12. Recording sheet for latency.

CHAPTER 4

Issues in Single Subject Research

IMPORTANT CONCEPTS TO KNOW

THE CONCEPTS OF PREDICTION, VERIFICATION, AND REPLICATION

Prediction

Verification

Replication

RELIABILITY AND VALIDITY

Reliability

Validity

ETHICS

Single subject research is an applied approach that is concerned with the demonstration of functional relationships between the independent and dependent variables. In fact, as you will see when you study each of the designs and their variations, this approach may demonstrate such relationships better than other approaches (e.g., group study approaches). Rather than striving to meet assumptions that allow for particular statistical inferences (e.g., with the use of analysis of variance) to demonstrate a functional relationship, single subject researchers try to demonstrate that relationship in a very direct fashion. That is, the effectiveness of single subject designs relies on demonstrating that changes in the dependent variable are directly attributable to the presence or absence of changes in the independent variable. Continuous measurement of the dependent variable and subsequent changes in accordance with the researcher's manipulation of the independent variable allows this direct demonstration within the chosen design. **Prediction, verification,** and **replication** of effects are present when this functional relationship exists. Also, the researcher must demonstrate **reliability** and **validity** as well as **ethical** and humane treatment. When all these effects are achieved, the researcher is able to make a strong case for the functional relationship between independent and dependent variables. We will discuss each of these issues as it relates to single subject research.

THE CONCEPTS OF PREDICTION, VERIFICATION, AND REPLICATION

The concepts of prediction, verification, and replication relate to the issues of reliability and validity as specifically applied to single subject research. When these concepts can be demonstrated within a single subject research design, the functional relationship between the independent and dependent variables is evident. Hence, the reliability and validity of the study are verified assuming the extraneous variables and systematic bias discussed earlier cannot be reasonably perceived to have accounted for the changes that have occurred. Each concept plays a unique part in this verification process, yet the concepts are interdependent. That is, the demonstration of each is critical but the presence of all is equally important. Each concept is related to changes in the dependent variable that are directly attributable to the independent variable. In other words, the changes that are present in the data path can be explained by systematic manipulations included in the study. The following discussions include a summary of Tawney and Gast (1984) with some of our own modifications.

Prediction

Prediction refers to the idea that if there is no effect attributable to the independent variable, the dependent variable's data path will remain unchanged. For example, a researcher has collected baseline data on an individual's target behavior. After stability has been achieved during the baseline phase, the intervention phase would be introduced. If the intervention had no effect on the dependent variable, one could logically assume that the data path from baseline to intervention phases would depict no appreciable change (see Figure 4–1). Therefore, one could *predict* the data path will remain unchanged despite a phase change. Should the data path change and that change be maintained, one could then reject the prior notion that phase change had no effect on the dependent variable (also assuming appropriate control of extraneous variables and systematic bias). When a data path changes predictably in conjunction with a phase change, it is possible that there is verification the intervention has an effect on the dependent variable or target behavior.

Verification

Verification is the confirmation that the dependent variable is changing in a predictable fashion as the independent variable is systematically applied (see Figure 4–1). For example, a baseline phase is completed and an intervention is introduced. As we have discussed, if the independent variable will have no effect, we could predict there will be no change in the data path with that phase change. We may predict conversely that the data are likely to reveal a change in the desired direction in the data path as a result of the implementation of the independent variable. When this happens, we have verified our hypothesis that the dependent variable will change predictably with the introduction of the independent variable. Replication is needed also to complete our demonstration of a functional relationship.

Replication

Replication refers to the repeating of the observed predictions and verifications within the same study. This concept is essentially what separates the single subject research designs from the typical teaching situation. For example, a practitioner gathers baseline data on math accuracy and implements a reinforcement program, and the desired changes are observed. Please note that one could state that both a prediction (base-

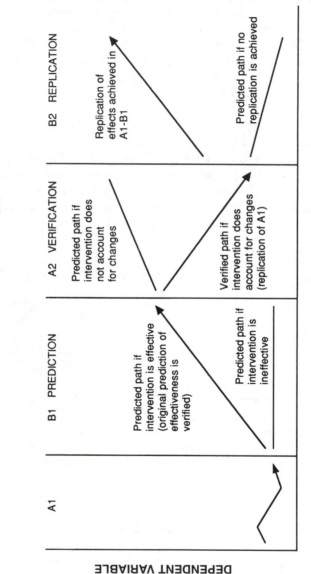

— Data path if prediction, verification, and replication are not achieved

→ Data path if prediction, verification, and replication are achieved

OBSERVATIONS

Figure 4-1. Example demonstrating prediction, verification, and replication within a withdrawal design.

line will remain unchanged if the reinforcement program is not started and the data will show improved accuracy when positive reinforcement is started) and a verification (the accuracy does in fact improve) are present. Replication of the effect of the independent on the dependent variable, however, is *not* present. For replication to occur, the researcher might return to baseline conditions (and one could predict the data will remain unchanged if the positive reinforcement is not actually accounting for the improved accuracy and we could predict that it will decrease if in fact positive reinforcement is accounting for the change) and measure the outcome. Should the individual's accuracy decrease with this phase change, we have verified the prediction. We may also allow the data path to return to the same or a similar level as during our original baseline. We then may reintroduce the intervention. This allows the researcher to replicate the original prediction and verification. If replication occurs (accuracy once again increases as a result of the introduction of the independent variable), we have built a stronger case for the demonstration of a functional relationship. This example would be an A-B-A-B, or withdrawal, design. In each of the chapters related to how to set up a particular design, we will discuss how prediction, verification, and replication are used to strengthen the case for influence of the independent variable on the dependent variable.

Replication has at least one other important connotation in single subject research. Because group experimental designs use a larger number of individuals as subjects who frequently are randomly assigned to treatment groups, there is an assumption that the influences of intraindividual variables are evenly distributed across groups (error variance in the parlance of parametric statistics). In other words, whatever peculiar or unique influences occur for each individual, they do not influence the overall outcome of the study because those influences are balanced by the size of groups and the random assignment of individuals to those groups. We have trouble making these assumptions when there is only an individual or a few subjects involved in a study. Perhaps positive reinforcement was effective only for this individual's math accuracy, or because it was in a particular setting, or because of the time of year, or the maturation of the individual, or a myriad of other conceivable influences. The more replications included within a study, the less changes in the dependent variable are attributable to extraneous or confounding variables. Also, the case for the power (or robustness) of an independent variable to influence a dependent variable is strengthened when other researchers seek to replicate effects with other individuals, with similar behaviors, in different settings, and so on. The more different studies replicate one another or achieve a similar and predictable effect, the greater confidence we may place in the intervention being used. The procedures discussed in Chapter 2, for example, have effects that have been replicated many times over and their power verified.

Prediction, verification, and replication are key elements to demonstrating a functional relationship between the independent and dependent variables. These concepts are linked to the concepts of reliability and validity in single subject research.

RELIABILITY AND VALIDITY

Reliability and validity may have some meaning to you already. In single subject research, we have three major areas of concern related to these concepts. First, **interobserver reliability** (sometimes referred to as interrater reliability or interobserver agreement) is important to establish confidence in the measurement of the dependent variable. Second, **internal validity** is important to establish the believability of the functional relationship and, therefore, establish confidence in the results and conclusions drawn. We will also discuss **external validity**, which is related to the confidence others may have that the same independent variable will yield similar results in similar studies (e.g., with different individuals, with different dependent variables, in different settings). External validity is also related to the concept of replication.

Reliability

In Chapter 3, we discussed the specifics for determining the interobserver reliability for the more standard methods of recording target behaviors used in applied behavior analysis (e.g., frequency, duration, latency). Interobserver reliability is not our only measurement concern, but the researcher should provide evidence that her or his measures of the dependent variable are accurate. As we outlined in Chapter 3, the researcher must identify and define the target behavior in such a way that there is confidence that at least two people can observe the individual and agree whether or not the behavior has occurred, or to what extent, or for how long, and so on. This process is essential to establishing reliability and also internal validity. Practitioners may frequently use observation to determine whether progress toward a goal has occurred, but they may rely on their own personal judgment regarding the individual's performance. This may result in subjective measures or observer drift. Establishing interobserver reliability helps to ensure that the process has been fair, ethical, and rigorous.

As the term would imply, interobserver reliability relies on the use of more than one observer. Typically, the researcher identifies at least two individuals (which may include herself or himself) who will be in-volved in measuring the dependent variable or at least are available to serve as observers for reliability purposes. More than two is advisable so that the loss of one observer will not disrupt the study. Once the ob-servers are identified, a training program is established in which the ob-servers gain practice in observing the individual and scoring the de-pendent variable. In our experience, this training process involves a number of steps. The researcher or practitioner must identify and define the target behavior. An example might be sitting in one's chair. After ob-serving the individual, the researcher may wish to operationally define sitting in one's chair so that minimal judgment is required to decide if in fact the individual is sitting in her chair (e.g., sitting might be defined as buttocks in contact with seat, the back in contact with the chair back, at least one foot on the floor, and the trunk and head erect and not in con-tact with any part of the chair or other furniture). Operational defini-tions were more fully described in Chapter 3, but the reader should un-derstand here that the target behavior should be so well defined that it is easy to determine if it has occurred and to what extent (e.g., when it began and ended). Defining the target behavior may require having oth-er observers also participate so that potential ambiguities and unusual occurrences or circumstances may be observed or anticipated. Some-times, videotapes of the individual may assist in defining the target be-havior and practicing observations and scoring the dependent variable without intruding in the experimental environment. Generally, it is im-portant to also define what are nonoccurrences of the target behavior. That is, the observers should practice recognizing when the target be-havior did not occur (e.g., the individual meets all aspects of the defini-tion of sitting in seat but both feet are propped up on a chair in front of her and hence is *not* sitting based on the definition). Observers should practice until they are very comfortable and efficient with recognizing the target behavior. This may take some time. Next, the researcher must select a system for measuring the target behavior. For example, if an in-terval system is used (see Chapter 3), more practice may be required be-cause of the more complicated procedures. Following practice sessions, the observers should compare results for each and every occurrence or measurement of the target behavior (or the dependent variable). They should reach an understanding of both why and why not the the target behavior had occurred. When disagreements occur, it is particularly im-portant to understand and reach agreement as to what the correct meas-urement was and why. This comparison process can take some time, but it also serves to more precisely define the target behavior, to refine the measurement procedure, and to provide confidence that a reliable sys-tem is in place. As the practice observations continue, interobserver reli-ability should be calculated among and between observers. The coefficients should be calculated in the more rigorous manner as discussed in Chapter 3 to ensure adequate reliability. In our experience, it also is critical that the researcher maintain an open mind and avoid being judgmental with observers. Although the researcher ultimately must make decisions as to what is being measured, how, and by whom, the input from the observers is invaluable. A researcher who adopts an attitude that the observer is always wrong whenever a disagreement in scoring occurs with the researcher is likely in for trouble. The researcher must remember that she or he needs good observers who are committed to performing their task with integrity and confidence. Those attributes are acquired through reinforcement, practice, and honest and open discussions when disagreements do occur. We cannot overemphasize this point, especially to the student-researcher who may be relying on peers to help with a study.

It should be noted that some experts (e.g., Barlow & Hersen, 1984) argue that observers should be naive to the intervention and purpose of the study, should not be involved in calculating interobserver agreement, and should be unaware of when reliability checks are scheduled. In our experience, the researcher herself or himself is frequently involved in data collection (which does have its own limitations in terms of introducing a possible bias), so such precautions often are not possible. However, if the researcher is not actually involved in the data collection, then such precautions may be advisable to strengthen internal validity.

Once interobserver agreement is ensured, the researcher and/or observers may begin collecting data. However, they must still be aware of reactivity and observer drift, which may serve to confound their observational procedures.

Reactivity

Reactivity refers to the individual being observed altering his or her behavior (i.e., target behavior) as a response to being observed. Using our previous example, the individual may immediately improve (or worsen) her performance on sitting in seat if she is aware of or suspects that she is being observed on that target behavior. Reactivity generally diminishes as the number of observations increases. Actual practice observations in the experimental setting can, therefore, reduce the possibility of reactivity when the official data collection begins, although the presence of observers regularly before the introduction of the independent variable may have an unknown and confounding result as well. Reactivity may also be overcome by extending baseline measurements until there is stability but also a reasonable assumption that the performance on the dependent variable truly represents previous levels un-affected by observer presence. The use of videotaping, audiotaping, or two-way mirrors may also help to avoid reactivity, although the presence of cameras, recorders, or large mirrors can also influence the individual. Once reactivity may be ruled out as a major contributor to performance on the dependent variable, the researcher must still continue to guard against observer drift.

Observer Drift

Observer drift refers to a change in interpretation of when the target behavior occurs or not (or at what level, or how intensely, or for how long, etc.) from the original operational definitions. Observer drift occurs generally when a number of observations have been made, particularly if the communication and comparison of scores among raters has not been regularly reviewed and discussed. In our example of sitting in seat, one observer may begin to score occurrences even if the individual has begun to slump over (i.e., not erect in trunk and head) and props herself with her hand with her elbow on the chair's armrest. After all, the observer may think, the individual is paying attention to what is going on and maybe she is a little tired, and her buttocks and back are in proper contact with the seat and both feet are on the floor. So, the observer scores the individual as sitting in her seat. Drift has occurred. If another observer was simultaneously scoring the individual's performance, they may very well disagree on what the actual performance was and therefore threaten interobserver reliability. In commonsense terms, observer drift occurs when one or more observers begin(s) to exert a personal definition or at least personal modification of the definition of the target behavior. As we have already suggested, the best guard against drift is regular communication and perhaps even repeating training exercises throughout the study to ensure all observers remain in agreement about the definition of the target behavior. If during a study interobserver reliability should fall below the 90% level in any observation session, the researcher should be alert to the possibility that drift may be occurring and take appropriate measures to avoid a serious lapse in reliability. If, as mentioned earlier, the observers are naive to the reliability checks and coefficients, then such measures might include additional training, ensuring observers have memorized operational definitions and observation procedures, and finally interviewing observers to ascertain any biases or other potential confounding variables that may influence their scoring (Barlow & Hersen, 1984).

Validity, like reliability, is of critical importance to single subject researchers. As with reliability, single subject research has some unique considerations in terms of validity. We will discuss these considerations as they regard internal and external validity.

Validity

As you may already be aware, there are several types of validity associated with measurement in particular (e.g., face validity, content validity, and predictive validity). These are frequently used when providing evidence that a test (e.g., an intelligence test or test of vocabulary knowledge) measures what it purports to measure. The reader should become familiar with the various types of validity and the concepts determining the validity of measurement procedures. These procedures are used less frequently in single subject research than in group studies, but understanding them is important. Internal and external validity are concepts that apply to both group and single subject research and are of primary concern to us.

Internal Validity

Internal validity refers to the degree to which the researcher has adequately controlled the independent, dependent, and extraneous (or confounding) variables so that changes in the dependent variable are directly attributable to the presence or absence or intensity of the independent variable. In simpler terms, the researcher convincingly demonstrates a functional relationship in that the treatment led to the individual changing his or her behavior. For example, a researcher is attempting to help an individual improve his articulation. The researcher implements a treatment that is intended to accomplish this objective. After several weeks of intervention within an appropriate design, the researcher's measurement of the individual's articulation does in fact verify that the target behavior is substantially improved. Examining the individual's life across those several weeks, there is no reason to suspect that any other factor or variable accounted for the improved articulation. As an example of diminished internal validity, let us examine the same example. In this case, the same substantial change in the target behavior is noted by the researcher. However, the individual reports he has been reading materials that tell how other people overcame their articulation difficulties and he was truly inspired by their examples. He also reports that his mother gave him these materials and that together they have prayed for divine assistance several times a week. The researcher must now acknowledge that the individual's reading, inspiration, and support from his mother may have at least contributed to the observed improvements.

If these inspirational activities had been going on for weeks, months, or even years before the outset of the study, the influence of the activities may be explained as potentially less or nonexistent. If, however, the inspirational activities commenced during the study, the researcher must be honest and acknowledge that the treatment alone may not account for changes in the target behavior (articulation). The control of extraneous or confounding variables is paramount to establishing a functional relationship between the independent and dependent variables.

Extraneous variables refer to virtually anything that may affect the demonstration of the functional relationship between the independent and dependent variables. In other words, the presence of these variables may elicit questions as to whether it was the influence of the independent variable alone that led to changes in the dependent variable (i.e., confound the interpretation and validity of your results and conclusions). Cooper, Heron, and Heward (1987) noted that the strength of an experimental design is evident to the extent that it reduces or eliminates the influence of confounding variables while still allowing the researcher to investigate the research questions. Some of these extraneous variables are commonly recognized among researchers. Two examples noted by Cooper et al. (1987) are attrition and maturation confounds. Interference from the use of multiple interventions and the extent to which the intervention is applied consistently and as planned (treatment integrity and treatment drift; Cooper et al., 1987) are also potential confounders. Measurement effects that were addressed in Chapter 3 may also occur. It is worth noting that the presence of extraneous variables may or may not influence the desired treatment outcomes. In other words, the goal of the study may be achieved (e.g., better accuracy on solving math problems or more fluent speech), but demonstrating that it was the influence of the systematic application of the independent variable (i.e., a functional relationship) may not be achieved. Several typical extraneous or confounding variables are discussed in the following passages.

History is used to refer essentially to the passage of time and both foreseen and unforeseen events that arise. For example, a researcher may begin an experiment in the fall of the year and conclude it in the winter. The change in seasons may have some influence on the individual who is changing his or her behavior. Or, the individual's parents may have decided to get divorced. Or, the individual may have started an after-school job that had an influence on her beliefs about herself so that her actions in the study setting change. Clearly, some events are beyond the control of the researcher. What the researcher must achieve is (a) obtaining as much information as possible that may shed light on changes in the individual's behavior (see Chapter 13 for qualitative measures discussion); (b) seeking to control any foreseen events; and (c) if possible, altering the presentation of the independent variable in such a way that changes in the dependent variable are more clearly linked to the independent variable than the other events.

Maturation is similar to history except that *maturation* refers to the natural development of an individual that occurs over time. In our example concerning accuracy in solving math problems, an individual might mature sufficiently during the length of an experiment so that her accuracy is improving because she is psychologically and cognitively better equipped to learn and excel rather than as a result of the use of positive reinforcement. Maturation is generally controlled by attempting to limit the length of a study so that such influences are minimized. Still, the researcher does not necessarily have control over the length of a study and must be aware if maturation forces are at work. The researcher can account for these influences by obtaining as much information as possible about the individual's behavior not only in the experimental setting but also in other settings. For example, if the individual began to excel in all areas of school, in her communication skill development, in her behavior at home, etc., there may be some reason to believe that positive reinforcement for improved math accuracy would hardly account for such universal changes. However, if the area of math accuracy improves while other areas of endeavor remain relatively unchanged, the researcher may be on firmer ground for ruling out the influence of maturation.

Attrition, as the term implies, is the loss of subjects during the course of a study. In experimental designs with large numbers of subjects, such events are not uncommon and, unless dramatic, tend to have little influence on the overall outcomes. In single subject research, the loss of an individual participant can be devastating. Later, we discuss the ethics of single subject research and, as a part of that discussion, we stress the need for informed consent. As part of the consent process, the researcher should stress the need for the individual (and his or her significant others) to commit to the behavior change. This is one reason why the social and ecological validities of desired changes are so critical. People must see clearly the worthiness of the outcomes of the study to be committed to seeing the study concluded. At times, attrition is unavoidable. We have had the unfortunate and sad instance of a participant dying during a study, another who required surgery and had to be hospitalized, and another whose family moved out of the state. Attrition can best be controlled by knowing with whom you are working and whether or not any conditions exist that may suggest the likelihood of such an event. We stress, however, that the presence of any of these extraneous variables does not constitute a valid reason to deny treatment to a person in need. Rather, they are controlled as best as possible and sometimes merely explained as well as possible following the intervention.

Multiple treatment interference is a very real threat in many single subject studies. Interference might occur when more than one independent variable (e.g., positive reinforcement followed by negative reinforcement) is used. For example, the negative reinforcement might be more effective when it is preceded by positive reinforcement than if it is the only treatment used. Also, it could be that positive reinforcement did have an effect (albeit not a powerful one) that is compounded when negative reinforcement is implemented. In other words, negative reinforcement appears to have an effect that could be partially attributable to positive reinforcement. Other times, a package treatment (or independent variable) is used (e.g., positive reinforcement plus verbal prompting plus response interruption). Because more than one intervention is being used, it may be difficult if not impossible for the researcher to accurately determine which of the components of the independent variable or variables actually accounted for changes in the dependent variable (Cooper et al., 1987). Cooper et al. also noted that researchers must ensure that the independent variable is carried out consistently by all involved and exactly as planned. Otherwise, the integrity of the treatment program may be jeopardized or treatment drift may occur. **Treatment drift** refers to individuals involved in administering the independent variable producing personal modifications (consciously or unconsciously) that may influence the impact of the independent variable on the dependent variable (Cooper et al., 1987). The same precautions used to control observer drift should be used to control any potential treatment drift.

Other extraneous variables are myriad and virtually infinite in number. They may be intrinsic to the individual or present in the setting. The researcher must be extremely careful that these inevitable influences have minimal impact on the study. More importantly, the researcher must be rigorous in her or his self-examination to ensure that she or he is not in some way influencing the outcome of the study in an undue way. Researchers may find themselves wanting so badly for an outcome to be achieved that she or he may be tempted at some level to arrange matters in such a way that those outcomes are more likely to occur. This could be done consciously (which would be very unethical) but is more likely to occur because the researcher did not carefully guard against such a possibility. For example, in our math accuracy example, we might select for our experimental setting one that we know is very well liked by the student and with a teacher who is so effective that the outcome is virtually guaranteed. Such arrangements are sometimes referred to as systematic bias. That is, the researcher has introduced some element to the experimental conditions that is likely to influence changes in the dependent variable regardless of the manipulation of the independent variable. Perhaps the best manner in which to guard against such bias is to apply the old adage "Two heads are better than one." The more people involved or at least reviewing the procedures used in the study, the less likely that such influences will go unnoticed before the implementation of the study. Although the impetus to improve individuals' lives through desired changes in behavior is admirable, the researcher must be careful that this desire does not unduly influence her or his actions.

External Validity

External validity refers to the degree to which the researcher may have confidence that she or he or other researchers will obtain the same or similar results if they use the same or very similar experimental procedures with other individuals, with other target behaviors, or in other settings. In simpler terms, the researcher must convince the reader that the treatment used will likely be effective if used by the reader under similar circumstances to those described by the researcher. When researchers conduct studies using the same experimental procedures as those in another study, we refer to this as replication. The more an experimental effect is replicated by the same or other researchers, the greater the external validity. However, as Johnston and Pennypacker (1980) noted, the term replication may be interpreted to mean the replication of the procedures rather than specifically replicating effects. That is, one cannot precisely replicate results, but one might obtain similar results from precisely replicating experimental procedures.

Cooper et al. (1987) and Sidman (1960) described two types of replication in establishing external validity, **direct and systematic replication**. In **direct replication** the researcher attempts to duplicate the procedures as precisely as possible. **Intrasubject replication** occurs when the same subject is used in the subsequent study. **Intersubject replication** studies involve maintaining every aspect of an earlier study but with different although similar subjects. Intersubject replication appears most frequently in the research literature (Cooper et al., 1987). For example, five different experiments may be conducted using the same procedures (and same independent and dependent variables) in the same setting with five different subjects. Some designs, such as multiple baseline across subjects, include intersubject replication as a typical aspect of a study.

Systematic replication involves varying the conditions from an earlier study but still obtaining similar results. For example, a researcher may use the same experimental procedures as those from an earlier study, but apply them in a different setting, or with subjects whose characteristics vary in some significant manner from the earlier study (e.g., applying the procedures with an individual with a different cultural and socioeconomic background from the subject in the earlier study yet both exhibit behavior disorders). Target behaviors, administration of the experimental procedures, or virtually any aspect of a study may be varied (Cooper et al., 1987). If such variations are used, and similar results are obtained, then the generality of the procedures (external validity) is enhanced. If, however, different results are obtained, one may be unable to discern which variation may have caused different results. For example, if the subject of a different cultural and socioeconomic background participated in a study involving the reduction of aggressive behaviors, but very different results were obtained, it may be difficult to determine exactly which variations may have influenced the outcomes. Cooper et al. noted that systematic replications may occur as researchers conduct a series of studies, or may be conducted by different researchers. These same authors stressed that, while the field of applied behavior analysis has moved increasingly toward studies involving socially significant behavior changes, it is still equally important to analyze procedures and results to make the best possible determination concerning which variables affect those changes. Although similar results may be obtained, knowing why those results were obtained is critical to expanding the knowledge base.

Over time, researchers have focused on other aspects of validity that may be discussed in texts concerned with group research procedures. Frequently, the educational significance of obtained results is considered. **Educational significance** refers to the concern that, although statistically significant results may be achieved, the results should merit conclusions that the interventions used also translated into real world significance. The question is asked, "Did the interventions result in outcomes that are meaningful to practitioners and to the lives of the participants in the study?" In single subject research, this question is equally important. It is also related to the ethical treatment of individual participants. Ethical treatment is critical to obtain informed consent of participants and/or those responsible for their well-being and to ensure research is conducted in a humane manner that results in educational significance. In single subject research, we may equate educational significance with the empirical and social validity of the study, which are closely related to the ethical treatment of human subjects.

ETHICS

Single subject studies may incorporate elements of qualitative and quantitative procedures. As in much qualitative research, single subject

research emphasizes change within the individual or individuals participating and the value placed on those changes by significant others.
Therefore, the need to obtain data that are not numerical is common in
single subject research. Interviews and observations with family members, teachers, and the subjects themselves may be used. The compilation and presentation of data from multiple sources to verify changes
and the social validity of those changes are found in single subject studies. As in much quantitative research, there is a focus on a target behavior or dependent variable by which changes in individuals can be objectively verified. Like quantitative group designs, single subject designs
may combine the performance of individuals on some measure to determine the effectiveness of interventions across a sample of individuals.

In short, single subject designs are versatile and flexible, allow for
the use of a variety of data collection and presentation techniques, may
involve an individual or a number of persons, focus on socially valid
changes, incorporate a wide variety of interventions and outcome measures, are applicable in educational and clinical settings, have been used
with people across all ages and with many types of strengths and challenges, and provide for both internal and external validity. Single subject designs also are relatively easy to understand.

Because single subject designs may incorporate robust and powerful methods for influencing the behavior of individuals, ethical concerns
are extremely important. Walker and Shea (1991) posed the following
questions for consideration:

- Who shall decide who will manage behavior?
- Who shall decide whose behavior is to be changed?
- Who will guarantee that the behavior manager behaves
  ethically?
- What type of interventions will be used?
- Who will determine if these interventions are ethical?
- What are the outcomes sought?

Walker and Shea also noted that these considerations are especially
critical when applied to children. They modified the above questions
with some additions to consider specifically working with children.
These include

- What is a child?
- Is a child free to make choices?
- Should a child be allowed to make choices concerning inter-
  ventions and treatments?

- Does a child behave in a manner that is observable and predictable in accordance with principles of applied behavior analysis?
- Can a child's behavior be changed by external forces?
- Can an educator modify a child's behavior?
- Can another child or parent modify a child's behavior?
- Who shall determine which and whose behavior is to be modified?
- Which interventions are to be applied in school or in other settings?
- Who will approve the use of these interventions and monitor their ethical use?
- What are the outcomes sought?

These questions pose both philosophical and ethical issues to be addressed by each single subject researcher. Walker and Shea suggested the following guidelines that they found in the research literature (cited in Walker & Shea, 1991):

- Explore alternative interventions before selecting aversives (Schloss & Smith, 1987).
- Consider potential side effects and injury that may occur as a consequence of any intervention (Sabatino, 1983).
- Determine whether the individual understands the treatment program (Hewett, 1978).
- Anyone involved in applying an intervention should be trained and comfortable with the procedures (Morris & Brown, 1983; Rose, 1989).
- Empirical evidence should be available that indicates the intervention is effective (Morris & Brown, 1983).
- Any formal plans (e.g., Individualized Education Program, Individualized Family Services Plan, Individual Written Rehabilitation Plan) should be consistent with the planned treatment and should be agreed to by the principals involved in those plans (Morris & Brown, 1983; Singer & Irvin, 1987).
- The planned intervention should be carefully monitored, its results should be documented, and it should be regularly evaluated (Morris & Brown, 1983).
- Informed consent should be obtained and include information about the nature of the program, benefits, risks, expected outcomes, and possible alternatives to the planned treatment (Axelrod, 1983; Kazdin, 1980; Morris & Brown, 1983; Rose, 1989; Singer & Irvin, 1987).

- The principle of normalization should be applied (Allen, 1969; Nirje, 1967). This principle demands that individuals with disabilities be given opportunities and treatments that are as close to normal as possible.
- The procedure used should be fair and appropriate to the degree of concern regarding the behavior targeted for change (Allen, 1969; Sabatino, 1983). In other words, are due process safeguards in place and will the outcomes result in an improved life for the individual whose behavior is changing (Walker & Shea, 1991)?
- The dignity and fundamental human worth of the individual should be protected (Allen, 1969). Do the proposed procedures embody respect for the individual as a human being (Walker & Shea, 1991)?
- Committee review of all procedures should occur (Rose, 1989; Singer & Irvin, 1987). Human rights committees and institutional review boards for studies involving human subjects are commonly found in school, residential, community agency, and higher education settings and may well be required by law. These committees may monitor the necessity, quality, and social validity of the procedures used. Peer review of procedures is also recommended (Axelrod, 1983).
- Finally, the principle of the least restrictive environment should be applied (Singer & Irvin, 1987). This principle may be viewed as applying the procedures in the least restrictive manner and environment, and such that outcomes of the research project increase the likelihood that the individual will remain in the least restrictive environment or will move to a less restrictive one.

When each of these points is addressed, the researcher or practitioner is establishing what some refer to as the empirical and social validity of the proposed study (Evans & Meyer, 1985). **Social validity** refers to the degree to which other people think that the targeted changes in behavior are important and that the methods used to encourage behavior change are acceptable. **Empirical validity** refers to the measurements that actually demonstrate that the proposed behavioral changes will indeed positively affect the individual's life (Evans & Meyer, 1985). Evans and Meyer noted that the charting of individual behavioral responses leaves much to be desired. Such measures do not answer whether clinically or educationally significant changes have occurred; if good or bad side effects have occurred; or whether the interventions used were appropriate, humane, and carried out in accordance with philosophical and legal assumptions regarding the rights of individuals (Evans & Meyer, 1985).

There are many issues in the use of applied behavior analysis that are discussed at greater length and detail in the research literature or in texts devoted to interventions using applied behavior analysis techniques. Although we discussed methods for changing target behaviors in Chapter 2, the reader is strongly advised to obtain any and all information relevant to the use of any particular procedure. Texts and articles related to group designs may include information (e.g., obtaining and selecting subjects when whole groups are to be treated as a single case) that may prove useful. Also, many organizations (e.g., the American Association on Mental Retardation) publish materials related to informed consent and the ethical treatment of individuals with disabilities. The reader is encouraged to avail herself or himself of these materials. This chapter should provide an overview of those issues relevant to single subject research.

Summary Checklist

Prediction—The idea that if the independent variable has no effect on the dependent variable, the data path will remain unchanged across phases.

Verification—The confirmation that the dependent variable is changing in a predictable fashion as the independent variable is systematically applied.

Replication—The repeating of the predictions and verifications within the same study.

Reliability—In single subject research, we are concerned primarily with interobserver reliability; the researcher must ensure observational procedures and results are reliable.

Reactivity—An individual altering his or her behavior as a result of being observed.

Observer drift—A change in interpretation of the agreed upon operational definition of the target behavior; this is a threat to reliability.

Internal validity—The degree to which the researcher has adequately controlled the independent, dependent, and extraneous variables so that there is confirmation of a functional relationship.

History—The passage of time and both foreseen and unforeseen events; this is a threat to internal validity.

Maturation—The natural development of the individual over time; this is a threat to internal validity.

Attrition—The loss of a subject during the course of a study; this is a threat to internal and external validity.

Interference from multiple treatments—Effects from previously used interventions (e.g., in an A-B-C design where interference from B might influence the outcomes in the C phase) or when package interventions are used (e.g., BC phase when it is difficult to determine whether B or C has the greater influence or if only the combination has the effect).

External validity—The degree to which the researcher (or consumer of the research) may have confidence that similar results will be obtained if the experimental procedures are used with other individuals, in other settings, with other behaviors, and so on.

Direct replication—Occurs when a researcher duplicates as precisely as possible the procedures used in a previous study and similar results are obtained.

Systematic replication—Occurs when experimental conditions are varied but similar results are obtained.

Ethics—There are many considerations in the use of applied behavior analysis and single subject research; empirical and social validity are equally important.

References

Axelrod, S. (1983). *Behavior modification for the classroom teacher.* New York: McGraw-Hill.

Allen, R. C. (1969). *Legal rights of the disabled and disadvantaged* (GPO 1969-0-360–797). Washington, DC: U.S. Government Printing Office.

Barlow, D. H., & Hersen, M. (1984). *Single case experimental designs: Strategies for studying behavior change* (2nd ed.). New York: Pergamon Press.

Cooper, J. O., Heron, T. E., & Heward, W. L. (1987). *Applied behavior analysis.* Columbus, OH: Merrill.

Evans, I. M., & Meyer, L. H. (1985). *An educative approach to behavior problems: A practical decision model for interventions with severely handicapped learners.* Baltimore: Brookes.

Hewett, F. M. (1978). Punishment and educational programs for behaviorally disordered and emotionally disturbed children and youth: A personal perspective. In F. Wood & K. Lakin (Eds.), *Punishment and aversive stimulation in special education* (pp. 101-117). Minneapolis: University of Minnesota.

Johnston, J. M., & Pennypacker, H. S. (1980). *Strategies and tactics for human behavioral research.* Hillsdale, NJ: Erlbaum.

Kazdin, A. E. (1980). *Behavior modification in applied settings* (2nd ed.). Homewood, IL: Dorsey Press.

Morris, R. J., & Brown, D. K. (1983). Legal and ethical issues in behavior modification with retarded persons. In J. Matson & F. Andrasik (Eds.), *Treatment issues and innovations in mental retardation*. New York: Plenum.

Nirje, B. (1967). The normalization principle and its human management implications. In R. Kugel & W. l. Wolfensberger (Eds.), *Changing patterns in residential services for the mentally retarded*. Washington, DC: President's Committee on Mental Retardation.

Rose, T. L. (1989). Corporal punishment with mildly handicapped students: Five years later. *Remedial and Special Education, 10*, 43–52.

Sabatino, A. C. (1983). Discipline: A national issue. In A. C. Sabatino & L. Mann (Eds.), *Discipline and behavior management* (pp.1–27). Rockville, MD: Aspen.

Schloss, P. J., & Smith, M. A. (1987). Guidelines for ethical use of manual restraint in public school settings for behaviorally disordered students. *Behavioral Disorders, 12*, 207–213.

Sidman, M. (1960). *Tactics of scientific research*. New York: Basic Books.

Singer, G. S., & Irvin, L. K. (1987). Human rights review of intrusive behavioral treatments for students with severe handicaps. *Exceptional Children, 57*, 298–313.

Tawney, J. W., & Gast, D. L. (1984). *Single subject research in special education*. Columbus, OH: Merrill.

Walker, J. E., & Shea, T. M. (1991). *Behavior management: A practical approach for educators*. Englewood Cliffs, NJ: Prentice-Hall.

PART 2

Overview and Application of Single Subject Designs

CHAPTER 5

Overview of Withdrawal Designs

The withdrawal design is widely recognized across disciplines as a basic experimental procedure for demonstrating treatment effects. For example, the withdrawal design has been used in several areas of special education, including those of communication disorders, deaf education, and visual impairment (Yaden, 1995). **Withdrawal** refers to the withdrawal of treatment during one or more phases of a study to demonstrate the effects that it has on the target behavior. This design also has been referred to as the equivalent time samples design (Campbell & Stanley, 1963), the interrupted time series with multiple replications design (Cook & Campbell, 1979), and the within series elements design (Barlow, Hayes, & Nelson, 1984). Its more common name is the reversal design, and it was initially described by Baer, Wolf, and Risley (1968). The term **withdrawal** is preferred, however, because it describes the mechanics of the design (withdrawal of intervention) rather than the intended outcomes of the design (reversing the direction of the target behavior). Nonetheless, the term **reversal design** is used extensively in the professional literature. The typical withdrawal design is usually designated by the letters A-B-A-B where A represents baseline and B represents intervention. There are many adaptations to this design that will be described later.

The withdrawal design is an important design because it allows the investigator to easily demonstrate cause-effect relationships between behavior and intervention (Tawney & Gast, 1984). Because of the nature of the withdrawal design, the effects of history and maturation are ruled out by demonstrating that the behavior change occurs only with the introduction or withdrawal of treatment. As Schloss and Smith (1998) stated, "the more times this effect is replicated, the less likely that maturation and history are causing the effects" (pp. 260–261).

Before discussing the mechanics of the withdrawal design, it is necessary to present information on the most basic single subject design, the A-B design.

THE A-B DESIGN

As noted, the A-B design is the most basic of the single subject designs. In fact, all other single subject designs can be viewed essentially as variations of the A-B design (also referred to as a teaching design; Alberto & Troutman, 1999). In the A-B design, the researcher collects baseline data (A) and then implements a treatment (B) to determine its effect on the target behavior. Unfortunately, it is also the weakest of the single subject designs because the functional relationship between the dependent and independent variables is not firmly established. Although changes in the target behavior might be attributed to the treatment, there are many other factors (e.g., maturation, practice effects) that could also play a role. To better establish the functional relationship between the target behavior and the treatment, a researcher might withdraw the intervention to see if the behavior changes toward or returns to the baseline level (A-B-A). Still better, the researcher might also reintroduce the treatment to determine if the pattern of behavior will again change (A-B-A-B). In this chapter, we will refer to the A-B-A-B design as the typical withdrawal design. Specifically, the A-B-A-B design includes the following steps: (a) baseline data are collected on a target behavior before an intervention is introduced (A1); (b) the intervention is introduced for a specific period of time and data are collected on the same target behavior (B1); (c) the intervention is withdrawn for a short period of time to determine if the target behavior reverses back to the baseline level (A2); and (d) the intervention is reintroduced to see if it once again affects the target behavior (B2). Figure 5–1 shows data that demonstrate the functional relation-

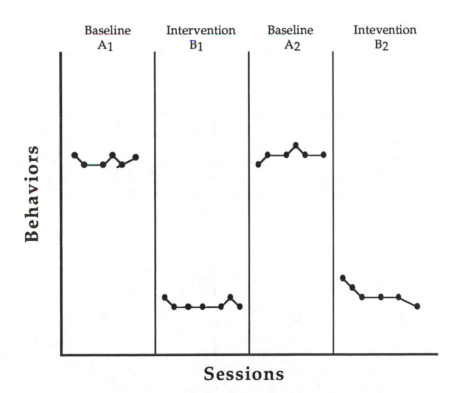

Figure 5–1. Data that indicate a functional relationship.

ship of the target behavior and the intervention. Note that the behavior increased during the presentation of the intervention and decreased during its withdrawal. Figure 5–2, on the other hand, shows data that do not demonstrate a functional relationship. In this case, the withdrawal of the intervention (A2) did not increase the target behavior.

MECHANICS OF THE WITHDRAWAL DESIGNS

In the most basic type of withdrawal design, experimental control is increased when the intervention is subsequently withdrawn so that baseline conditions are again in effect resulting in an A-B-A design. The goal is to show that there is a functional relationship between the target behavior and the intervention. In other words, the behavior will change as a function of the presence or absence of the intervention. Although it shows more experimental control than the A-B design, the A-B-A design is still not recommended in educational or clinical settings because the

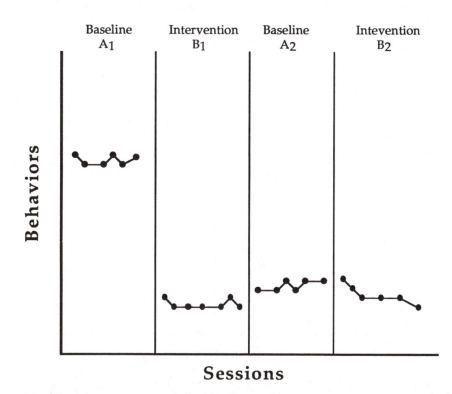

Figure 5–2. Data that do not indicate a functional relationship.

experiment concludes with the subject in a nontreatment phase. Further, if the intervention is shown to be successful (i.e., reverses to baseline levels), the subject will be left at the pretreatment level. Nonetheless, the use of A-B-A designs is reported in the professional literature and should be addressed in a discussion of withdrawal designs.

The A-B-A Design

In the first step in an A-B-A design, the investigator must precisely define both the target behavior to be altered and the treatment to be implemented. The next step is to collect baseline data (A) for at least 5 consecutive days (Alberto & Troutman, 1999) or until a stable baseline trend is established. In other words, the data should be either stable or going in an undesired direction (Schloss & Smith, 1998). The third step is to introduce the treatment (B) or intervention and collect continuous data either until a specific criterion has been met (e.g., reduction of out-of-seat behavior to 25% or less) or until a stable mode of responding in the desired direction is recorded. The last step is to withdraw the treatment or return to the baseline phase (A). The logic of this design is that if the target behavior improves in the desired direction during the intervention phase and changes toward baseline levels once the treatment is withdrawn, then the investigator can conclude that the treatment was indeed responsible for the improvement of the target behavior.

The following is a hypothetical example of an A-B-A design.

Johnny, a 7-year-old student with a mild behavioral disorder, has a history of not staying in his seat during instruction time. His special education teacher wanted to improve his in-seat behavior. She decided to use a reinforcer (play time) in her classroom to increase Johnny's target behavior during instruction time. After carefully defining both the target behavior (in-seat behavior) and the intervention (play time) she began to collect data. During the baseline phase (A) Johnny got out of his seat frequently and wandered around the classroom. A stable baseline trend was established after 5 consecutive days; the teacher then introduced the treatment (B). For every 5 min Johnny stayed in his seat during his 50 minute instruction time, he would earn 1 min play time for a total of a possible 10 min. During this intervention phase she collected data for 10 days. During this time, for the most part, Johnny stayed in his seat to earn his play time. During the 3rd week, for 5 days, she did not give Johnny the opportunity to earn time to play, thus there was a return to the baseline condition (A). During this period, Johnny again got out of his seat and wandered around the classroom. These data are graphically presented in Figure 5–3.

This design allows the teacher to conclude that the intervention was indeed responsible for the change in Johnny's in-seat behavior. However, this design ends in a baseline phase where he was out of his seat during the instruction time. To avoid this negative situation, an A-B-A-B design, a more clinically appropriate design that reintroduces the treatment, should be used.

The A-B-A-B Design

As explained previously, the investigator must precisely define a target behavior and the intervention to be used before collecting data. The

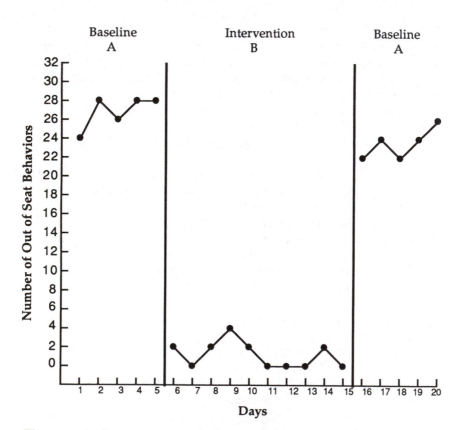

Figure 5–3. Example of data from an A-B-A design.

common four-phase A-B-A-B withdrawal design involves a no-inter-vention baseline (A1) and an intervention phase (B1), with each phase (A2 and B2) being repeated. Introducing the intervention twice to com-pare the target behavior with two baseline phases is done to strengthen or validate the functional relationship between the target behavior and treatment.

Consider the following example.

Carla, a 6-year-old student with autism, has a moderate vocab-ulary but has limited verbal skills. She frequently uses body lan-guage or points to objects rather than using oral language when interacting with adults. The speech and language clinician (SLC) wanted to increase Carla's verbalizations for communication purposes. She decided to use verbal praise combined with a raisin as positive reinforcers for Carla's verbalizations. During the first baseline (A1), the SLC collected data on the total num-ber of verbalizations in a 30-min free time period. During the first intervention phase (B1), the SLC provided the reinforcers after each verbalization and collected data. During the second base-line (A2) phase, the reinforcers were withdrawn. As can be seen in Figure 5–4, the pattern of the second baseline (A2) data closely resembles the pattern of Carla's first baseline (A1) data. The SLC was able to assume that there was a functional rela-tionship between the use of the reinforcers and Carla's increased verbal responses. However, to further establish the functional relationship and leave Carla in a more clinically appropriate situation, the SLC reintroduced her treatment (B2) and collected data. Figure 5–4 shows that Carla's verbal responses increased to a level consistent with the first interven-tion phase (B1).

PREDICTION, VERIFICATION, AND REPLICATION

The issues of prediction, verification, and replication can be easily de-scribed for the typical withdrawal, or A-B-A-B, design. After stable base-line (A1) data are collected, one would **predict** that the same pattern would remain under the same conditions (A2). However, if the treat-ment (B1) has an effect, one would predict that a different pattern would emerge. **Verification** occurs first when the change from baseline to in-tervention phase results in a change in responding. Then, again, it oc-curs when return to the baseline condition (A2) results in a pattern sim-ilar to the original baseline condition (A1). Finally, **replication** occurs

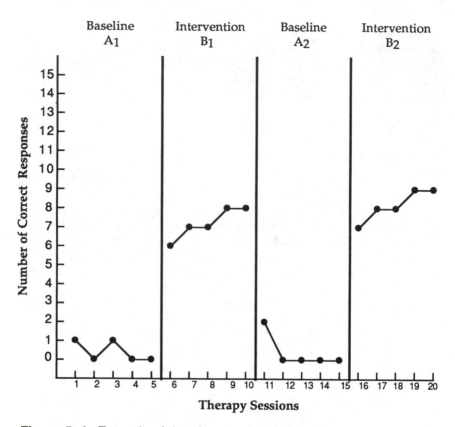

Figure 5–4. Example of data from an A-B-A-B design.

when the second treatment phase (B2) results in a similar response pattern as the previous treatment phase (B1). These concepts can be better understood by referring back to Figure 5–1. As will be discussed later in this chapter, some withdrawal designs might include the reintroduction and withdrawal of the intervention more than once. This further strengthens the evidence of prediction, verification, and replication.

ADVANTAGES OF THE WITHDRAWAL DESIGN

As noted earlier, the withdrawal design is one of the easiest single subject designs to implement. It can be used when the withdrawal of a particular treatment will reverse the target behavior to baseline, or preintervention, levels. This means that the target behavior itself must be reversible. Unfortunately, this is often neither possible nor desirable. For example, if a target behavior is learned (e.g., reading), it is not likely or desirable that it would be unlearned when the intervention is withdrawn. There are also times when the target behavior might be maintained after the treatment is withdrawn because of factors in the natural environment. For example, a student is shown to be verbally abusive to his peers (A1) and treatment is introduced that reduces his verbal abuse (B1). After the treatment is withdrawn (A2), however, the behavior remains at a reduced level. It is possible that the reduction of verbal abuse was maintained because it resulted in the student receiving positive reinforcement from, and engaging in positive interactions with, his peers. In addition to the target behavior being reversible, the nature of the treatment must also be reversible. For example, if a student was taught a mnemonic strategy to increase memory skills, then it is unlikely that removal of the treatment will decrease the memory skills. In this situation, the treatment has been learned or internalized, thus affecting the target behavior.

If the criteria for reversibility of the behavior and treatment can be met, the withdrawal design is a powerful design that documents the functional relationship between the independent and dependent variables. As Cooper, Heron, and Heward (1987) noted, "when an investigator can and does reliably turn the target behavior on and off by presenting and withdrawing a specified variable, a clear and convincing demonstration of experimental control is made" (p. 177). This is particularly true when the treatment is presented and withdrawn a number of times in the same study. This is referred to as the repeated withdrawal design and is discussed later in this chapter. The alteration of baseline and treatment conditions also provides direct evidence of prediction, verification, and replication of treatment effects. Finally, the possibility that confounding variables are responsible for treatment effects is minimized given the nature of the design (Alberto & Troutman, 1999).

In summary, the withdrawal design can be used in the following situations:

- When a clear functional relationship between the independent and dependent variables needs to be demonstrated;

- When the nature of the target behavior is such that it can be reversed when the treatment is withdrawn;

- When the nature of the treatment is such that its effects are not present on the target behavior after it is withdrawn;

- When withdrawal of treatment does not compromise ethics.

DISADVANTAGES OF THE WITHDRAWAL DESIGN

Even though the withdrawal design is both powerful and easy to implement, it has several disadvantages. As discussed, there are practical and ethical issues related to the required reversibility of the target behavior in order to demonstrate its functional relationship with the independent variable. In a very real sense, the goal of the withdrawal design is antithetical to educational or clinical goals. It is certainly desirable once a behavior has changed in a more positive direction that it continue in that direction or stay at that level. In fact, maintenance of treatment effects is an important goal in and of itself. One compromise that has been suggested is that treatment can be reintroduced after the behavior returns to only one third to two thirds of its baseline level (Sulzer-Azaroff & Mayer, 1977). In this way, the subject does not have to spend as much time in a nontreatment phase. Conversely, if this procedure is used, evidence of the functional relationship between the behavior and treatment is weakened.

Another disadvantage, reported by Yaden (1995), has to do with what is called **resentful demoralization** (Cook & Campbell, 1979). Although it refers to the attitudes of individuals who are subjects in control groups, this term could be extended to those involved in withdrawal designs as well. Essentially, it means that individuals' behaviors during subsequent baseline conditions might be negatively affected by resentment over having the treatment withdrawn. In addition, many teachers and clinicians are hesitant to withdraw effective intervention for the sake of experimental control. Another, and perhaps the greatest, concern is of an ethical nature when using the withdrawal design with dangerous behaviors, such as physical violence or self-abuse. Particularly for behaviors such as these, removal of a successful treatment would be highly questionable.

In summary, the major disadvantages of the withdrawal design have to do with the following situations:

- When the target behavior is not reversible;

- When the treatment effects will continue after the treatment is withdrawn;

- When it is not educationally or clinically desirable for the behavior to return to baseline levels;

- When the target behavior is such that withdrawal of effective treatment would be unethical (e.g., dangerous behavior).

ADAPTATIONS OF THE
TYPICAL WITHDRAWAL DESIGN

Because of the basic, almost simplistic, nature of the withdrawal design, there are many adaptations that are frequently used and reported in the professional literature. Some of these allow the introduction of more than one treatment, the use of combinations of treatments, the repeated introduction and withdrawal of various treatments, or the elimination of the initial baseline data phase.

The B-A-B Design

There are times when the collection of initial baseline data is either impossible or inappropriate. As noted previously, if an investigator is working with an individual whose behavior results in physical harm or danger to self or others, then an A-B-A or A-B-A-B design should not be used due to ethical reasons. In this situation the B-A-B design can be used to determine the effectiveness of an intervention on the target behavior. In this design, the experiment begins with the application of the independent variable (B phase). Once this intervention phase produces stable responding at an acceptable (usually predetermined) level, the treatment is withdrawn. If the behavior reverts or moves toward the preintervention level in the absence of the treatment (A phase), the intervention is reintroduced to demonstrate the functional relationship between the behavior and the intervention.

Consider the following example.

Mark is a 15-year-old boy with severe mental retardation. His major behavior problem is biting others when he comes into contact with adults. His special education teacher was very concerned about everyone's safety and wanted to eliminate his biting behavior. After a series of meetings with concerned individuals, she sought assistance from a behavior therapist to determine a method to control his dangerous behavior. After learning about Mark's condition, the therapist began his experiment with the application of a piece of rock candy paired with praise as a reinforcer. Using differential reinforcement of other behavior (DRO), the therapist decided that, for every 5-min interval in which Mark did not attempt to bite others during his 30 min of therapy time, he would earn one reinforcer, for a possible total of six. This intervention phase (B) lasted for 15 sessions. During this period, for most of the time, Mark earned his reinforcer by not attempting to bite adults. During the withdrawal phase, for 3 sessions the therapist did not give Mark the opportunity to earn his reinforcer. During this time, Mark's biting behavior moved toward the pretreatment level. The therapist then reintroduced the treatment (B) and noticed that Mark's biting behavior decreased to the level observed during the first treatment phase (see Figure 5–5).

As stated earlier, the B-A-B design is preferable over the A-B-A design because the study ends with the intervention condition in effect. However, to evaluate the treatment effectiveness, the "B-A-B design is the weaker of the two because it does not enable assessment of the effects of the independent variable on the preintervention, or natural, rate of occurrence of the target behavior" (Cooper et al., 1987, p. 175). Again,

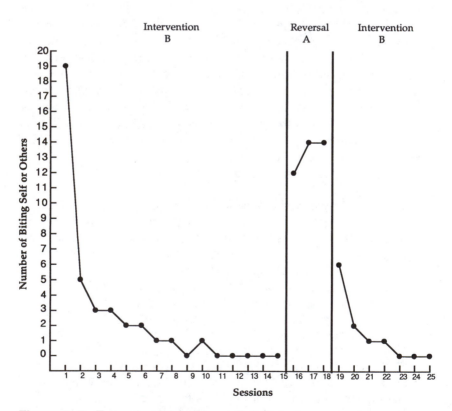

Figure 5–5. Example of data from a B-A-B design.

that is why the A-B-A-B design demonstrates the most experimental control of the three designs.

The A-B-A-B-A-B Design (Repeated Withdrawals)

In this design, the treatment variable is introduced and withdrawn repeatedly. For example, the A-B-A-B design previously described could be extended to include additional withdrawals and presentations of the same treatment. These repeated withdrawals increase our confidence in the functional relationship between the treatment and the target behavior. Theoretically, the more times the treatment is applied and withdrawn (with the predicted pattern demonstrated), the more there is evidence of experimental control. Again, the issue of ethics and treatment efficacy must be considered. For example, a researcher must decide when a clear functional relationship has been established so that it is no longer necessary to continue the withdrawal phases. In other words, if experimental control is demonstrated, is it ethical to continue the withdrawal condition?

A-B-C Design (Changing Conditions)

In the A-B-C design, the researcher can evaluate the effectiveness of more than one treatment. Thus, A would represent baseline, B would indicate Treatment 1, and C would indicate Treatment 2. This design is frequently used educationally, when a treatment is introduced and not found to be effective, so that another is tried. Any number of treatment conditions could be introduced (A-B-C-D or A-B-C-D-E) with the goal to end the design in an effective treatment condition. Alberto and Troutman (1995) made the following comments about the changing conditions design:

1. It reflects reality because teachers often keep trying different interventions until one works.
2. Change in behavior should be seen within five sessions of any given intervention.
3. As with an A-B design, a functional relationship between the dependent and independent variables cannot be made.
4. Behavior change may be the result of a cumulative effect of the treatments rather than the effect of any one treatment.

To address the most obvious limitation of the changing condition design (lack of experimental control), Alberto and Troutman recommend that baseline conditions should be reinstated before the introduction of a new treatment. This is sometimes described as the multiple treatment design (Cooper et al., 1987).

The A-B-A-C Design (Multiple Treatments)

One of the major advantages of withdrawal designs, in general, is their flexibility. At times, due to several reasons, the investigator may choose to or have to change the nature of the treatment, even after the experiment has started. This change can be accomplished through the use of the A-B-A-C design without validity being compromised (Yaden, 1995). In this design, the C phase may be an alteration to the original treatment introduced in the B phase or it may represent a new treatment altogether. In this design the investigator collects baseline data (A), introduces the intervention variable (B), and then withdraws it as in an A-B-A design. Next the investigator introduces a second intervention (or significant alteration of the first). The obvious advantage of this design over the A-B-C is that the functional relationship can be better established because of the return to the baseline.

There are an endless number of adaptations of this design. For example, the experimenter could evaluate the effects of three interventions (A-B-A-C-A-D) or even more. It is also possible that the experimenter might combine treatments (A-B-A-C-A-BC-A-BC). For example, the B phase might be the use of modeling, the C phase the use of prompts, and the BC phase a combination of the two. Cooper et al. (1987) noted several considerations when using a multiple treatment design:

1. Make sure that only one variable at a time is changed from one phase to the next.
2. Be aware of the limitations of the functional relationships established. For example, in an A-B-A-B-C design (where A = baseline, B = Treatment 1, C = Treatment 2), the relationship of B to A can be established, but *not* the relationship of C to A. In this example, sequencing effects (B-C) might mask the true relationship of C to the baseline condition (A). This is similar to the problems in an A-B-C design.
3. Note that the time necessary to complete many experiments using a multiple treatment design with many phases can result in threats to internal validity such as maturation.
4. Understand that a treatment that is offered only in combination with another cannot be adequately evaluated for its effectiveness alone. Consider the previous example where the B phase was modeling and

C was the use of prompts. An A-B-A-BC-A-BC design would not allow the experimenter to evaluate the effectiveness of the use of prompts alone.

Summary Checklist

Basic goal—Demonstration of a functional relationship between the target behavior and intervention by withdrawing (and reintroducing) the treatment.

A-B design—Sometimes called the teaching design; baseline (A) data are collected and a treatment (B) is introduced; very little experimental control.

A-B-A design—There is a return to baseline condition after the treatment phase; better demonstrates functional relationship between behavior and treatment; subject is left in baseline condition.

A-B-A-B design—Typical withdrawal design adds a second treatment phase; more evidence of a functional relationship is provided; subject is left in the treatment phase.

Prediction—After baseline data are stable, the prediction would be that the same or a similar pattern would emerge in other baseline conditions; conversely, a different pattern should emerge during treatment phases.

Verification—This occurs when treatment results in a change in the target behavior and the return to baseline condition results in a similar pattern as the previous baseline condition.

Replication—This occurs when the return to the treatment phase results in a similar pattern as the previous treatment phase.

Advantages of withdrawal design—Easy to implement; a powerful design to demonstrate the functional relationship between target behavior and the treatment; has many possible variations.

Disadvantages of withdrawal design—Often times the target behavior is not reversible; returning to baseline condition is not clinically or educationally desirable; often times the treatment effects remain after it has been withdrawn.

Adaptations

B-A-B—Used when collection of initial baseline data is either impossible or inappropriate; subject is left in treatment condition.

Repeated withdrawals—Involves the repeated application and withdrawal of the treatment (e.g., A-B-A-B-A-B); increases evidence of functional relationship; additional baseline phases can raise ethical concerns.

Changing conditions—Allows the evaluation of more than one treatment (e.g., A-B-C); evidence for functional relationship is weak.

Multiple treatments—Allows the evaluation of more than one treatment with reintroduction of baseline condition(s) (e.g., A-B-A-C); more experimental control than changing conditions; many variations possible.

References

Alberto, P., & Troutman, A. (1995). *Applied behavior analysis for teachers* (4th ed.). Columbus, OH: Merrill.

Alberto, P., & Troutman, A. (1999). *Applied behavior analysis* for teachers (5th ed.). Columbus, OH: Merrill.

Baer, D .M., Wolf, M. W., & Risley, T. R. (1968). Some current dimensions of applied behavior analysis. *Journal of Applied Behavior Analysis, 1,* 91–97

Barlow, D. H., Hayes, S. C., & Nelson, R. O. (1984). *The scientist practitioner: Research and accountability in clinical and educational settings.* New York: Pergamon Press.

Campbell, D. T., & Stanley, J. C. (1963). *Experimental and quasi-experimental designs for research.* Chicago: Rand-McNally.

Cook, T. D., & Campbell, D. T. (1979). *Quasi-experimentation: Design and analysis issues for field settings.* Chicago: Rand-McNally.

Cooper, J., Heron, T., Heward, W. (1987). *Applied behavior analysis.* Columbus, OH: Merrill.

Schloss, P. J., & Smith, M. A. (1998). *Applied behavior analysis in the classroom* (2nd ed.). Boston: Allyn & Bacon.

Sulzer-Azaroff, B., & Mayer, G. R. (1977). *Applying behavior analysis procedures with children and youth.* New York: Holt, Rinehart & Winston.

Tawney, J., & Gast, D. (1984). *Single subject research in special education.* Columbus, OH: Merrill.

Yaden, D. B. (1995). Single subject experimental research: Applications for literacy. In S. B. Neuman & S. McCormick (Eds.), *Single subject experimental research: Applications for literacy* (pp. 32–46). Newark, DE: International Reading Association.

CHAPTER 6

Application of Withdrawal Designs

For each chapter focusing on different single subject designs, an application chapter is included. These chapters summarize the results of studies published in the professional literature that use each designated design. Users of this textbook are encouraged to read the original study that is referenced to more fully understand the intricacies of the research designs.

In the previous chapter we described the different types of withdrawal or reversal designs and their variations. Withdrawal designs are important single subject designs because they allow the investigator to demonstrate a strong functional relationship between treatment and changes in behavior. In this chapter we will provide specific examples from the professional literature for each of the basic types of withdrawal designs and two examples for adaptations of the withdrawal designs.

THE A-B-A DESIGN

Nientimp, E. G., & Cole, C. L. (1992). Teaching socially valid social interaction responses to students with severe disabilities in an integrated school setting. *Journal of School Psychology, 30,* 342–354.

Research Question

In this study, the investigators evaluated the effectiveness of a teaching procedure called constant time delay to teach appropriate social interaction skills to students with severe disabilities.

Subjects

The subjects were two boys, ages 12 years 0 months and 13 years 4 months. Both were labeled as autistic and had a history of aggressive, self-injurious behavior. The subjects were verbal, but their verbalizations were often prompt-dependent and/or echolalic.

Setting

This study was conducted in a self-contained special education classroom that had three other students with similar disabilities. The subjects had attended special schools and it was their first year in an integrated middle school setting.

Dependent Variables

The dependent variables were the subjects' responses to social greetings. These responses included (a) correct responses, given by the subject within 5 s after the greeting was initiated; (b) error responses, defined as no response within 5 s after the greeting was initiated; (c) echolalic responses, when the subject repeated all or part of the peer- or teacher-initiated greetings; and (d) prompted correct responses, defined as responses where the subjects exhibited the response only after the prompt.

Independent Variable

The independent variable implemented by the classroom teacher was a constant time delay procedure. During this procedure, greetings were presented to the subject, and the trainer provided the correct response if the subject gave an incorrect response or failed to respond. If the subject correctly responded, verbal praise (e.g., "That's good, saying hello") was provided.

The Design

The authors used an A-B-A withdrawal design and replicated the study across subjects to evaluate the treatment effects.

The Intervention

Each day, the trainer initiated a social greeting to a subject and paused for 5 s. If the subject responded correctly within 5 s, the subject received verbal praise. If an error or echolalic response was received, the trainer firmly stated "No" and provided the correct response. If the subject failed to provide a correct response again, the trainer provided the correct response (e.g., "Hi"). On the other hand, if the subject correctly repeated the response after the prompt, the trainer provided verbal praise. Each subject was provided 10 trials in which to respond to five different greetings. Each training session lasted about 10 min.

Obtaining the Data and Plotting the Results

Baseline data were collected for 4 days before the intervention began. During daily training sessions the first author recorded the subjects' responses as correct, error, echolalic, or prompted correct after the trainers initiated the greetings. Baseline conditions were later reinstated to determine if the subjects' responses would return to preintervention levels. Data were plotted on graphs to determine if the time delay teaching procedure produced improvement on these subjects' responses.

Results

The investigators reported that the correct responses for social greetings increased and echolalic responding decreased considerably for both participants during the treatment phase. Figures 6–1 and 6–2 display the data for these participants. As can be seen in Figure 6-1, Subject 1 averaged 5% correct responses and 85% echolalic responses during baseline. During the constant time delay phase, his correct responses increased to 70% and echolalic responding decreased to 21%. Subject 2 averaged 8% correct responses, 22% echolalic, and 70% error responses during baseline. During intervention, his correct responding increased to 100% and echolalic responding decreased to 0%.

Why Use an A-B-A Design?

The investigators were interested in determining the impact of a constant time delay procedure across subjects. By using this design, they were able to clinically test the teaching procedure and establish a functional relationship between the intervention and subjects' responses to social greetings.

Limitations of the Study

Although the participants showed increased social responses and decreased echolalic responding during intervention, their response level was similar to the intervention phase when the intervention was withdrawn. Moreover, the study ended in a baseline phase, so ethical issues should be considered. The fact that the behaviors did not return to preintervention levels is positive from a therapeutic point of view (and negated the need to reintroduce intervention). However, this lack of reversal of the data is undesirable for demonstrating a functional relationship.

Summary

A summary of the relevant dimensions of this A-B-A study can be found in Table 6–1.

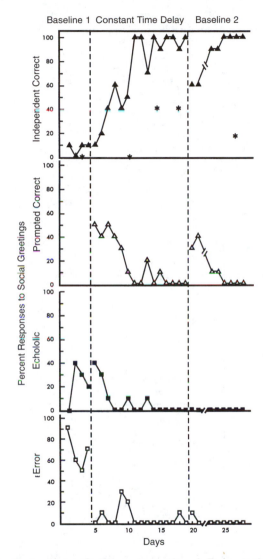

Figure 6–1. Data from Subject 1 in the A-B-A study. *Note.* From "Teaching Socially Valid Interaction Responses to Students With Severe Disabilities in an Integrated School Setting," by E. G. Nientimp and C. L. Cole, 1992, *Journal of School Psychology, 30*, p. 349. Copyright 1992 by Pergamon Press. Reprinted with permission.

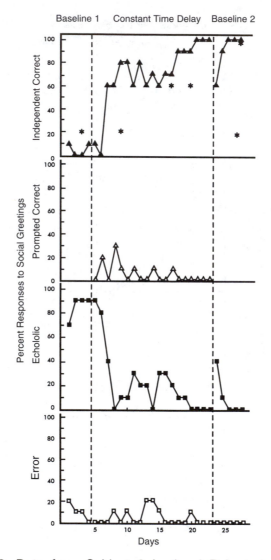

Figure 6–2. Data from Subject 2 in the A-B-A study. *Note.* From "Teaching Socially Valid Interaction Responses to Students With Severe Disabilities in an Integrated School Setting," by E. G. Nientimp and C. L. Cole, 1992, *Journal of School Psychology, 30*, p. 350. Copyright 1992 by Pergamon Press. Reprinted with permission.

Table 6–1. Summary of "Teaching Socially Valid Social Interaction Responses to Students With Severe Disabilities in an Integrated School Setting."

Feature	Description
Type of design	A-B-A design
Goal of study	Determine effectiveness of a teaching procedure (constant time delay) to increase social interaction skills in young children
Subjects	Two boys with autism
Setting	Self-contained special education classroom in a middle school
Dependent variables	Responses to social greetings (correct responses, error responses, echolalic responses, and prompted correct responses)
Independent variable	Constant time delay procedure
Results and outcomes	Constant time delay procedure increased correct responses for social greetings and decreased echolalic responding in both subjects

THE A-B-A-B DESIGN

Muir, K. A., & Milan, M. A. (1982). Parent reinforcement for child achievement: The use of a lottery to maximize parent training effects. *Journal of Applied Behavior Analysis, 15,* 455–460.

Research Question

The investigators evaluated a reinforcement program in which parents earned lottery tickets and won prizes when their preschoolers with disabilities achieved mastery of language skills in a home-based early intervention project.

Subjects

The subjects in this study were two girls and one boy ranging in age from 2 years to 2½ years at the beginning of the study. Two of the subjects had cerebral palsy and one had a diagnosis of developmental delay with a seizure disorder. Each subject was identified as language delayed and did not vocalize, imitate, or follow instructions.

Setting

The actual study took place in the subjects' homes. Two of the subjects lived in low-rent housing projects and one in a small house in an impoverished area. All contacts between the therapist and family took place in the homes.

Dependent Variables

The dependent variables were the children's responding to name, waving bye-bye, clapping, pointing to pictures, and following directions during receptive language tasks. Also included were the children's responses to expressive tasks such as imitating vowel sounds and words, and naming objects. The series of language tasks were arranged in a developmental sequence.

Independent Variable

Reinforcement through delivery of lottery tickets that could be exchanged for prizes was used as the independent variable in this study. Lottery prizes consisted of toys and household merchandise as well as complimentary meals from local restaurants. Parents earned their reinforcement contingent on actual improvements in their children's behavior. Interestingly, the authors note that the concept of a lottery would suggest that the parent may or may not receive the reinforcement for successful change in the target behavior. They used continuous reinforcement to deliver the prize after each lottery ticket won during the first and second home visits. The schedule was thinned to an FR-2 and then an FR-3 (the parents received the prize after every second and third visit, respectively, after they earned a ticket).

The Design

An A-B-A-B design consisting of baseline and lottery phases was replicated across three subjects to assess the effects of the lottery program.

Although the use of more than one subject is not requisite, the demonstration of the functional relationship is further strengthened if replicated across subjects.

The Intervention

During the therapist's initial home visits, the subjects' language level was established by having the parent give a prompt to respond to each task and seeing if they responded. If the child provided the desired response on two of the three trials, mastery was assumed and another prompt to a different task was given. Three tasks were identified for the next home visit in which the subject failed to meet the two-thirds correct response criterion. These three tasks were used to determine the effectiveness of the intervention program. Each mother was given a lottery ticket each time her child mastered a task (the child correctly performed a task within 5 seconds on two out of three trials), for a maximum of three tickets for each week.

Obtaining the Data and Plotting the Results

During the therapist's home visit, each mother was asked to test for mastery of each task three times in random order while the therapist scored the child's performance. It was the children's performance during these trials that was used to assess the effects of the procedures. Data for each subject were recorded as the cumulative number of tasks mastered to determine if the intervention produced mastery of language skills (see Figure 6–3).

Results

The results indicated that each subject responded differently, yet positively, to the treatment. Subject 1 (Alice) mastered 3 tasks during Baseline 1 and 2 tasks in 10 sessions during the second baseline. During the two lottery phases, she mastered 9 tasks and 10 tasks, respectively. Subject 2 (Benny) mastered only 1 task during the first baseline phase and did not master any during the second baseline phase. However, he mastered 9 tasks during the first lottery phase and 7 tasks during the second lottery phase. Subject 3 (Candy) mastered 1 task during the first six baseline visits and none during the second baseline phase, but mastered 5 tasks each during the first and second lottery phases. All these tasks are reported in cumulative numbers, thus providing an example of cumu-

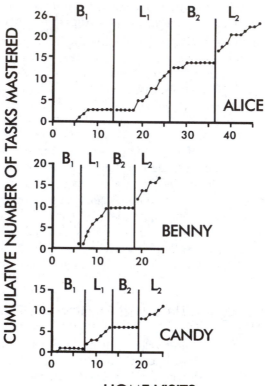

Figure 6–3. Data from the subjects in the A-B-A-B study. *Note.* From "Parent Reinforcement for Child Achievement: The Use of a Lottery to Maximize Parent Training Efforts," by K. A. Muir and M. A. Milan, 1982, *Journal of Applied Behavior Analysis, 15,* p. 459. Copyright 1982 by the Society for the Experimental Analysis of Behavior. Reprinted with permission.

lative graphing. Note that this type of recording does not demonstrate a reversal when the baseline condition is reinstated. Rather, it results in a leveling off of the data, indicating that no progress was made during that condition.

Why Use an A-B-A-B Design?

As noted in the previous chapter, providing the same treatment twice to compare the target response with two baseline phases replicated the functional relationship between the target behavior and treatment. Clearly, this design is more powerful than the A-B-A design to evaluate the effectiveness of a procedure. Also, the study ends with the treatment phase in effect.

Limitations of the Study

In this study, parents were reinforced for improving their child's language skills. This type of intervention may lead to criticism because parents were given external reinforcement for something they should be doing anyway. However the authors provide a rationale by stating that "the ultimate choice is between achieving an optimal level of progress for the children or of sacrificing them on the altar of these quasi-humanistic biases" (p. 460). The authors do acknowledge this limitation and encouraged the parents to maintain intervention efforts in the absence of reinforcement.

Summary

A summary of the relevant dimensions of this A-B-A-B study can be found in Table 6–2.

THE A-B-A-C DESIGN

Handen, B. C., Parrish, J. M., McClung, T. J., Kerwin, M. E., & Evans, L. D. (1992). Using guided compliance versus time out to promote child compliance: A preliminary comparative analysis in an analogue context. *Research in Developmental Disability, 13,* 157–170.

Research Question

This study was an effort to determine whether guided compliance was a better procedure for promoting child adherence to adult requests than a traditional time-out procedure.

Table 6–2. Summary of "Parent Reinforcement for Child Achievement: The Use of a Lottery to Maximize Parent Training Effects."

Feature	Description
Type of design	A-B-A-B design
Goal of study	Determine effectiveness of parental reinforcement to increase language skills in their young children
Subjects	Two girls and one boy ranging in age from 2 years to 2½ years who had no vocalization or imitation skills
Setting	Subjects' homes
Dependent variables	Receptive tasks (wave bye-bye, imitate, point to pictures) and expressive tasks (vowel sounds, name objects)
Independent variable	Lottery tickets and prizes
Results and outcomes	Subjects responded positively and gained more tasks during lottery phases

Subjects

The subjects were five children (four males, one female) ranging in age from 3 years 8 months to 6 years 4 months. All the subjects were classified as having mild developmental disabilities. Three of the subjects were functioning in the mild range of mental retardation; other disabilities reported were language delays and early signs of nonspecific learning disabilities.

Setting

The study was conducted in a small individual treatment room furnished with a one-way mirror, a worktable, and two chairs. For each session, the subjects were brought into this room, given requests, and allowed to play with books, blocks, puzzles, cars, and trucks without restrictions.

Dependent Variable

The dependent variable under investigation was child compliance behavior to adult requests. The authors defined compliance as "satisfactory completion of a requested task within 10 seconds of the request" (p. 161). Examples of the compliance requests are "Give me the _____,″ and "Put the _____ on the _____.″

Independent Variables

The independent variables were guided compliance (B), a technique that incorporates physical guidance, and time-out (C). Subjects were reinforced with praise for compliance during both intervention conditions.

The Design

The impact of guided compliance and time-out on all subjects' compliance responses was evaluated using an A-B-A-C design, with the order of the multiple treatments counterbalanced across subjects.

The Intervention

During all experimental sessions, the experimenter established eye contact, called the subject by name, and then issued a request. During the guided compliance phase, if the subject responded to a request within 10 s, verbal praise was provided and the child was allowed to play until the next request at the beginning of the subsequent minute. If noncompliance resulted, praise was withheld and the subject was physically guided to complete the task. During the time-out phase, the subject was also praised and allowed to play until the next request if he or she responded to a request within 10 s. If noncompliance resulted, the subject was placed in a chair facing a corner in the room for 30 s (if the subject refused to stay in the seat, then the subject was held gently in the chair). Subsequent to this time-out, the next request was initiated. Also, at the conclusion of training phases, five generalization requests were given in 1-min intervals.

Obtaining the Data and Plotting the Results

The observer recorded each compliance trial as correct (compliant) or incorrect (noncompliant). Data were collected on one subject at a time. Ten requests were presented at a rate of about one per minute; the subjects were instructed to respond while the observer collected data on each response. Data for each subject were placed on x-y graphs to determine the effectiveness of the intervention procedures in increasing compliance. For the purpose of visual inspection, as a representative sample, data for Subject 1 are shown in Figure 6-4.

Results

During baseline the overall mean percentage (*M*) of compliance (i.e., within a phase) was below 41% for all subjects. During time-out the mean percentage of compliance was 85% (range 71–92%), and during guided compliance the mean percentage of compliance was 59%. Figure 6–4 shows the mean percentage of compliance recorded by the observer across conditions for Subject 1. As can be seen, Subject 1 exhibited no change in compliance rates over baseline (*M* = 47%) with guided compliance (*M* = 48%). However, following a return to baseline, presentation of time-out led to a considerable increase in compliance rate (*M* = 71%).

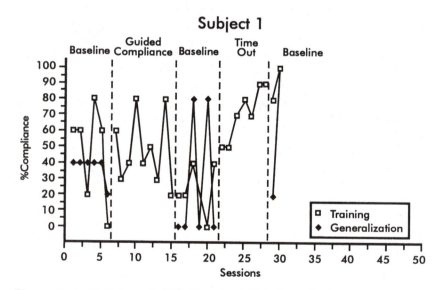

Figure 6–4. Data from Subject 1 in the A-B-A-C study. *Note.* From "Using Guided Compliance Versus Timeout to Promote Child Compliance: A Preliminary Comparative Analysis in an Analogue Context," by B. C. Handen, J. M. Parrish, T. J. McClung, M. E. Kerwin, and L. D. Evans, 1992, *Research in Developmental Disabilities, 13*, p. 164. Copyright 1992 by Pergamon Press. Reprinted with permission.

This graph depicts why overall means and ranges can be useful in evaluating results when data are highly variable.

Why Use an A-B-A-C Design?

Clearly, the researchers were interested in determining the effects of two behavior management procedures to increase compliance behavior of children with developmental disabilities. This design allowed the investigators to test more than one independent variable after each baseline phase. Also, by using more than one subject, the researchers were able to counterbalance the presentation of the two procedures to help avoid sequencing effects.

Limitations of the Study

As stated earlier, Subject 1 made no change in compliance rates during baseline and guided compliance phases. This may have been due to the subject's inability to discriminate among the treatment conditions, or as the authors described, "guided compliance may have served on occasion to maintain noncompliance among these children" (p. 167–168).

Summary

A summary of the relevant dimensions of this A-B-A-C study can be found in Table 6–3.

THE A-B-A-B-A-B DESIGN

Carnine, D. W. (1976). Effects of two teacher-presentation rates on off-task behavior, answering correctly, and participation. *Journal of Applied Behavior Analysis, 2,* 199–206.

Research Question

In this study, the author examined the effectiveness of slow-rate presentation versus fast-rate presentation of two teachers on students' off-task behavior, correct answering, and participation during a beginning reading class.

Table 6–3. Summary of "Using Guided Compliance Versus Time Out to Promote Child Compliance: A Preliminary Comparative Analysis in an Analogue Context."

Feature	Description
Type of design	A-B-A-C design
Goal of study	Determine effectiveness of guided compliance and time-out procedure to promote child adherence to adult requests
Subjects	Four boys and one girl ranging in age from 3 years 8 months to 6 years 4 months who had developmental disabilities
Setting	A treatment room (2.6 m × 2.9 m) in an outpatient clinic; it had a one-way mirror, a worktable, and two chairs
Dependent variable	Compliance behavior
Independent variables	Guided compliance and time-out procedures
Results and outcomes	Time-out procedure produced more compliance by all subjects than the guided compliance procedure

Subjects

The subjects participating in this study were a boy and a girl judged by the classroom teachers as being the poorest readers and the most off-task from three first-grade classrooms. On the Wide Range Achievement Test, they scored at the 2nd and 8th month of kindergarten (k.2 and k.8) in reading, respectively.

Setting

The subjects received 30 min of reading instruction each day in a classroom. The classroom was organized into small groups of four, and the subjects were seated in the order of subject, nonsubject, subject, and nonsubject throughout the study period.

Dependent Variables

The dependent variables were off-task behavior, correct answering, and participation. Off-task behavior was defined as leaving the chair to engage in an inappropriate behavior, blurting out, inappropriate talking, and other disruptive behavior such as foot tapping. Participation was defined as the subject's responding within 1 s after the teacher's cue to answer, whether or not the answer was correct. A correct answer was scored if the subject provided the right answer even if it was given after 1 s (i.e., a nonparticipation).

Independent Variables

Independent variables were the rate of presentation (fast vs. slow) of the Level 1 DISTAR reading program.

The Design

Teachers delivered slow-rate presentation during the A condition of the A-B-A-B-A-B design and fast-rate presentation during the B condition. Once every 90 s the teachers praised the subjects if they had responded to a question or were on task. This is an example where the baseline condition was somewhat different from a typical one.

The Intervention

During slow-rate presentation, there was a delay between the subjects' response and introduction of the next task. In fast-rate presentation, there was no delay. Teachers used a fixed-interval 90 s schedule in all phases of the study to praise the subjects. During the first four phases, a certified special education teacher made the presentations. During the last two phases, a student teacher made the presentations because the first teacher took another job.

Obtaining the Data and Plotting the Results

As noted previously, the subjects' correct responses were recorded. Similarly, their off-task behaviors were recorded if they engaged in undirected activity. If the subjects responded within 1 s after the teacher's cue to answer, it was recorded as participation regardless of correctness of the answer. One subject was rated on all the dependent variables for 10 consecutive tasks and then the second subject was rated for the next 10 consecutive tasks. Two data collectors used stopwatches to record data. Each subject's percent occurrence of off-task, answering correctly, and participation are depicted in Figures 6–5 and 6–6.

Results

Results indicated that fast-rate presentation decreased the subjects' off-task behavior and increased their correct answering and participation behavior. As can be seen in Figures 6–5 and 6–6, both subjects responded positively to slow- and fast-rate presentations. However, Subject 1 was much more responsive to fast-rate presentation than slow-rate presentation. For Subject 2, off-task behavior was decreased during fast-rate presentation, although answering correctly and participation did not seem to be influenced as much by the rate of presentation.

Why Use an A-B-A-B-A-B Design?

The author's goal was to determine which of the two presentation methods would be effective in decreasing students' off-task behavior and increasing correct answering and participation during instruction. This design is very flexible and it allowed the teachers to repeat each phase three times to establish functional relationships between presentation rates and subjects' responses. Unfortunately, it was not clear whether or not the A condition (slow-rate presentation) was being used in the classroom before the beginning of the study. If it was it would essentially be a baseline condition. If it was not, then there really was no baseline phase.

Limitations of the Study

In most special education classrooms, students are given ample time to provide correct responses. One limitation of this study was that during the fast-rate presentation the children were rushed into providing responses immediately after hearing a question. This approach could force anybody to answer quickly without thinking through the answer and make errors or not participate at all. Another limitation of this study was that the author did not discuss the purpose of the study or the effects of

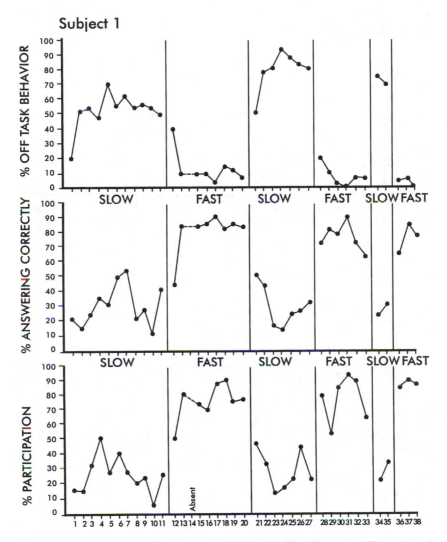

Figure 6–5. Data from Subject 1 in the A-B-A-B-A-B study. (The dotted lines indicate when Subject 1 was absent.) *Note.* From "Effects of Two Teacher-Presentation Rates on Off-Task Behavior, Answering Correctly, and Participation," by D. Carnine, 1976, *Journal of Applied Behavior Analysis, 2*, p. 204. Copyright 1976 by the Society for the Experimental Analysis of Behavior. Reprinted with permission.

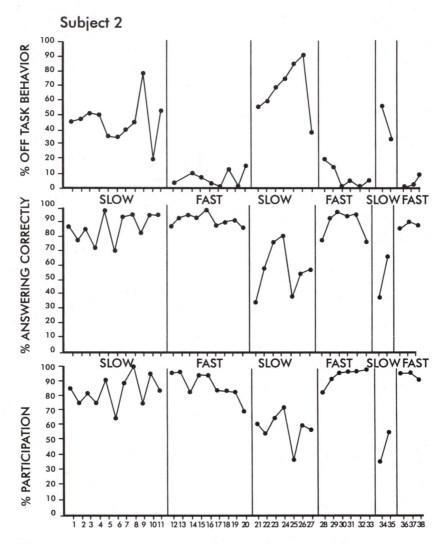

Figure 6-6. Data from Subject 2 in the A-B-A-B-A-B study. *Note.* From "Effects of Two Teacher-Presentation Rates on Off-Task Behavior, Answering Correctly, and Participation," by D. Carnine, 1976, *Journal of Applied Behavior Analysis, 2*, p. 205. Copyright 1976 by the Society for the Experimental Analysis of Behavior. Reprinted with permission.

presentation rates with the teachers. Finally, the previously mentioned concern about the nature of the baseline condition is a limitation.

Summary

A summary of the relevant information about this design can be found in Table 6–4.

Table 6–4. Summary of "Effects of Two Teacher-Presentation Rates on Off-task Behavior, Answering Correctly, and Participation."

Feature	Description
Type of design	A-B-A-B-A-B design
Goal of study	Examine effectiveness of slow-rate presentation versus fast-rate presentation on students' off-task behavior, correct answering, and participation during reading class
Subjects	Two low-functioning subjects with off-task behaviors
Setting	A classroom
Dependent variables	Off-task behavior, answering correctly, and participation
Independent variables of a reading program	Slow-rate presentation and fast-rate presentation
Results and outcomes	Fast-rate presentation decreased off-task behavior and increased both correct answering and participation for both subjects

Withdrawal designs may be used in a variety of situations. As we have noted, however, the ethics involved in withdrawing an intervention and the possibility of irreversibility of the intervention sometimes make their application problematic. For these and other reasons, additional designs have been devised. One example is the multiple baseline design, which is probably the most commonly used design found in the literature. As the reader shall see in the next chapter, multiple baseline designs help overcome the problems associated with withdrawal designs.

CHAPTER 7

Overview of Multiple Baseline Designs

IMPORTANT CONCEPTS TO KNOW

THE BASIC MULTIPLE BASELINE DESIGN

MECHANICS OF THE MULTIPLE BASELINE DESIGN

Prediction, Verification, and Replication

Covariance Among Dependent Variables

ADVANTAGES OF THE MULTIPLE BASELINE DESIGN

DISADVANTAGES OF THE MULTIPLE BASELINE DESIGN

THE DIFFERENT MULTIPLE BASELINE DESIGNS

Multiple Baseline Across Behaviors

Multiple Baseline Across Settings

Multiple Baseline Across Subjects

ADAPTATIONS OF THE MULTIPLE BASELINE DESIGN

Multiple Probe Design

Delayed Multiple Baseline Design

Multiple baseline designs are A-B designs that are replicated within the same study. The three major types of multiple baseline designs are multiple baseline across behaviors, settings, and subjects. In the basic multiple baseline design, the researcher takes repeated measures of baseline performance concurrently on two or more baselines. When a stable, predictable baseline is obtained, the researcher implements the intervention (independent variable) and records the results over a period of time to determine the effects of the intervention. Typically, a criterion is established a priori to establish a dependent variable level at which one may judge the intervention or treatment has been successful in altering the dependent variable, or the researcher may simply apply the independent variable until a stable performance is obtained on the dependent variable following the introduction of the intervention. Therefore, a changing criterion is sometimes included within a multiple baseline design (see Chapters 11 and 12). A withdrawal may also be included following an intervention phase within a multiple baseline design. The process is repeated for each baseline.

THE BASIC MULTIPLE BASELINE DESIGN

Multiple baseline designs may be the most appropriate single subject designs to use for a variety of reasons (Baer, Wolf, & Risley, 1968). These include the following: (a) when withdrawal or reversal designs may not be feasible due to ethical concerns about withdrawing treatment that is working; or (b) there may be practical considerations, such as more than one person or setting needing interventions; or (c) in those cases where the independent variable (treatment) should not be withdrawn or the achieved target behavior cannot be reversed (e.g., allowing verbal threats to once again increase after a decrease has been obtained, learning to match consonant sounds with the appropriate alphabet letter), it may be more appropriate to implement a multiple baseline design. Multiple baseline designs are versatile, are relatively easy to understand, and are generally practical in real world settings (Cooper, Heron, & Heward, 1987).

Because multiple measures are used to obtain data over two or more baselines (and usually three or more; Barlow & Hersen, 1984), the end result appears visually as a series of A-B designs stacked on top of one another. The dependent variable may actually consist of two or more technically different behaviors (Cooper et al., 1987). The reader may find this somewhat confusing. Actually, in a multiple baseline across behaviors design, two or more target behaviors of the same individual receive the same treatment in the same setting. In the multiple baseline across settings design, the researcher is applying the same intervention to the target behavior in two or more settings. In a multiple baseline across subjects design, the researcher is applying the same intervention to the target behavior of two or more individuals in the same setting. Many experts (e.g., Alberto & Troutman, 1999; Cooper et al., 1987) prefer to conceptualize each baseline (be it different behaviors in the same individual, different settings where the same individual's target behavior is occurring, or different individuals exhibiting the target behavior in the same setting) as a different target behavior or dependent variable. This concept is used because each baseline followed by intervention is treated as a separate applied behavior analysis (Cooper et al., 1987). Therefore, we will discuss the designs in terms of recording and intervening with the first, second, and third dependent variables (i.e., behaviors, settings, or individual subjects). Keep in mind that this is convenient for the sake of discussion. In reality, the same method for recording the target behavior is used with each baseline and intervention (Alberto & Troutman, 1999). See Figure 7–1 for a depiction of the various designs and what variables actually remain the same and which change based on the design used.

MECHANICS OF THE MULTIPLE BASELINE DESIGNS

Assume three dependent variables have been chosen. After baseline data have been obtained for all three dependent variables, the researcher implements the intervention for the first dependent variable while maintaining baseline conditions for the other two. When the criterion is obtained on the first behavior, in the first setting, or with the first individual subject following intervention, the intervention may be implemented and analyzed as to its effect on the second dependent variable. Meanwhile, baseline conditions are maintained with the third dependent variable. This is then followed by introducing the intervention to the third dependent variable after it is clear that the intervention is working with the second dependent variable (see Figure 7–2). Subsequent dependent variables, if any, would continue with the same format and design. Frequently, a follow-up stage or a generalization phase is included to ensure that the effects of the independent variable are maintained over time, settings, behaviors, and/or individuals.

Prediction, Verification, and Replication

Beginning the collection of baseline data simultaneously across all dependent variables adds an important feature to multiple baseline designs.

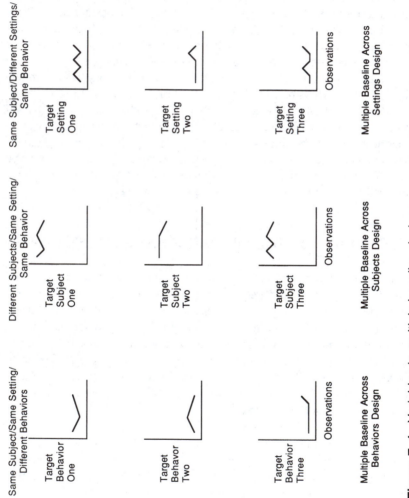

Figure 7–1. Variables in multiple baseline designs.

148

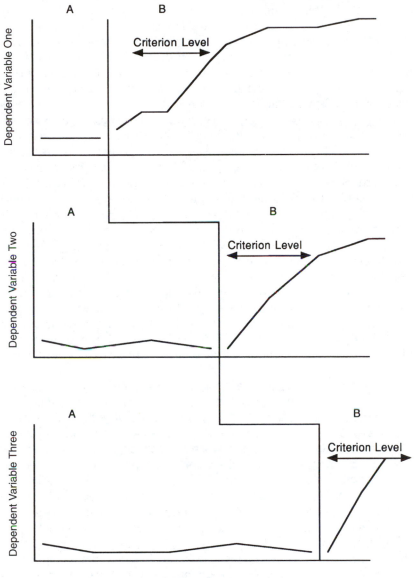

Figure 7–2. Typical multiple baseline design.

It allows the researcher to infer a verification of the prediction that the baseline behaviors would have remained stable and unchanged if the intervention had not been implemented (Kucera & Axelrod, 1995). As discussed in Chapter 4 (and here we have modified the discussions of Cooper et al., 1987 and Tawney & Gast, 1984), verification is evident if the data path changes in a predictable manner through a phase change, as from baseline to intervention. In other words, if the data path line remains constant across the baseline and intervention phases, then the independent variable yields no effect on the dependent variable (i.e., no change in the target behavior when the intervention is implemented) and there is not verification. If there *is* a change in the data path, then the possibility exists that the independent variable is responsible for the change and there is verification that the data path has changed with the introduction of the treatment. In a multiple baseline design, replication of this prediction and verification may occur when the data paths of subsequent dependent variables follow patterns similar to the first (and subsequent) variables. According to Cooper et al. (1987), inferences can be made concerning the complementary roles of prediction and verification in multiple baseline designs. First, if potential confounding variables are held constant across all variables and target behavior remains unchanged from Dependent Variable 1 to Variables 2 and 3 (and so on), then the prediction is valid. Second, if changes in the independent variable occur with Dependent Variable 1, the observed changes in that target behavior are brought about by the independent variable because only that dependent variable was exposed to the independent variable. In other words, baseline levels of each dependent variable remain stable and then change when and only when the independent variable is introduced.

> For example, a student's recognition of inflectional endings is stable. Following the introduction of the intervention or treatment, however, recognition of the ending *s* increases while the other two baselines (ending *ed* sounds and those representing spelling changes) remain unchanged. Once criterion is obtained for *s* endings, the independent variable is introduced with recognizing *ed* endings. The *s* endings continue to maintain criterion levels or improve while the *ed* recognition behavior begins to increase. Meanwhile, the recognition of spelling changes remains stable at baseline levels. Once criterion is achieved with *ed* endings, the intervention may be introduced to the third dependent variable. The first two dependent variables should continue to maintain or improve. The recognition of endings representing spelling changes also should change in a manner similar to those first two dependent variables. Replication is achieved when similar results ultimately are obtained with each dependent variable following the introduction of the same independent variable (see Figure 7–3).

This form of replication provides a convincing argument for the presence of a functional relationship between the dependent and inde-

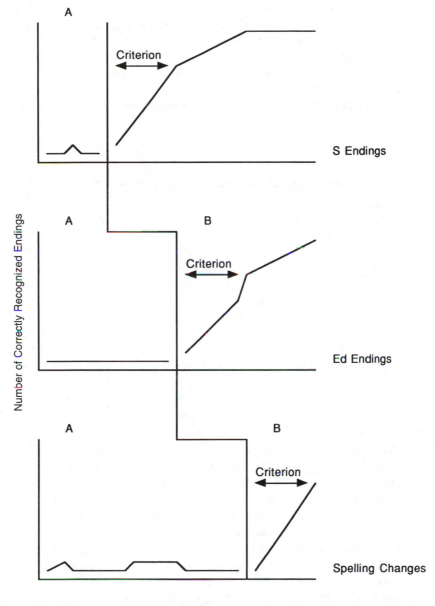

Figure 7–3. Example demonstrating functional relationship within a multiple baseline design.

pendent variables. It is important to note the importance of maintaining stability of the extraneous variables that have the potential to influence results across variables. The only changes that should be evident are found in (a) the target behaviors (and again those may be behaviors, settings, or different individuals) that have been designated as the dependent variables (these will be discussed in following sections) and (b) the treatment, or independent variable. Other variables, such as environment and time, should remain constant to ensure that the results can indeed be attributed to the independent variable (Cooper et al., 1987).

Covariance Among Dependent Variables

It is also important to note the relationship among the dependent variables. Realizing that variables in the treatment may covary, it is important to select dependent variables that exhibit some degree of independence (Tawney & Gast, 1984). In our example, if a student was likely to improve recognition of ending *ed* sounds and/or spelling changes when the independent variable is introduced to improve recognition of *s* endings, then these dependent variables would likely covary (or change at the same time and in the same direction). These variables would not be considered sufficiently independent of one another for research purposes because one could not achieve the desired replication of effects across the dependent variables (see Figure 7–4 for an example of covariance among dependent variables). This independence is important in maintaining experimental control, yet selecting independent variables that are completely unrelated would also be undesirable.

For example, the dependent variables in a multiple baseline design such as hitting children on the playground, eating too quickly at lunch, and starting work on time are all behaviors that through some type of intervention one might aim to improve, but one *might* not expect them to change in response to the same independent variable. For example, intervention designed to teach this student to obtain attention in more adaptive manners might decrease hitting, but may not result in similar changes in eating too quickly or starting work on time. Also, in our example, measurement of the dependent variables would probably not be the same. Whereas hitting might be measured through frequency, one would likely measure eating too quickly through a duration procedure and starting work on time through a latency procedure.

It is necessary that each of the dependent variables be measured using the same method of recording behavior (Alberto & Troutman, 1999)

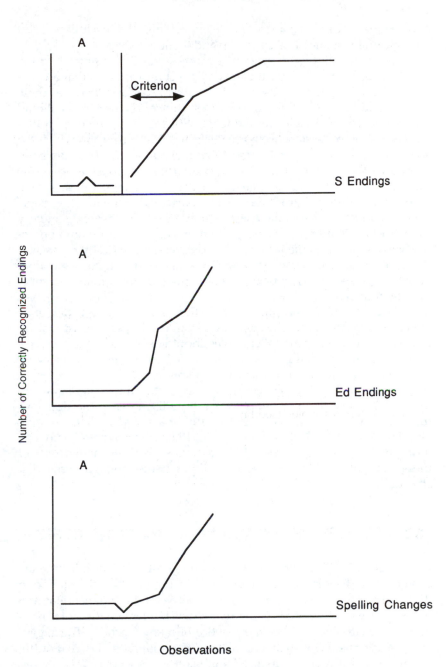

Figure 7–4. Example of covariance among dependent variables.

and the researcher have a reasonable expectation that each dependent variable will respond similarly to the independent variable.

Therefore selecting dependent variables that are completely unrelated can present as many problems as selecting variables that are significantly interrelated (Barlow & Hersen, 1984). A balance between these two areas of concern will produce the best choice. The researcher should select dependent variables (individuals with the same behavior, different behaviors in the same individual, or different settings in which the same individual exhibits the same behavior) that are functionally similar so that they would likely change similarly in response to the same treatment while at the same time not be likely to change until that treatment is specifically introduced to the particular dependent variable (e.g., *ed* endings and spelling changes may very well respond similarly to instruction that improves recognition of *s* endings but would be unlikely to change until the instruction is delivered specifically for each of those behaviors). Tawney and Gast (1984) referred to these dependent variables (or baselines) as being at once functionally similar and functionally independent of one another. Again, these dependent variables must be measurable using the same method for recording behavior as well so that results are easily compared from one dependent variable to the next. Also, the dependent variables should be measured concurrently and the possible influences of other variables should be reasonably equal for each dependent variable (Cooper et al., 1987).

In addition to these concerns, the researcher must also be aware that the various design options available will influence the decisions made regarding experimental procedures. As noted earlier, multiple baseline designs typically involve multiple baselines across behaviors, individuals, or settings. Although the basic design is unchanged, each of these particular variations has its unique issues and concerns that should be addressed.

ADVANTAGES OF THE MULTIPLE BASELINE DESIGN

Cooper et al. (1987) outline several advantages to the multiple baseline design. First, the withdrawal of an effective treatment is not required to demonstrate the functional relationship between the independent and dependent variables. Second, the sequential implementation of the independent variable parallels the practice of many teachers. Third, generalization of behavior change is monitored through the design. Fourth, the design is easily conceptualized and used.

A multiple baseline design should be used in the following situations:

- When withdrawal designs are not feasible due to ethical concerns;

- When there is more than one target behavior, setting, or individual in need of treatment;

- When the effects of the independent variable cannot be withdrawn or reversed.

DISADVANTAGES OF THE MULTIPLE BASELINE DESIGN

Cooper et al. (1987) also noted that multiple baseline designs have their limitations. These include the possibility of covariance and the aforementioned result that a functional relationship is not clearly demonstrated. Second, verification is reliant on dependent variable levels not changing until the independent variable is introduced and then changing in a similar manner to any previously treated behaviors. Cooper et al. argued that this is a weaker design than a withdrawal/reversal design where the relationship between the independent and dependent variable is more directly observed. Third, the multiple baseline design does yield data related to general effectiveness of the independent variable in treating various behaviors, in different environments, or with various individuals, but allows us to analyze the dependent variable less so than other designs might allow because the treatment is applied in only one intervention phase as a rule. Finally, implementing a multiple baseline design can be time consuming and may require substantial resources because two or more dependent variables are being measured simultaneously. Despite these limitations, the multiple baseline design remains a commonly used design and one that lends itself well to clinical practice where intervention is required for multiple behaviors, multiple individuals, or the same behavior in multiple settings requires intervention.

The multiple baseline design should not be used in the following situations:

- When selected target behaviors are not functionally similar nor independent of one another;

- If there is only one individual, in one setting, and/or one target behavior selected for treatment;

- When more than one intervention phase is desirable to demonstrate the functional relationship;

- When constraints on resources make implementation impossible.

THE DIFFERENT MULTIPLE BASELINE DESIGNS

Because multiple baseline designs have variations within the basic design itself, we have constructed this chapter somewhat differently from those explaining the other single subject designs. First, we will discuss the variations of the basic design that are commonly found in the literature (across behaviors, settings, or individual subjects). Second, we will discuss adaptations (i.e., multiple probe, and delayed multiple baseline) of the basic design that may be applied to any of these first three variations.

Multiple Baseline Across Behaviors

Generally with the multiple baseline across behaviors design, three or more behaviors are identified that are exhibited by the same individual in the same setting and then systematically subjected to the same intervention or independent variable. The behaviors selected as targets need to be both functionally similar and functionally independent (Tawney & Gast, 1984). That is, the behaviors should be similar enough that the same treatment or intervention is likely to influence the occurrence of each in a similar fashion (e.g., increase, decrease, or maintain the level of each dependent variable). At the same time, the behaviors should be unlikely to change (i.e., covary) until the intervention is actually introduced to influence that specific dependent variable. For example, a student in a class might exhibit physical aggression, verbal threats, and vandalism. One might reasonably expect that these behaviors would be functionally similar (e.g., each involves abuse of another person or property). However, one might be less certain that if physical aggression is treated, verbal threats and vandalism would not covary when aggression alone is treated. If they do not covary, then the behaviors are functionally independent. This type of covariance is of special concern with a multiple baseline across behaviors design because achieving functional similarity and independence among target behaviors is not necessarily easy. In fact, doing so a priori may be difficult (Tawney & Gast, 1984). From a treatment or outcomes perspective such covariance is not necessarily undesirable; however, from a research perspective, the establishment of a functional relationship between the independent variable and dependent variables becomes problematic. The researcher will not have a clear demonstration that the dependent variables or target behaviors change when and only when the independent variable is systematically applied to each. Hersen and Barlow (1975) noted that incorporating as many target behaviors as reasonable might assist in addressing this problem. That is, if one uses four or more baselines, the likelihood that all would covary would be reduced. However, one might equally argue that the more target behaviors included, the greater the likelihood that at least two will covary (Hersen & Barlow, 1975). One possible advantage to covariation is that the researcher may assess and subsequently analyze concomitant changes that occur when the treatment is introduced to a specific dependent variable. For example, the researcher may indeed discover that verbal threats diminish when the independent variable is applied to physical aggression. Yet, the third baseline (vandalism) remains unchanged during the treatment of physical aggression. This does suggest generality of treatment as noted earlier (Cooper et al., 1987) but, again, may not allow one to carefully analyze the direct influence of the treatment on verbal threats, and it may weaken the demonstration of the functional relationship.

The critical issues in implementing a multiple baseline across behaviors design include

1. selection of an individual participant who displays multiple behaviors (at least two but preferably three or more for a convincing argument for a functional relationship) in a single setting that require intervention;
2. functional similarity and functional independence of those behaviors as one might be able to determine a priori;
3. a reasonable expectation that the same variables (extraneous or systematic) will exert equal influence on each of the dependent variables;
4. selection of a treatment or independent variable that can be expected to produce a similar and independent effect on each of the dependent variables;
5. a consistent recording procedure for each of the target behaviors and a criterion level for decision making; and

6. confidence that the resources and time needed to record multiple baselines and subsequent intervention will be maintained throughout the study.

The following scenario serves as an example of the use of a multiple baseline across behaviors design.

> Mrs. Davis has been working with Steve for several weeks now in her classroom. Steve has exhibited a number of behaviors that interfere with his learning and the learning of those around him, and, if untreated, may ultimately result in referral for evaluation for a behavior disorder. He has pinched other students, has repeatedly told others he would "get them" after school, and has made obscene gestures when he is upset or angry with others. Mrs. Davis has requested that Dr. Lester assist her in intervening. After using anecdotal recording, the two agree on operational definitions for Steve's kicking, threatening, and gesturing behaviors. They also want to ensure that any intervention attempted will be successful before investing all their time and effort, so they wish to use it with the more severe target behavior first (pinching) before investing in using it with each of the other behaviors. They implement baseline recording on each of the three target behaviors in the classroom. Once stable responding is achieved, they implement their intervention (differential reinforcement of other behaviors with response interruption) with the pinching target behavior. The frequency of pinching abruptly decreases to zero levels after six sessions. Meanwhile, baselines have been maintained on threatening and gesturing and those behaviors have remained stable. Next, the two implement the intervention on threatening and that target behavior changes to zero levels after only four sessions. Pinching has remained at zero levels and gesturing continues to exhibit a steady baseline. Finally, the intervention is implemented with gesturing, which decreases to zero levels after only three sessions. Both kicking and threatening have remained at zero levels. See Figure 7–5 for a depiction of this study.

A major advantage of the multiple baseline across behaviors design is that generality of intervention effects for similar behaviors within the same individual can be demonstrated. The major disadvantage is the aforementioned possibility of covariance among behaviors, which weakens the demonstration of a functional relationship.

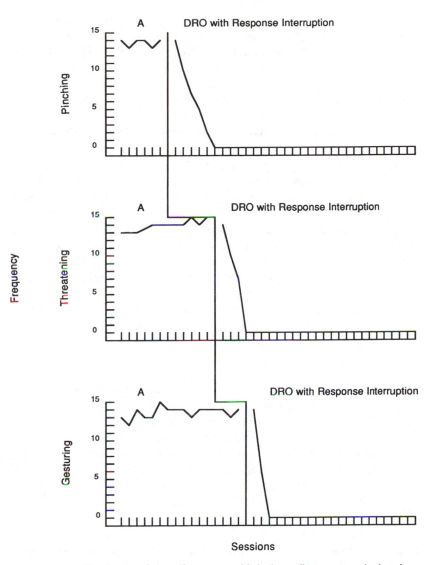

Figure 7–5. Example of data from a multiple baseline across behaviors design. DRO = differential reinforcement of other behavior.

Multiple Baseline Across Settings

The multiple baseline across settings design is similar to the across behaviors design in that only one subject is identified. The researcher identifies two or more settings (again, generally at least three) in which the individual emits the same behavior. The same subject is treated for the same behavior in different settings. For example, a student might be treated for aggressive behavior in the classroom, in the school halls, and in the cafetorium. Settings need not be literally interpreted, however, to mean different physical environments. Settings may include functionally similar situations that are still independent of one another. For example, a student's fluency might be addressed in whole group, cooperative group, and presentation situations. The physical environment may not actually change although the situations may be different enough that the researcher may not expect the behavior to change in any of those situations until the intervention is applied. The intervention is applied after baseline data have been obtained in all settings, but initially applied in only one setting. When criterion or an acceptable level of responding is achieved in the first setting, the researcher implements the intervention in the second setting. Following acceptable responding in the second setting, the intervention is applied in the third setting. Baselines are maintained in settings during intervention in prior settings. Intervention is maintained in prior settings as it is applied in subsequent settings (or some follow-up or maintenance phase is in effect in the prior setting if optimal responding has already been achieved).

Critical issues in the implementation of the multiple baseline across settings design include

1. selection of an individual subject who displays the same target behavior in multiple settings;
2. selection of settings that are functionally similar but also independent of one another as one may best determine a priori;
3. a reasonable expectation that the same variables will be exerting the same influence in each of the settings;
4. selection of a treatment or independent variable that can be expected to produce similar effects in each setting;
5. a consistent recording procedure for each setting and a criterion level for decision making; and
6. confidence that the resources and time needed to record data in multiple settings will be maintained throughout the study.

The following scenario serves as an example of the use of a multiple baseline across settings design.

Mr. Stephens, Mrs. Roberts, and Mr. Michaels have all been working with Sara since she arrived at the high school 2 months ago. Each of the teachers works on a team that serves 10th-grade students including Sara, who has mild mental retardation and is included in their classes. In one meeting, they all express concern that Sara is consistently slow in beginning work. Each notes that she usually falls behind almost immediately because she dawdles at getting her class materials out and therefore is not focusing on what the teacher and other students are saying. She sometimes wanders slowly to her desk as the bell rings, further compounding her problem. Dr. Lester is asked to assist the team in implementing a program. Each teacher wishes to help Sara change her behavior, but they agree as a team to try the intervention (differential reinforcement for lowering the latency spent from when the bell rings to beginning work) in one class at a time to ensure it is effective. After beginning work has been clearly defined, baseline measures are taken in each class. The baselines are all steady. Mr. Stephens first implements the intervention and Sara achieves the criterion level of responding (1 min latency) in four sessions. Meanwhile, her latency for beginning work has continued at higher and steady levels in Mrs. Roberts' and Mr. Michaels' classes. Next, Mrs. Roberts implements the intervention and Sara's latency falls to the acceptable level of 1 min within five sessions. Her beginning work has continued to remain within the 1 min latency in Mr. Stephens' class and her baseline continues to be higher and steady in Mr. Michaels' class. Finally, Mr. Michaels implements the intervention and obtains a result similar to that achieved in the first two settings. Figure 7–6 depicts the data from this example.

A major advantage to the multiple baseline across settings design is that generality of intervention effectiveness with the same individual in different settings may be demonstrated. A major disadvantage is that extraneous variables that may influence responding in different settings may be difficult to control or predict. The presence of different people, times of the day, instructional or clinical activities, and so on, all may have some unforeseen influence on the individual's responding. The more control the researcher may exert over such possible influences, the greater the likelihood that a functional relationship may be demonstrated.

Multiple Baseline Across Subjects

The multiple baseline across subjects design differs from those for multiple behaviors or settings in that more than one subject participates. In this design, two or more (again, three or more is desirable) individuals are identified who emit the same target behavior in the same setting.

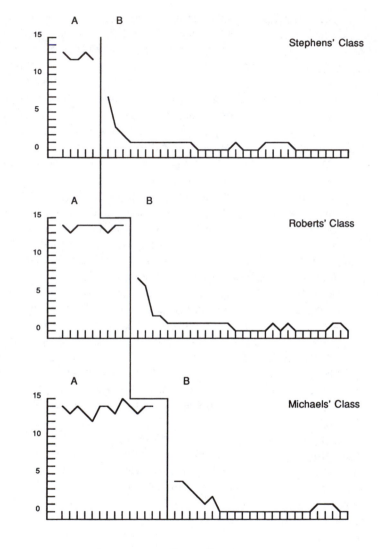

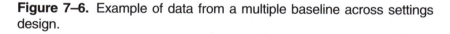

Figure 7–6. Example of data from a multiple baseline across settings design.

The baseline measures reflect the responding of the multiple subjects. For example, three subjects may exhibit an articulation problem (or verbal threats or inaccurate math problem solving, etc.) in the same setting. The subjects should be enough alike that one might reasonably expect each to respond similarly to the same intervention yet independent enough of one another that one is not likely to change his or her behavior as a result of perceiving changes in one of the other subject's behavior (covariance). All other variables are held as constant as possible. One should be aware that same target behavior need not be literally interpreted to mean *exactly* the same behavior. Such an example might include one student who is disruptive by making noises, one who is disruptive by talking out during instruction, and a third student who disrupts by talking to classmates during instruction. Although these target behaviors of different individuals are not *exactly* the same, they may be functionally similar yet still independent of one another. The researcher should logically be able to operationally define the target behavior of disrupting class in such a manner that each of the individual responses given would be examples of the target behavior.

The critical issues in implementing a multiple baseline across subjects design include

1. selection of individual participants who display the same target behavior in the same setting;
2. selection of individuals who are similar enough to one another to expect each would change his or her behavior in response to the same intervention and yet not likely to change his or her behavior until the intervention is specifically implemented to treat his or her behavior;
3. a reasonable expectation that the same variables will exert the same influence on each of the subjects;
4. selection of an independent variable that is likely to have a similar effect on each subject;
5. a consistent recording procedure for all subjects' behavior and a criterion level for decision making; and
6. confidence that the resources will be available to maintain data collection and intervention across the life span of the study.

An example of the use of a multiple baseline across subjects design follows.

Mrs. Ziegler, a speech and language clinician, works with Ed, Charles, and Lydia each day in their regular sixth-grade class. Each has difficulty with writing personal stories that can be followed well by others. After operationally defining storytelling, Mrs. Ziegler and the teacher decide to try teaching the students a strategy by which they can construct personal stories. They also decide they want to try the intervention with only one student at a time to ensure it is effective. They take baseline measures on the permanent products obtained from each student's written stories. Each consistently exhibits a number of errors in storytelling. The intervention is implemented with Ed first. Within five sessions where he has received the strategy instruction, Ed reduces his error level to an acceptable level of two per story. Meanwhile, both Charles and Lydia continue to make many errors for each story they write. Next, Charles is taught the strategy. He improves to a two errors or fewer level of responding in only three sessions. Ed continues his improved performance and Lydia continues to exhibit a steady and high level of errors. Finally, Lydia is taught the strategy and she too improves rather quickly. All students continue to maintain their performance. Figure 7–7 depicts the results of this study.

A major advantage to the multiple baseline across subjects design is that it allows the researcher to demonstrate the effectiveness of an intervention with more than one individual who displays a similar need for behavior change. A major disadvantage is that covariance among subjects may emerge if individuals learn vicariously through the experiences of other subjects. Identifying multiple subjects who are functionally similar yet independent of one another can prove difficult.

Clearly, the multiple baseline design is versatile and has many potential applications. Still, a primary difficulty in implementing these designs is the availability of time and resources to maintain multiple baselines and data collection across behaviors, settings, or individuals. This can be prohibitive, so researchers have developed adaptations to the multiple baseline design that help to overcome this difficulty.

ADAPTATIONS OF THE MULTIPLE BASELINE DESIGN

There are two major adaptations of the multiple baseline design that are relevant to this discussion. These are the multiple probe and delayed multiple baseline designs. However, these adaptations may also include problems that potentially weaken the possibility of demonstrating the functional relationship between the independent and dependent variables.

Multiple Probe Design

The multiple probe design (Horner & Baer, 1978) may be used as an adaptation to designs addressing multiple behaviors, settings, or individuals. The primary variation in the multiple probe design is to de-

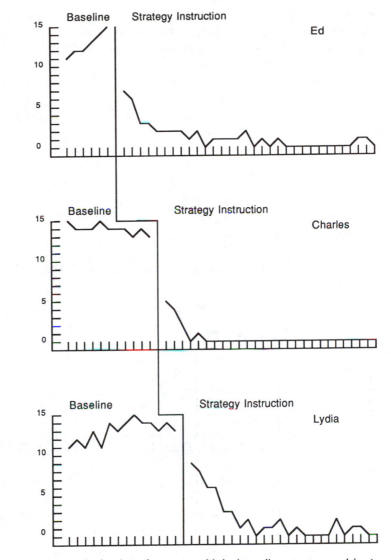

Figure 7–7. Example fo data from a multiple baseline across subjects design.

crease the collection of data across multiple baselines (and possibly during follow-up or maintenance phases). In this adaptation, the researcher collects data across the multiple baselines at the study's outset, but does not maintain continuous recording of all baseline measures before the introduction of the intervention. Rather, the researcher makes periodic recordings of baseline levels to ensure that no significant changes have occurred before the introduction of the intervention (see Figure 7–8 which uses data from a previous example in this chapter modified to demonstrate a multiple probe design). The periodic measures are referred to as probes, hence the design's name. The periodic probes may

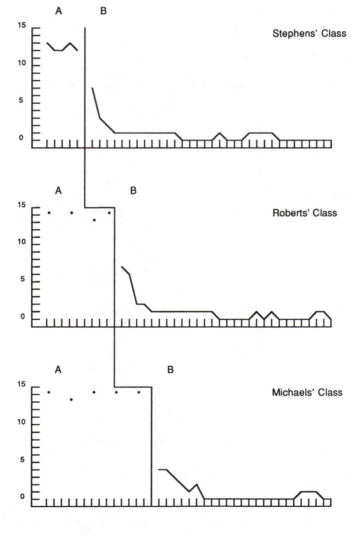

Figure 7–8. Example of data from a multiple probe design.

be used because they reduce the need for resources that may be unavailable to maintain continuous recording of behavior during baseline phases, or because baseline measures are causing severe reactivity, or because there is a strong a priori assumption of stability (e.g., the target behavior is not likely to be emitted until the intervention is introduced, as it does not yet exist in the individual's behavioral repertoire; Horner & Baer, 1978). Also, once optimal or criterion responding is achieved during an intervention phase, the researcher may resort to data probes to ensure that changes are being maintained. This last procedure is used commonly within many designs and is not unique to the multiple probe design.

Prediction, verification, and replication are achieved through the same processes discussed with the basic multiple baseline design, with one noteworthy element. Because there is not continuous recording of baseline data, the researcher should be aware that the demonstration of a functional relationship between the independent and dependent variables is at greater risk. For example, if one or more of the probes of a baseline measure appeared inconsistent with other probes, one may have difficulty explaining this phenomenon or providing an adequate argument that covariance was not occurring, or that a stable baseline level of responding had been achieved. Also, this lack of continuous measurement of data may make a subsequent change in responding following the intervention less obvious.

The critical issues in implementing a multiple probe design are the same as those for multiple behaviors, settings, and individuals. The major advantage to the multiple probe design is that fewer resources are required. The major disadvantage is that the functional relationship may be more difficult to demonstrate. The researcher may wish to take several precautions. First, the researcher must ensure that an adequate number of probes are conducted so that one may easily infer that those probes do represent a true depiction of baseline responding. Second, should a probe result in a measurement that significantly deviates from other measures, the researcher may need to implement continuous recording for that baseline (or at least more frequent measures) to obtain insight into why this may be occurring and to establish a true baseline level of responding (Horner & Baer, 1978). Third, the researcher may wish to conduct a short but continuous baseline measure for each behavior, setting, or individual just before the introduction of the independent variable to assist in establishing a better depiction of baseline level responding. Although in the latter two instances the advantage of reduced need for resources may be diminished or forfeited, the greater disadvantage of failure to demonstrate a functional relationship between independent and dependent variables may be avoided.

Delayed Multiple Baseline Design

The delayed multiple baseline design also may be used across behaviors, settings, or individuals. This design may be employed when inadequate resources are available for continuous recording of baselines, but is usually used when either of two following contingencies arise (Cooper et al., 1987). First, the researcher begins the study with the intention of using a withdrawal design. Some unforeseen occurrence makes the use of such a design impossible (e.g., other persons concerned with the outcomes of the study are concerned about introducing a withdrawal phase). In this situation, the researcher may attempt to salvage the ability to demonstrate a functional relationship by introducing the intervention following a baseline on another behavior, in another setting, or with another individual. Second, new behaviors, settings, or individuals could emerge during the study that are in need of similar treatment. For example, a student may begin to display a new behavior that is functionally similar to but independent of the target behavior. An individual may begin emitting the target behavior in settings where it had not previously occurred. Another individual who had not previously done so may begin to emit the same target behavior. Also, other settings or individuals in need of treatment may become available if principals concerned with the original study are convinced that the treatment is effective and should be applied with other behaviors, settings, or individuals. In these contingencies, the delayed multiple baseline design is probably not planned a priori, which presents a separate difficulty with prediction, verification, and replication.

Following is an example of a delayed multiple baseline design.

Ms. Johnson is a first-year teacher who works with fourth-grade students. She has had considerable difficulty in managing Robert's behavior. Mr. Hilary has been asked to assist her with her problem. After observing and recording ABCs in the class, the two agree that Robert is a student with learning difficulties whose behavior is much in need of changing. Robert is very disruptive by making loud and inappropriate comments during class. Mr. Hilary and Ms. Johnson have agreed to use differential reinforcement of other behavior to diminish disruptive talking out. After four sessions, the disruptive behavior has dropped to an acceptable level of no more than one response per class period. Unfortunately, Robert has begun disrupting in Ms. Davis' music class now, where heretofore he had been quite pleasant. Mr. Hilary confers with Ms. Davis and the two measure baseline levels of disruptive behavior, implement the intervention, and meet with success in only five sessions. Meanwhile, the low level of responding has been maintained in Ms. Johnson's class.

Finally, Robert begins to exhibit the same disruptive behavior in physical education with Coach Michaels. Again, Mr. Hilary obtains baseline data and the intervention is again successful and continues to be so in all settings. In this scenario, new settings emerged that were not evident at the outset of the study. Figure 7–9 depicts the results of this delayed multiple baseline study.

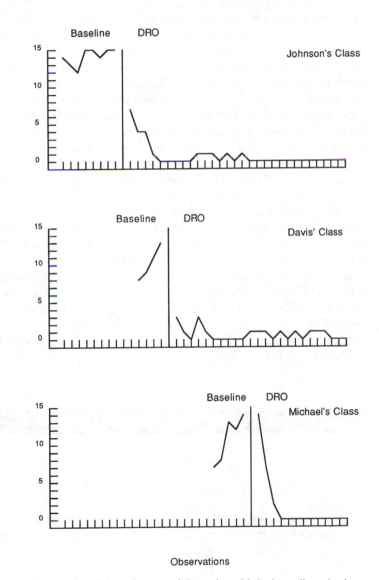

Figure 7–9. Example of data from a delayed multiple baseline design.

The major advantages to the delayed design is that it may allow the use of fewer resources and it may allow the researcher to extend the study to new behaviors, settings, and individuals that had not been targeted a priori. Cooper et al. (1987) noted three limitations to delayed designs. First, delaying treatment for other behaviors, in other settings, or with other individuals may be problematic, although this difficulty is inherent in multiple baseline designs in general. Second, fewer data points may have been gathered and the length of the various baselines may differ. Third, the use of delayed baselines when new behaviors, settings, or individuals emerge may mask the effects of the independent variable on the dependent variable. That is, the researcher is less likely to demonstrate that each baseline remains unchanged even when the treatment is introduced to other baselines. The fact that new possibilities emerge may suggest some influence occurring in the study that the researcher may have difficulty explaining. As Cooper et al. (1987) stressed, the best use of the delayed multiple baseline design may be to add tiers to an already existing multiple baseline design, which enhances further the demonstration of a functional relationship established during the course of the study as originally planned.

Multiple baseline designs are versatile and relatively easy to understand. They are found frequently in the literature and are perhaps the most common design in use today. As the reader will note in Chapter 8, pure designs are not always found when one reviews a study in which a multiple baseline design was used. Changing criteria, changing conditions, and even withdrawals are sometimes found, in addition to the alternatives discussed here in Chapter 7. Do not let these variations throw you as you review the research literature. Rather, take note of how well these designs may be manipulated and altered to meet the needs of individuals in many settings.

Summary Checklist

Basic goal of multiple baseline design—Demonstration of a functional relationship between the target behavior and intervention by replicating the intervention effects with two or more behaviors, in two or more settings, or with two or more individuals.

Basic design—The basic multiple baseline design includes two or more A-B designs where baseline data are simultaneously measured and the intervention is introduced to one behavior, in one setting, or with one individual at a time.

Prediction—After baseline data are stable, the prediction would be that there would be no change in the data path for the dependent variables if there was no intervention effect.

Verification—When the intervention is implemented, the data path changes predictably for the dependent variable.

Replication—The prediction and verification are repeated for each dependent variable.

Covariance—This occurs when baseline measures change in the same direction as during an intervention phase although the intervention has not yet been implemented with that dependent variable; this is a threat to internal validity.

Advantages—Withdrawal of treatment is not required; sequential implementation of the independent variable parallels the practice of teachers; generalization of behavior change is monitored within the design; the design is easily conceptualized and used.

Disadvantages—Possibility of covariance of dependent variables; the demonstration of the functional relationship is not as direct as in a withdrawal design; there is typically only one intervention phase with each dependent variable, reducing the opportunities to study the functional relationship; requires substantial resources to maintain multiple baselines and is time consuming.

Multiple baseline across behaviors design—The same intervention is applied to similar behaviors in the same individual in the same setting.

Multiple baseline across settings design—The same intervention is applied to the same behavior in the same individual in different settings.

Multiple baseline across subjects design—The same intervention is applied to the same or similar behaviors, in the same setting, to different individuals.

Adaptations

Multiple probe design—May be adapted to any of the basic designs; data probes are taken during baselines rather than continuous measurement; reduces need for resources; potentially leads to problems if probes are too infrequent or do not suggest steady baseline responding.

Delayed multiple baseline design—Used when a withdrawal design no longer is possible or when other behaviors, settings, or individuals emerge that are in need of intervention; baselines are not measured simultaneously; potential problems in demonstrating a functional relationship.

References

Alberto, P. A., & Troutman, A. C. (1999). *Applied behavior analysis for teachers* (5th ed.). Englewood Cliffs, NJ: Prentice-Hall.

Baer, D. M., Wolf, M. W., & Risley, T. R. (1968). Some current dimensions of applied behavior analysis. *Journal of Applied Behavior Analysis, 1,* 91–97.

Barlow, D. H., & Hersen, M. (1984). *Single-case experimental designs: Strategies for studying behavior change* (2nd ed.). New York: Pergamon Press.

Cooper, J. O., Heron, T. E., & Heward, W. L. (1987). *Applied behavior analysis.* Columbus, OH: Merrill.

Hersen, M., & Barlow, D. H. (1975). *Single-case experimental designs: Strategies for studying behavior change.* New York: Pergamon Press.

Horner, R. D., & Baer, D. M. (1978). Multiple-probe technique: A variation of the multiple baseline. *Journal of Applied Behavior Analysis, 11,* 189–196.

Kucera, J., & Axelrod, S. (1995). Multiple-baseline designs. In S. B. Neuman & S. McCormick (Eds.), *Single-subject experimental research: Applications for literacy* (pp. 47–63). Newark, DE: International Reading Association.

Tawney, J. W., & Gast, D. L. (1984). *Single subject resesarch in special education.* Columbus, OH: Merrill.

CHAPTER 8

Application of Multiple Baseline Designs

In this chapter we will discuss studies related to multiple baseline designs. The studies will demonstrate multiple baseline designs across behaviors, across settings, and across subjects. In the interest of space, we have not included adaptations. There are examples in the literature, although multiple probe and delayed multiple baseline designs in particular are less common than the basic design examples presented here.

We will determine whether each study is designed to increase or decrease behavior and whether the study addresses outcomes related to academic, social, behavioral, linguistic, or physical needs. The background for the studies will be presented in a chart that describes the subjects, research question(s) presented in the study, setting, independent and dependent variables, results, limitations, and any interesting aspects of the study related to the use of the design.

MULTIPLE BASELINE ACROSS BEHAVIORS DESIGN

Hargrove, P. M., Roetzel, K., & Hoodin, R. B. (1989). Modifying the prosody of a language-impaired child. *Language, Speech, and Hearing Services in the Schools, 20,* 245–258.

Research Question

The investigators determined if a behaviorally based treatment can affect or modulate prosody of a child with language impairments.

Subject

The subject in this study was a 6-year-old male who had been receiving services for language dysfluencies and unintelligible speech from the age of 3½ years. Nonlinguistic development was essentially normal except for a heart murmur and recurrent middle ear infections. Although progress had been realized, the child's spontaneous speech was still characterized by prosodic problems.

Setting

The setting for the study was the child's home. The trainer for the study was a graduate student in speech-language pathology who administered the training and probe procedures for each of the sessions. The trainer had herself received practice in administering the intervention before the study began. Videotaping was used as a part of the practice sessions. The training was administered twice daily over a 9-day period in 2 consecutive weeks. No other speech or language training was offered to the child during this period.

Dependent Variable

The dependent variable in this study was the prosodic performance of the child. The criterion established was 78% correct performance on a targeted contradiction type (subject, verb, or object) on a posttraining session probe task or completion of seven consecutive training sessions regardless of percent correct. The seven-session criterion was used because of concerns about involving the child in an extended study. Four elements, including use of stress, intonation, and syntactic structures were used to determine correctness of responses.

The child's performance on the probe tasks is depicted in Figure 8–1 which includes percent of correct responses on subject, verb, and object contradictions during baseline, and treatment and a final no-treatment phase for each target behavior. The subject training sessions encompassed Sessions 4–9, the verb training sessions occurred during Sessions 10–16, and the object training sessions were from Sessions 17–21.

Independent Variable

The independent variable consisted of training and reinforcement elements. Positive verbal feedback, token reinforcement, and a variety of cues were used during the intervention. Verbal feedback and tokens were delivered for correct responses following presentation of the discriminative stimulus (an enactment and a question). If a response was incorrect, the trainer used a variety of cues to elicit the target response. The training procedures were expected to provide generalization of target responses to the probe tasks.

Design

A multiple baseline across behaviors design was used to test the effectiveness of the intervention with three functionally similar yet independent behaviors of the same subject in the same setting. The intervention was sequentially applied as the criterion level of performance

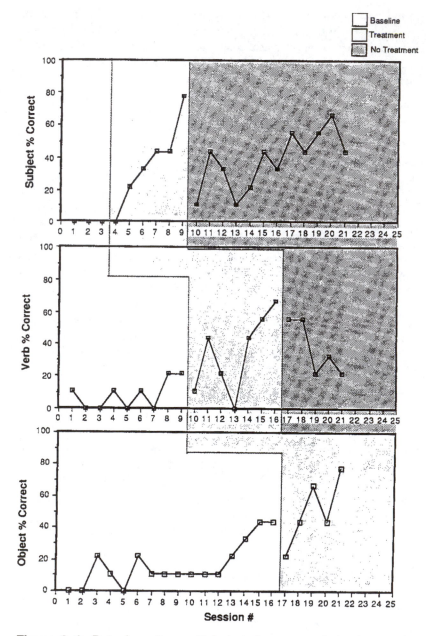

Figure 8–1. Data from the multiple baseline across behaviors study. *Note.* From "Modifying the Prosody of a Language-Impaired Child," by P. Hargrove, K. Roetzel, and R. Hoodin, 1989, *Language, Speech and Hearing Services in Schools, 20*, p. 253. Copyright 1989 by the American Speech, Language, and Hearing Association. Reprinted with permission.

was met on the preceding target behavior. Treatment was also discontinued with a target behavior once criterion was achieved.

Intervention

This intervention involved the controlled sequential training of sentences that were organized in blocks by subjects, verbs, and objects. The child was taught to label lexical items in the tasks. The trainer provided an enactment and then asked the child a question in which one of the block elements (subject, verb, or object) was incorrect. The desired targeted response would be the contradiction of the trainer's question (e.g., Trainer: "Is Ann holding the pen?"; Child: "No, Bob is holding the pen."). The order of the blocks and the order of the sentences within the blocks were randomly determined. Each training session used 27 target sentences that represented various permutations of the subjects, verbs, and objects. Probe sessions (which immediately followed the training) also consisted of 27 different but similar permutations. During the probe task the trainer withheld feedback regarding response accuracy.

Obtaining the Data and Plotting the Results

The data obtained consisted of the subject's performance on probe tasks that involved the use of subject, verb, and object contradictions. Data were plotted on x-y graphs which in turn were used to determine the subject's performance with these untrained stimuli.

Results

The results from this study indicated that prosody was modifiable through the intervention. The program's success is demonstrated by noting the progress of the subject. The performance of the subject on the probes reached a 78% level of accuracy on two of the behaviors and 67% on the third (when training was terminated due to reaching the seven consecutive training session constraint). Given that the primary purpose of the study was to investigate if the prosodic skills of a child with language impairments would improve using a specific treatment procedure, the results support rapid improvement, although maintenance of the performance was unstable. Interobserver agreement concerning implementation of the independent variable was 100% (although adherence to the training procedures was rated at 98.1%–100%). Interobserver agreement concerning the correctness of the child's responses during probes was 76% (87% for intraobserver agreement). The authors noted that the 76% level of agreement may have been due to the trainer being more lenient in assessing the correctness of the child's responses.

Why Use a Multiple Baseline Across Behaviors Design?

The investigators were interested in determining if a subject could improve prosodic performance using contradictions related to subjects, verbs, and objects. Using an across behaviors design would permit performance on these three speech parts to be treated as separate behaviors. An important component of across behaviors designs is selecting behaviors that are functionally independent of one another yet similar enough that they are likely to change for the same treatment. The lack of covariance among the targeted responses before implementation of the training procedure strengthens the argument for internal validity.

Limitations of the Study

The limitations of this study include the lack of identification of the *training* components or combination of components that might have been responsible for changes. For example, the trainer was allowed to select from a variety of cues following an incorrect response during the training phase of the intervention (training loosely). However, as noted, data indicated that the trainer adhered to the procedures as they were defined. The generalization from training to probe conditions was substantial, although the gains were not fully maintained. Among the modifications, suggestions included implementing a longer training phase, more vigorous criterion, or addition of a maintenance phase.

Summary

A summary of the relevant components of this study demonstrating an across behaviors multiple baseline design is found in Table 8–1. This study demonstrates how similar behaviors may be changed in the same subject in the same setting.

Table 8–1. Summary of "Modifying the Prosody of a Language-Impaired Child."

Feature	Description
Type of Design	Multiple baseline across behaviors
Goal of study	Determine if a behaviorally based treatment can affect or modulate prosody of a child with language-impairments
Subject	Six-year-old male receiving services for language dysfluencies
Setting	The child's home
Dependent variable	The prosodic performance of the child
Independent variable	Positive verbal feedback, token reinforcement, and a variety of cues along with specific training
Results and outcomes	The performance by the subject on the probe items reached a 78% level of accuracy on two of the behaviors and 67% on the third over the 18 training sessions that were implemented over a 9-day period

MULTIPLE BASELINE ACROSS SUBJECTS DESIGN

Yoder, P. J., Yarren, S. F., Kim, K., & Gazdag, G. E. (1994). Facilitating prelinguistic communication skills in young children with developmental delay: II. Systematic replication and extension. *Journal of Speech and Hearing Research, 37,* 841–851.

Research Question

Several questions were presented in the study that were addressed through the following hypotheses: (a) modified milieu teaching facilitates the increased use of intentional requests in both intervention (with staff) and generalizaton (with mothers) sessions; (b) mothers, who were naive to the intervention, would linguistically map a greater number and proportion of the children's communicative acts during the intervention phase than during the baseline phase; and (c) classroom teachers and mothers would be more likely to linguistically map intentional than preintentional communication acts. Here, we will focus primarily on the first hypothesis.

Subjects

The subjects in this study were 4 children with mental retardation between the ages of 21 and 27 months who were recruited from a university-based school for toddlers and preschoolers with developmental disabilities. Using standardized data from infant development and communication behavior scales as well as baseline and other data, the subjects were identified as communicating well below levels expected for their chronological ages including absence of speech and delayed production of intentional requesting.

Setting

The setting for the study was a university-based early intervention program designed for children from birth to 3 years. Children in the program were identified as being at risk for developmental delays. All sessions, including baseline and intervention sessions, occurred in a playroom that was furnished with age-appropriate materials.

Dependent Variable

Data were collected on a range of adult and child behaviors. However, we will focus on the data concerning child behaviors. Subjects' behaviors were coded for intentional prompted and self-initiated requests, other intentional communication (e.g., comments, protests, greetings), and preintentional signals. The investigators used videotaping to aid in data collection. Whether by direct observation or videotape, 10-min samples of behavior were coded. Subjects' intentional requests were recorded with interventionists (circles in Figure 8–2) and with mothers (triangles in Figure 8–2). See Figure 8–2 for the graphic depiction of the results of this study. The subjects are noted by the letters A–D.

Independent Variable

The milieu teaching method was used to increase the intentional requesting of the four children in the study. Fading of prompts was used as part of the teaching procedure. Presumably, the activities in which the children were engaged and the attention received from staff and mothers provided reinforcement.

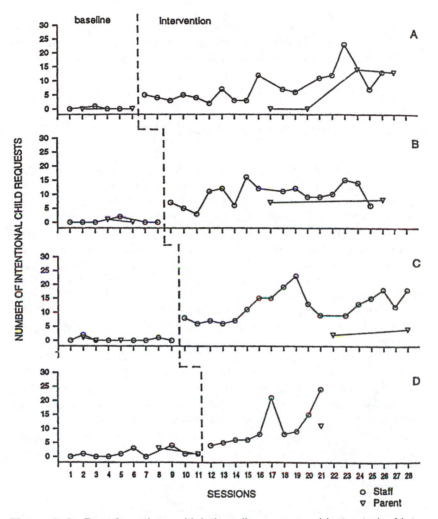

Figure 8–2. Data from the multiple baseline across subjects study. *Note.* From "Facilitating Prelinguistic Communication Skills in Young Children with Developmental Delay: II. Systematic Replication and Extension," by P. Yoder, S. Warren, K. Kim, and G. Gazdag, 1994, *Journal of Speech and Hearing Research, 37*, p. 847. Copyright 1994 by the American Speech, Language, and Hearing Association. Reprinted with permission.

Design

A multiple baseline across subjects design was used to evaluate if an intervention aimed at teaching intentional requesting to the 4 subjects in the study would be effective. Following the baseline period, the intervention was sequentially used with the subjects. The researchers used abrupt changes in the level of responding and slope of the data path as indicators of intervention effects rather than a specific criterion level to determine when to implement the intervention with the next subject.

Intervention

Two staff members who had been trained in the milieu teaching method implemented the intervention with the subjects. During the baseline sessions with staff members, communication with the 4 subjects was not encouraged, although there were many opportunities for interactions to occur. In sessions with the mothers, the parents talked to and played with their children. The baseline lengths varied with each child, but in all cases the staff sessions preceded the mothers sessions, and staff sessions were more numerous than those with the mothers. The data derived from sessions with mothers were used to assist in evaluating generalization and transactional effects. Teaching sessions were conducted 4 days per week for 25 min each. The number of teaching sessions varied with the 4 subjects. During the intervention sessions, efforts were made by the trainers to engage the subjects in an activity that would sustain their interest. Once it was clear that the subject was attentionally engaged in the activity, the trainer used various direct prompts to teach requesting (e.g., stopping a routine and asking a child, "What do you want?"; i.e., continue the activity). When appropriate, the trainer provided direct questioning, demonstrations, or physical assistance to initiate or complete the requesting acts. As the children acquired the target behavior, fewer prompts were used until intentional requesting could be elicited by simply stopping the routine.

Obtaining the Data and Plotting the Results

The results were displayed on x-y graphs that included the number of child intentional requests to staff and mothers. The number of intentional requests and communicative acts increased in all 4 subjects during the intervention stage.

Results

The results of this study indicated that the modified milieu teaching approach is an effective method for facilitating intentional, prelinguistic requesting in young children with mental retardation. This intervention was successful in facilitating generalized prelinguistic communication in the subjects' interactions with their mothers, as well as with their teachers (although these data are not included here). It is also of interest that the researchers used nonparametric statistical analyses to determine that both teachers and mothers linguistically mapped intentional communicative acts more than preintentional acts (the aforementioned adult behaviors that were coded and related to the other two hypotheses). The mean interobserver agreement for intentional requesting across all subjects was 90.9%.

Why Use a Multiple Baseline Across Subjects Design?

The researchers chose this design for several reasons. First, it was easier to observe the effects of the intervention across subjects using this design. Second, other designs would have been inappropriate. For example, a withdrawal design might not have been possible in that once the requesting had increased, it might have been difficult to reverse this behavior in order to demonstrate a functional relationship. Third, the staggered introduction of the intervention helped build a strong case for verification and replication within the design itself. This may have been more efficient and less intrusive to the subjects than some other design. Finally, it was anticipated before the study that there would be a functional relationship between the intervention and the subjects' performance on the basis of previous research conducted in the area of the milieu approach.

Limitations of the Study

The researchers noted several limitations of the study. First, it was difficult to get the mothers into the clinic for the intervention sessions. In addition, the effects of the generalization with the mothers were not expected to be immediate due to the level of retardation of the students. For this reason, the generalization sessions were scheduled late into the intervention. It was also noted that, for future research, an extended study with control and experimental groups might strengthen the validity of the findings. Although small groups are a strength of single subject research designs, such a small group (4 subjects) can affect degree of confidence in the generalizability of the intervention.

Summary

A summary of the relevant dimensions of the multiple baseline across subjects design can be found in Table 8–2. The reader should keep in

Table 8–2. Summary of "Facilitating Prelinguistic Communication Skills in Young Children With Developmental Delay: II. Systematic Replication and Extension."

Feature	Description
Type of design	Multiple baseline across subjects
Goal of study	Determine effectiveness of the modified milieu method for increasing intentional requests; other hypotheses were posited although not focused on here
Subjects	Four children between ages 21 and 27 months with mental retardation
Setting	University-based early intervention program
Dependent variable	Subjects' behavior for intentional prompted and self-initiated requests and other intentional communication and preintentional signals; other data were recorded although not focused on here
Independent variable	Modified milieu teaching approach
Results and outcomes	The modified milieu teaching approach is an effective method for increasing intentional requesting and facilitating generalized communication in the subjects' interactions with their mothers

mind that we have discussed the results primarily in reference to the children's targeted behavior.

MULTIPLE BASELINE ACROSS SETTINGS DESIGNS

Cushing, L. S., & Kennedy, C. H. (1997). Academic effects of providing peer support in general education classrooms on students without disabilities, *Journal of Applied Behavior Analysis, 30,* 139–151.

Research Question

The research question in this study focused on whether peer support provided by students without disabilities to students with disabilities would have positive or negative effects on academic engagement and associated measures for the peers without disabilities.

Subjects

The subjects in the part of the study being presented here were two 11-year-old students, Louie and Leila. It should be noted that the study included other student dyads, although, for our purposes, we are focusing on only one because of the design used. Leila was identified as a student with moderate intellectual disabilities and Louie was identified as a peer to work with Leila. Louie was selected because he was in the same classes as Leila, he had previously expressed a desire to work with a student with disabilities, and his engagement in class activities was below average. Leila was identifed as sociable but she had a limited vocabulary and articulation difficulties. Louie was identified as being occasionally disruptive, was not turning in assignments, was receiving very low grades, and had difficulty paying attention.

Setting

The study was carried out at a suburban intermediate school with 1,100 students from diverse backgrounds. Students in the school who were eligible for special education were provided with services while participating full-time in general education settings. The English, science, and social studies classes served as the three experimental settings.

Dependent Variable

The dependent variable in this study was percentage of time academically engaged for Louie, which was defined as attending to ongoing classroom activities, engaging in work-related assignments, or both. A 1-min momentary time-sampling recording procedure was used (the subject was observed for 1 s at the end of each min throughout the 55-min class periods). The observers were special education personnel who had been trained in the use of the observational system. A graphic depiction of the results of this study is presented in Figure 8–3. The broken line in the data path included in the social studies graph indicates an absence for Louie.

Independent Variable

The independent variable was the peer support system of academic engagement that included Louie's participation with Leila, training and

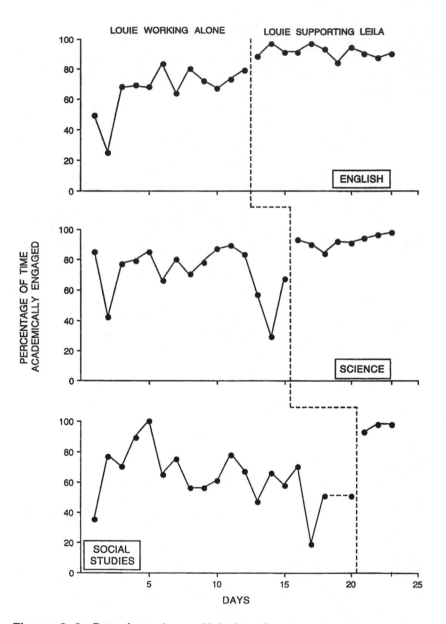

Figure 8–3. Data from the multiple baseline across settings design. *Note.* From "Academic Effects of Providing Peer Support in General Education Classrooms on Students Without Disabilities," by L. F. Cushing and C. H. Kennedy, 1997, *Journal of Applied Behavior Analysis, 30*, p. 146. Copyright 1997 by Society for the Experimental Analysis of Behavior. Reprinted with permission.

supervision by a special education teacher, and supervision by the general education teacher. More specifically, Louie worked with Leila on assignment completion, classroom participation, and adaptation of assignments. Special education personnel commented on Louie's performance approximately once every 10 min. Assistance was provided by personnel if Louie had difficulty with course content or adapting content, and brief daily feedback was provided regarding his performance. In addition, general education teachers were asked to praise Louie at least once in each class when he was serving as a peer support.

Design

A multiple baseline across settings design was used within this study for this particular student dyad (other designs were used with other dyads). The intervention was sequentially applied in each setting as Louie's academic engagement increased from baseline levels.

Intervention

The intervention applied in this study was the peer support provided to Leila by Louie. This support centered around special education personnel teaching Louie how to interact with Leila, including behavioral management strategies, adapting assignments to meet Individualized Education Program goals, and communication strategies. For example, Louie was taught to adapt assignments through verbal descriptions, modeling, and praise for correct performances. He also took notes for Leila and revised those notes to accommodate her. Training in adapting assignments was provided by special education personnel and occurred over several days.

Obtaining the Data and Plotting the Results

The percentage of time academically engaged for Louie when he worked alone was recorded across different settings, which included his English, science, and social studies classes. These data served as baseline measures, and observations were conducted under routine class conditions. The baseline data were compared to the observations conducted when Louie served as a peer supporter for Leila in each of the three settings. The number of observations conducted during baseline and peer support varied for each setting.

Results

The results indicated that the percentage of time in which Louie was academically engaged increased during the periods he was serving as a peer support for Leila. Also, a Likert-type scale was used to measure adults' perceptions of Louie's classroom performance. These data also indicated consistent overall increases for Louie across a variety of behaviors, including listening to and following directions, participating in activities, completing assignments, bringing supplies, and following rules. The data from this scale were intended to lend increased validity to the quantitative changes observed.

Why Use a Multiple Baseline Across Settings Design?

For this study, it would have been a less convincing demonstration of a functional relationship if observations were conducted in only one setting. Because the settings were similar but functionally independent of one another, the multiple baseline design offered the advantages of providing intervention in all settings of need without having to withdraw treatment. It is worth noting that covariance among the dependent variables was not evident, particularly in the social studies class, which was the last setting in which the intervention was implemented. There was also a notable increase in percentage of time engaged immediately following implementation of the intervention, particularly in the last two settings. This strengthened the demonstration of the functional relationship.

Limitations of the Study

One limitation of the study is the selection of students used for the study. The authors contend that because the sample of students was so selective, the robustness of the findings requires systematic replication across a variety of students without disabilities. Another area of concern is whether positive effects would occur for students who are already performing at high levels in general education classes. In this case, Louie was not performing to his perceived potential, and, as a result, there was an expectation that this intervention would result in improvement.

Summary

This study is summarized in Table 8–3. Please note that withdrawal designs were also included in this study, although we chose to focus on

Table 8–3. Summary of "Academic Effects of Providing Peer Support in General Education Classrooms on Students Without Disabilities."

Feature	Description
Type of design	Multiple baseline across settings
Goal of study	Peer support provided by students without disabilities to students with disabilities will have positive effects on academic engagement and associated measures for the peers without disabilities
Subjects	Two 11-year-old students, Louie (student without disabilities) and Leila
Setting	Suburban intermediate school with 1,100 students from diverse backgrounds; English, science, and social studies classes
Dependent variable	Percentage of time academically engaged for Louie, defined as involvement in ongoing classroom activities and/or work-related assignments
Independent variable	The peer support system of academic engagement that included participation with student with disabilities and training and/or supervision from special education and general education teachers
Results and outcomes	The percent of time in which Louie was academically engaged increased during the periods he was serving as a peer support for Leila

Louie and Leila because this represented a multiple baseline across settings design.

Multiple baseline designs are versatile and relatively easy to understand. Yet, the time and resources required to conduct multiple baseline studies are sometimes problematic. In addition, there may be no other behaviors, settings, or individuals available who are in need of the intervention. At times, the need to identify an effective intervention as quickly as possible is very important. For these reasons, other designs may be appropriate, including the alternating treatments design discussed in the following chapter.

CHAPTER 9

Overview of Alternating Treatments Designs

The alternating treatments design allows for the comparison of the effects of two or more independent variables (treatments) on the same behavior. This is a very important design for educators and clinicians who frequently are concerned with which of several intervention procedures is the most effective. The alternating treatments design has also been referred to as the multielement design (Ulman & Sulzer-Azaroff, 1975) and the multiple schedule design (Hersen & Barlow, 1976). It has also been erroneously called the simultaneous treatments design (Kazdin & Hartmann, 1978) or the concurrent schedule design (Hersen & Barlow, 1976). These latter designs are actually a modification of the alternating treatments design and are discussed later in this chapter.

The basic use of the alternating treatments design requires the "rapid alternation of two or more distinct treatments (i.e., independent variables) while their effects on a single target behavior are noted" (Cooper, Heron, & Heward, 1987; p. 181). In fact, the treatments can be alternated within sessions, across different times of the same day, or across different days. There are two important points that should be made about the alternating treatments design. First, the presentation of the treatments should be counterbalanced. If, for example, there were three treatments (A, B, and C), they could be presented randomly (e.g., ABBCAB-CAC) or in blocks. There are six possible blocks of the three treatments: ABC, BCA, CAB, ACB, BAC, CBA. The researcher would make sure that each treatment (or block of treatments) is presented the same number of times (Alberto & Troutman, 1999). It is important to note that *all* aspects of the treatment should be counterbalanced. For example if the treatments are given at different times of the day or by more than one person, then those aspects of the study should be counterbalanced as well. The second important point is that the subjects should be able to discriminate between or among the treatment conditions. This is made easier if the treatments are sufficiently different from one another. In some cases the nature of the treatment will help the subject discriminate (e.g., use of a worksheet vs. manipulatives to increase math computation skills). It might also be necessary to use verbal cues (e.g., "Today you will receive bonus points for completing your science workbook assignment"). Other means such as cue cards or signs can also be used. The important issue is that a distinct stimulus should be associated with each treatment (Cooper et al., 1987).

One interesting characteristic of the alternating treatments design is that, unlike typical single subject designs, it does not require the collection of baseline data. Neuman (1995) pointed out, however, that whenever possible baseline data should still be collected. There are, in fact, three different types of the basic alternating treatments designs, two of which incorporate baseline data and one of which does not. The three types are the alternating treatments without baseline, baseline followed by alternating treatments, and baseline followed by alternating treatments with a final treatment phase. It should also be noted that the alternating treatments design is frequently used in conjunction with other single subject designs. For example, the first phase of a study might use an alternating treatments design to determine which of several interventions is the most effective. Next, a withdrawal design (discussed in Chapter 5) might be used to further establish the functional relationship between the most effective treatment and the target behavior.

ALTERNATING TREATMENTS WITH NO BASELINE DESIGN

As noted previously, it is not necessary to collect baseline data when using the alternating treatments design. Thus, the treatment phases can be implemented immediately. It should be emphasized, however, that many individuals who use this design actually include a type of baseline data by having a no-treatment phase as one of the alternating treatments. This is sometimes referred to as the alternating treatments with a control condition design (Alberto & Troutman, 1995). Cooper et al. (1987) cautioned, however, that a no-treatment condition should not be considered the same as a preintervention baseline condition. When the no-treatment phase is alternated with various treatment phases, there may be multiple treatment interference (Barlow & Hayes, 1979), in which the effects of one condition carry over or in some way affect the other condition(s). This could result in the data from the no-treatment phase being different from baseline data recorded before any treatment is introduced. The issue of multiple treatment interference was discussed in Chapter 4 and is described in more depth later in this chapter.

The following is an example of an alternating treatments design with no baseline. Note that in this example a no-treatment condition was included.

Jimmy and Sue are two 5-year-old students with mild autism who have minimal but evident and emerging verbal skills. They frequently use more negative statements (e.g., "Not like you" and "Shut up") than positive sentences (e.g., "Like to play?" and "What's your name?") when interacting with their peers. The teacher wanted to increase the number of positive statements made by the two students. She decided to determine the effectiveness of the use of verbal praise versus a token system as reinforcers for positive sentences. She had noted that both of these approaches had seemed to work in the past but was unsure of their relative effectiveness. After carefully defining what was to be considered positive statements, she randomly assigned three treatment conditions: no reinforcer for a positive statement (A), verbal praise for a positive statement (B), and presentation of a token for a positive statement (C). The various contingencies and data collection were initiated during the 30-min free-play time that was scheduled each day. She carefully explained the token system that had been used in the class before, which used a reinforcement menu individualized for each student. At the beginning of the day, the teacher told the student which condition would be in effect. For example, "Today, I am going to tell you what a great job you are doing every time you say something nice to your classmates" or "Today I am going to give you a token so you can earn something on your wish list every time you say something nice to your classmates."

As noted, it is important that the treatments be randomly assigned or counterbalanced in some way to avoid order effects. Data would then be collected to determine which of the three treatment conditions was the most effective. These data are graphically presented in Figure 9–1. This same design could also be used by omitting the no-treatment phase and just comparing the two treatment conditions, although it would not provide the valuable information regarding treatment versus no-treatment gains.

BASELINE FOLLOWED BY ALTERNATING TREATMENTS DESIGN

It is generally agreed that, whenever possible, initial baseline data should be collected before introducing the alternating treatments. Although not a requirement, ideally, as in other single subject designs, the baseline data should demonstrate a stable rate of responding. There are two situations, however, when this might not be possible or educationally or clinically appropriate. The first is when the nature of the target behavior is so severe that, ethically, baseline data should not be collected. An example of this would be self-abusive behaviors in a child. Because of the nature of the target behavior, it would be more ethical to start treatment immediately. This is similar to the situation in which a B-A-B design is used (discussed in Chapter 5). The second occasion when baseline data do not have to be stable is when the trend is moving in a countertherapeutic direction. Suppose, for example, that the frequency of a target behavior, verbal insults, did not stabilize under baseline conditions. In fact, it increased at a rather steady rate. Then the collection of baseline data could be stopped and the intervention phase introduced.

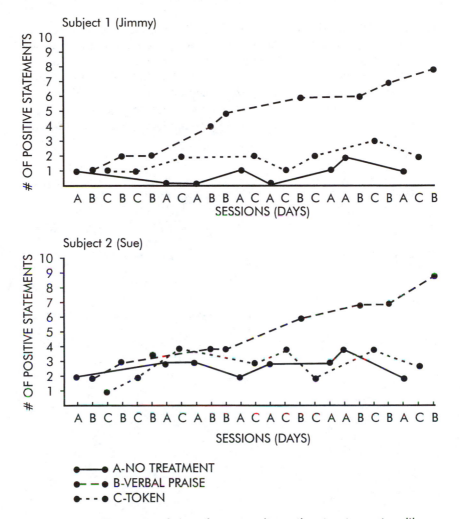

Figure 9–1. Example of data from an alternating treatements with no baseline design.

Tawney and Gast (1984) outlined four steps to follow when using the baseline followed by alternating treatments design. First, researchers should carefully define the independent and dependent variables. Second, they should determine a schedule for counterbalancing the presentation of the treatments. Third, they should collect baseline data for the dependent variable for a number of sessions. It is important to note that, although it is preferable, the baseline phase does not have to be stable before introducing the treatment. Finally, researchers should introduce the treatments in their predetermined order. Another option is to continue collecting baseline data by using a no-treatment condition as one of the alternating treatments. This becomes an even more powerful design. An example of data collected using the baseline followed by alternating treatments design using the previously described study is presented in Figure 9–2. The major difference is that the baseline data are gathered before the introduction of any treatment phase. The other dif-

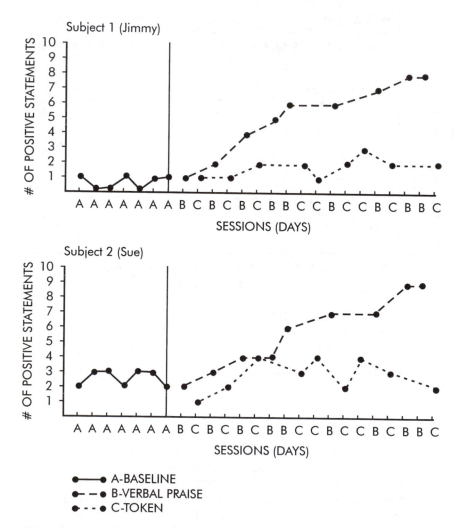

Figure 9–2. Example of data from a baseline followed by alternating treatments design.

ference from the data depicted in Figure 9–1 is that the no-treatment condition is eliminated.

BASELINE FOLLOWED BY ALTERNATING TREATMENTS AND A FINAL TREATMENT PHASE DESIGN

For both scientific and ethical reasons, it is important to continue the most effective treatment after that determination has been made. Thus, using this design, the researcher would first collect initial baseline data, then introduce the alternating treatments to determine which is the most effective, and, finally, continue the study using only the most effective treatment. Data using the baseline followed by alternating treatments and a final treatment phase are presented from the previously described study (see Figure 9–3). Note that once the determination was made that verbal praise was, in fact, the most effective treatment, it was used exclusively in the final treatment phase. In this way, the time and effort of planning and implementing the less effective token system could be eliminated.

PREDICTION, VERIFICATION, AND REPLICATION

There are some pros and cons of the alternating treatments design when it comes to prediction, verification, and replication. On the one hand, Alberto and Troutman (1999) stated that the determination of a functional relationship between the dependent and independent variables is relatively weak compared to reversal and multiple baseline designs. Also, the possibility of multiple treatment interference might produce carryover effects that obscure the relationship of the dependent variable to the various treatments. Also, as with other single subject designs, external validity is an area that should be specifically addressed. It is important to replicate the results of alternating treatments designs with different subjects, different experimenters, and/or different conditions.

On the other hand, Cooper et al. (1987) argued that the very nature of alternating treatment designs addressed each of the three issues in the following way.

1. Prediction—Each data point serves as a predictor of future behavior under the same treatment.
2. Verification—Each successive data point serves to verify previous predictions of performance under the same treatment.

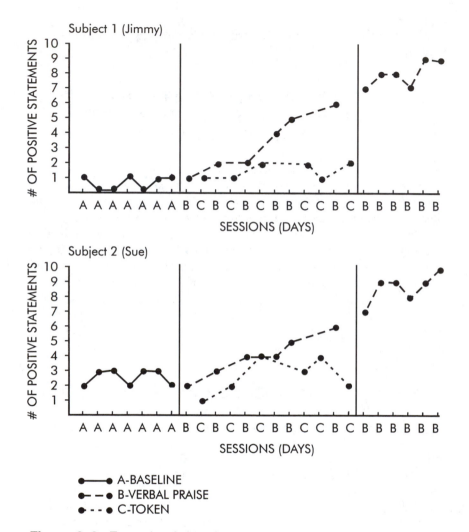

Figure 9–3. Example of data from a baseline followed by alternating treatments and a final treatment phase design.

3. Replication—Each successive data point replicates the differential effects produced by the other treatments.

Consider, for example, the data for Jimmy presented in Figure 9–1. Draw a vertical line after the 9th day or data point (after each condition has been presented three times). The last data point for each condition serves as a **predictor** for the next data point for each condition. If you then draw another line after the next set of data points (4 days later), it can **verify** the previous prediction. As you look at the rest of the data points over time, you notice the same trend continue as the three sets of data points separate. This provides **replication** of the relative effects of the different treatments.

Neuman (1995) also pointed out that the alternating treatments design may have good internal validity for two reasons. First, the patterns of response vary with the alternating treatment conditions, so there is minimal overlap among data in the conditions. Second, if one treatment is consistently associated with an improved level of responding, then the design demonstrates good experimental control. A flip side to the possible negative effect of multiple treatment interference is the possible positive effect of eliminating sequence effects through the treatment counterbalancing. What is clear is that the use of the alternating treatments design, like all single subject designs, should be based on a careful match of the dependent and independent variables.

ADVANTAGES OF THE ALTERNATING TREATMENTS DESIGN

There are many advantages of using an alternating treatments design. As noted previously, it is ideal for the teacher or clinician who is interested in determining which of several interventions is the most effective. In fact, because the treatments are alternated rapidly, the determination of their relative efficacy can usually be made faster than when using other designs. This process is especially fast if baseline data are not collected before the introduction of the interventions. It should be kept in mind, however, that researchers who want to make a stronger case for the effectiveness of the treatments should collect those pretreatment data.

Another advantage of the alternating treatments design is that the baseline data do not need to be stable before the intervention can be initiated. As noted in Chapter 4, stability of baseline is an important prerequisite for prediction, verification, and replication for most single subject designs. This is not always possible, however. Cooper et al. (1987) noted that it might be difficult to obtain stable baselines for many dependent variables merely because the behaviors change as a function of being introduced to the independent variable. This could also be viewed as practice effects. Suppose, for example, that a teacher was interested in determining the effects of a phonics versus a whole language approach on word identification. If the student first reads lists of words to establish a baseline, it is possible that the student's word identification skills might actually improve during the baseline condition due to practice effects (particularly if this was a skill that the student hadn't spent much time practicing). This could result in a baseline that never stabilizes. Again, because a stable baseline is not a prerequisite for the alternating treatments design, it might be a better choice when using dependent variables that are more susceptible to practice effects.

Some single subject designs (e.g., the A-B-A-B or A-B-A-C) require withdrawal of a treatment to demonstrate that a functional relationship exists between the independent and dependent variable(s). This is an ethical concern that is avoided when using the alternating treatments design because no withdrawal of treatment is necessary. In addition, because the determination of the most effective treatment can often be made quickly, less time may be spent administering an ineffective treatment. This could be accomplished by using the baseline followed by alternating treatments and a final treatment phase design. Again, the alternating treatments design seems to be a good design to use in an educational or therapeutic setting.

Another point, previously mentioned, is that the counterbalancing used in the alternating treatments design helps to eliminate sequencing effects. Suppose that an A-B-A-C withdrawal design discussed in Chapter 5 was used in our previously described study to determine the effects of verbal praise (B) versus tokens (C) to increase positive statements (with the A condition representing baseline). It is possible that the presentation of the verbal praise phase (B) might have an effect on the student's behavior in the token phase (C). Similarly, if the treatments had been presented in the other order, with the token phase preceding the verbal praise phase, then the first treatment condition might have an effect on the second. By using an alternating treatments design this problem could be avoided because the B and C phases (or the A, B, and C phases) would be counterbalanced.

In summary, the following guidelines can help to determine when an alternating treatments design should be used:

- When you want to determine the relative effectiveness of more than one treatment on a given behavior;
- When baseline data are either unavailable or might be unstable;
- When the treatments are sufficiently different from each other;
- When the subjects can discriminate the treatment conditions;
- When the effects of sequencing the interventions might obscure the results.

DISADVANTAGES OF THE
ALTERNATING TREATMENTS DESIGN

Although the advantages of the alternating treatments design are numerous, there are disadvantages as well. As noted previously, one major concern when using this design is the possibility of multiple treatment interference. In fact, the very nature of the alternating treatments design that requires the rapid alteration of interventions can lead directly to this situation. Multiple treatment interference results in the masking of the effects of a specific treatment because other treatments might influence, confound, or carry over. Also, as noted earlier, multiple treatment interference can even have an effect on the no-treatment condition, thus making that condition different from a true, preintervention baseline condition. It is possible to minimize multiple treatment interference in an alternating treatments design, however. First, if the various treatments are considerably different from one another then the likelihood of multiple treatment interference is minimized. Take, for example, a situation in which a researcher was interested in reducing the number of temper tantrums in a student with Down syndrome. He chose two types of time-out as the treatments. The first, contingent observation, allowed the student to see and hear what was going on in the classroom but not to receive any reinforcement. The second type, exclusionary time-out, allowed the student to hear what was happening in the classroom but not to see what was going on or to receive any reinforcement. The chance of multiple treatment interference would be greater in this situation than if contingent observation and a more dissimilar treatment such as differential reinforcement of other behavior (DRO) was used. Another suggestion to help decrease the possibility of multiple treatment interference is to include the presentation of the most effective treatment at the end of the design. This was discussed earlier as the baseline with alternating treatments and a final treatment design. In this way, the effects of the final treatment in isolation will help to eliminate the multiple treatment interference (Cooper et al., 1987).

A related issue has to do with reversibility. As was noted earlier, the withdrawal of treatment to demonstrate that the target behavior reverses toward baseline levels is not a requirement in the alternating treatments design. However, if dependent variables are chosen in which reversibility is not expected or desired, then the alternating treatments design would not be appropriate. Suppose, for example, that a teacher was interested in teaching phonics using two different methods. Once the student correctly learned a sound-symbol relationship, it is both likely and desirable that it would be retained, so the differential treatment effects could not be determined adequately.

Another disadvantage of the alternating treatments design is that it would be inappropriate to use with individuals who may not have the ability to discriminate between or among the treatment conditions. As noted earlier, this is a prerequisite for the use of the design. For example, its use with an individual with severe cognitive limitations who would have to discriminate among relatively subtle treatment conditions might not be appropriate. In addition, alternating treatments designs are not effective for evaluating independent variables that produce change slowly or that need to be administered over a continuous period of time (Neuman, 1995). In fact, the treatments should be able to produce change session by session. Consider the following two examples to demonstrate this point. The first example would be appropriate for an alternating treatments design, whereas the second would not be.

Example 1: Ms. Smith is a third-grade teacher for students with learning disabilities. She has two students in her class who perform poorly in the area of mathematics computation because they frequently perform the wrong operation (e.g., adding instead of multiplying, subtracting instead of adding). Ms. Smith wanted to see which of two interventions would be most effective. On worksheets of 25 problems the two students often would make between 7–10 mistakes because they performed the wrong operation. The first intervention involved the use of color-coded operation signs (e.g., blue +, red −, green ×) to serve as a visual cue to remind them which operation needed to be performed. The second intervention involved the use of a visual reminder "THINK SIGN" written at the top of the worksheet.

Example 2: Mr. Norris is a seventh-grade math teacher. He has three students who are having great difficulty converting fractions to percentages. He has been working on this skill with the students for over 3 weeks with little success. He decided to try two different approaches to teaching this skill. The first involved having the students memorize a conversion chart that showed the various fractions presented as percentages. The other was the use of a mnemonic device to teach the process of "Divide Top By Bottom, Multiply Times Hundred." To do this he made up the acrostic "Detroit Tigers Bat Boy Makes The Hit." The students used the first letter of each word in the saying to help remember the correct process to use.

In Example 1, an alternating treatments design could be used. Ms. Smith could have collected baseline on a series of worksheets and then randomly assigned the students to the two treatment conditions. The students should be able to discriminate the two interventions and had in their response repertoire the ability to perform differently in each session. Even here, however, the possibility of multitreatment interference is evident. It is possible that the effects of one intervention might carry over to the other.

In example 2, an alternating treatments design would probably not be the best choice. First, the students did not have the dependent variable—conversions of fractions to percentages—in their repertoire. Therefore it is unlikely that the behavior could change from session to session, at least initially. It would be necessary for the students to first learn the skill over repeated trials. Second, the goal of the mnemonic strategy intervention is for the students to remember it and use it whenever a fraction-to-percentage conversion is required. Thus the possibility of multiple treatment interference is not only possible but expected.

Other disadvantages of the alternating treatments design relate to its implementation and interpretation. Regarding implementation, Cooper et al. (1987) suggested that because this design uses *rapidly* alternating treatments, it is somewhat artificial and not typical of the method in which treatments are typically presented in the natural environment. They also pointed out that (a) it is often difficult to do the necessary counterbalancing in most natural settings and (b) typically a maximum of three treatments can be evaluated. Interpretation of data from an alternating treatments design can sometimes be ambiguous, particularly if the data paths overlap. The question becomes "How superior does one treatment need to be to assume that there are significant differences?" As will be discussed in Chapter 13, there are ways of determining statistical significance in single subject designs, although for most practitioners the question is more related to practical significance. Alberto and Troutman (1999) did state that in order to assume that one treatment is more effective than the other(s) when interpreting information from an alternating treatments design, their data paths must be separate except at the beginning of the study. Figure 9–4 shows an example of both ambiguous and unambiguous results. Note that in the data set representing ambiguous results, it is still possible to determine that using an intervention (either B or C) was better than using none (A). The superiority of B or C could not be determined, however.

In summary, the following are examples of instances when an alternating treatments design is not the most appropriate to use:

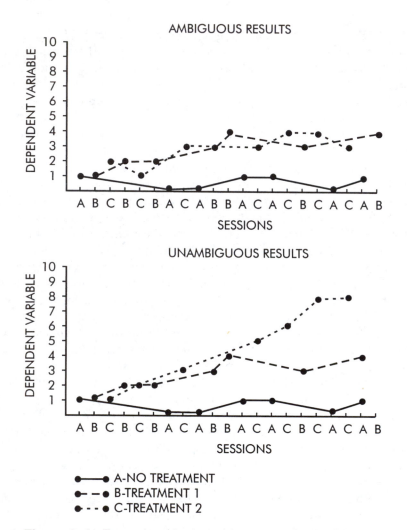

Figure 9–4. Example of both ambiguous and unambiguous results using an alternating treatments design.

- When the treatments might interact, thus obscuring the results;

- When the subjects cannot discriminate the treatment conditions;

- When the treatments typically produce slow behavior changes;

- When the treatments need to be administered over a continuous period of time to be effective;
- When it becomes difficult to counterbalance the various aspects of the study.

ADAPTATIONS OF THE ALTERNATING TREATMENTS DESIGN

Simultaneous Treatment Design

The major adaptation of the alternating treatments design is the **simultaneous treatments design** (Kazdin & Hartmann, 1978), also called the concurrent schedules design (Hersen & Barlow, 1976). As noted previously, these terms have been used erroneously to describe the alternating treatments design. The use of the simultaneous treatments design, in fact, is relatively rare in the professional literature. As the name implies, in this design the treatment conditions are presented *at the same time* instead of being alternated. The simultaneous treatments design actually has several advantages over other single subject designs (Tawney & Gast, 1984). First, it best approximates the conditions of the natural environment. Second, it takes less time to determine treatment effectiveness than other designs, including the alternating treatments design. Conversely, the use of this design requires more skill, planning, and organization than the use of other designs. It is a difficult task to systematically analyze the effects of several interventions presented at the same time.

The following example shows both the value of the simultaneous treatments design and the challenge that is present in its planning.

Ms. Ziegler, a general education teacher, and Ms. Massey, a special education teacher, were teamed together in a ninth-grade inclusion classroom. There were 20 students in the class, including 2 with learning disabilities, 1 with behavior disorders, 1 with mild mental retardation, and 3 who were receiving speech and language services. Joey, the student with behavior disorders, would frequently curse at the teachers, disrupting the classroom. Ms. Ziegler and Ms. Massey requested a meeting with the school psychologist to discuss some type of intervention plan. They mutually agreed to determine which of two intervention procedures—verbal reprimand or contingent exercise—

would be most effective in reducing Joey's cursing behavior. The school psychologist suggested that both teachers collect baseline data for a week, noting each instance of cursing behavior directed at each teacher during the day. During the 2nd week, Ms. Ziegler verbally reprimanded Joey's cursing behavior. This consisted of her saying loudly and abruptly "No Joey, do not curse." Also during the 2nd week (at the same time Ms. Ziegler was using verbal reprimands), Ms. Massey initiated the contingent exercise condition. During this condition, every time Joey cursed he was instructed to sit down and stand up 10 times. This procedure has been shown to be effective with cursing behavior (Luce, Delquadri, & Hall, 1980). The 3rd week, Ms. Ziegler provided the contingent exercise treatment while Ms. Massey used verbal reprimands. This continued for 2 more weeks, with each teacher providing each of the two interventions for a week.

In the above example, the treatment conditions were presented to the student at the same time rather than being alternated. In other words, both the verbal reprimand and contingent exercise conditions were presented simultaneously. The goal was to determine, over time, which treatment becomes superior, regardless of the teacher who is implementing it.

Adapted Alternating Treatments Design

Another version of the basic alternating treatments design that has been used in the professional literature is called the **adapted alternating treatments design** (Sindelar, Rosenberg, & Wilson, 1985). In this design, each intervention is applied to different behaviors that are considered to be of equal response difficulty but functionally independent. Unfortunately, the process of equating the behaviors can be time consuming and problematic, although it is a very important prerequisite to the use of this design. Holcombe, Wolery, and Gast (1994) noted that grade levels or other normative data might be used to help equate the dependent behaviors. For example, if a student had a very similar standard score on an achievement test measuring both written spelling and math computation, those two behaviors might be targeted for an adapted alternating treatments design. If two interventions were being evaluated (e.g., use of worksheets vs. flash cards), then each behavior would receive each treatment in a random order for the same number of sessions. If one treatment is shown to be more effective with both behaviors, it would provide additional evidence of a functional relationship.

Summary Checklist

Basic goal—Comparison of the effects of two or more treatments on the same behavior.

Alternating treatments with no baseline—Treatments are presented randomly to the subjects across different days, across times of day, or within sessions; preintervention baseline data are not collected, although a no-treatment phase (A) can also be alternated (e.g., BACBABCAC).

Baseline followed by alternating treatments—Baseline data are collected before the presentation of the treatments; provides additional information about changes from pretreatment to treatment.

Baseline followed by alternating treatments and a final treatment phase—Ends in a final treatment phase that has been determined to be the most effective during the study.

Prediction—Each data point in each condition serves as a predictor for future behavior under the same condition.

Verification—Succeeding data points in each condition verify the prediction made from the previous data points.

Replication—The differential effects of the treatment are demonstrated if the trend continues.

Advantages of the alternating treatments design—Good to use when determining which of two or more treatments is effective; collection of baseline data not necessary; avoids sequencing effects found in other single subject designs.

Disadvantages of the alternating treatments design—The possibility of multiple treatment interference when the treatments interact, thus obscuring the results; not good for behaviors that change slowly; sometimes difficult to implement (e.g., counterbalancing the treatments).

Adaptations

Simultaneous treatments design—Also called the concurrent schedules design; treatment conditions are presented simultaneously rather then being alternated; somewhat difficult to plan and implement.

Adapted alternating treatments design—Intervention is applied to multiple behaviors that are similar in nature but functionally independent.

References

Alberto, P., & Troutman, A. (1995). *Applied behavior analysis for teachers* (4th ed.). Columbus, OH: Merrill.

Alberto, P., & Troutman, A. (1999). *Applied behavior analysis for teachers* (5th ed.). Columbus, OH: Merrill.

Barlow, D., & Hayes, S. (1979). Alternating treatment design: One strategy for comparing the effects of two treatments in a single behavior. *Journal of Applied Behavior Analysis, 12,* 199–210.

Cooper, J., Heron, T., & Heward, W. (1987). *Applied behavior analysis.* Columbus, OH: Merrill.

Hersen, M., & Barlow, D. (1976). *Single case experimental designs: Strategies for studying behavior change.* New York: Pergamon Press.

Holcombe, A., Wolery, M., & Gast, D. (1994). Comparative single subject research: Description of designs and discussion of problems. *Topics in Early Childhood Special Education, 14,* 119–145.

Kazdin, A., & Hartmann, D. (1978). The simultaneous treatment design. *Behavior Therapy, 9,* 912–922.

Luce, C., Delquadri, J., & Hall, R. (1980). Contingent exercise: A mild but powerful procedure for suppressing inappropriate verbal and aggressive behavior. *Journal of Applied Behavior Analysis, 13,* 583–594.

Neuman, S. (1995). Alternating treatments designs. In S. Neuman & S. McCormick (Eds.), *Single subject experimental research: Applications for literacy* (pp. 64–83). Newark, DE: International Reading Association.

Sindelar, P., Rosenberg, M., & Wilson, R. (1985). An adapted alternating treatments design. *Education and Treatment of Children, 8,* 67–86.

Tawney, J., & Gast, D. (1984). *Single subject research in special education.* Columbus, OH: Merrill.

Ulman, J., & Sulzer-Azaroff, B. (1975). Multielement baseline design in educational research. In E. Ramp & G. Semb (Eds.), *Behavior analysis: Areas of research and application* (pp. 371–391). Englewood Cliffs, NJ: Prentice-Hall.

CHAPTER 10

Application of Alternating Treatments Designs

In the last chapter we described the different types of alternating treatments designs. The alternating treatments design is an important single subject design that is used to determine the effects of more than one treatment (independent variable) on the same behavior (dependent variable). In this chapter we will provide specific examples from the professional literature for each of the three basic types of alternating treatments designs.

ALTERNATING TREATMENTS
WITH NO BASELINE DESIGN

Caldwell, M. L., Taylor, R. L., & Bloom, S. R. (1986). An investigation of the use of high- and low-preference food as a reinforcer for increased activity of individuals with Prader-Willi syndrome. *Journal of Mental Deficiency Research, 30,* 347–354.

Research Question

In this study, the investigators determined the effectiveness of using high- and low-preference food for increased exercise in individuals with Prader-Willi syndrome (PWS). PWS is a disorder characterized by varying levels of cognitive deficits, extreme obesity, and inappropriate food-related behaviors. One area in which there have been conflicting reports is the lack of food preferences for individuals with PWS.

Subjects

The subjects were 11 adolescents and young adults with PWS (6 males, 5 females) ranging in age from 14 to 32. The IQs of the subjects ranged from 54 to 83. Although only one subject is necessary to use an alternating treatments design, the use of multiple subjects increases the external validity of the study.

Setting

The subjects were participating in a 5-week residential training program that focused on weight management and the development of appropriate social and leisure skills. The subjects resided in a university dormitory during the program, and all activities related to the study were conducted on the university campus.

Dependent Variables

The study was composed of two phases. In the first, the investigators determined what, if any, food preferences each subject had. As noted, previous research had produced equivocal results in this area. These investigators did find that each subject showed a definite preference for snack foods (pretzels, candy, potato chips) over healthy foods (carrots, oranges, apples). The caloric amount of each type of food was the same. The second phase used the alternating treatments design to determine if the food reinforcers could be used to increase activity levels of the subjects. Specifically, the dependent variable was the number of "activity units" that were generated by each subject. An activity unit was defined as engagement in a prescribed activity (e.g., walking, bicycling, swimming) for a 20-min period. Up to six activity units could be earned each day.

Independent Variables

The subjects were assigned to two treatment conditions and a no-treatment condition. These were high-preference food reinforcement, low-preference food reinforcement, and no food reinforcement.

The Design

The three treatment conditions were randomly assigned to 20 sessions (days). The following order was determined using A as the high-preference food condition, B as the low-preference food condition, and C as the no-food condition: ABCAABBCCCABACBBACBA.

The Intervention

Each day the subjects were told which treatment condition was in effect. Posters were also used throughout the day as a reminder. They were given several opportunities throughout the day to earn up to six activity units that could be traded for the reinforcer under effect in the treatment condition for that day. The activity unit consisted of a 20-min supervised exercise program. Each activity unit expended approximately 80-150 calories, whereas the food reinforcers were only approximately 30 calories. Consequently there was a net loss of calories for each exchange. The study was conducted over a 20-day period. Four staff members and a program director supervised all the activities.

Obtaining the Data and Plotting the Results

The collection of data consisted of simply determining how many, if any, activity units were earned each day. Data for each subject were placed on x-y graphs to determine if any treatment condition consistently produced more activity units.

Results

The investigators found that the data from the 11 subjects clustered into four patterns. For 3 subjects, there was little or no effect under any of the three treatment conditions. For another subject, the results were unclear, with increases noted for both the high- and low-preference foods. For 2 other subjects, the high-preference food condition was superior to low-preference, although the low-preference food condition was higher than the no-treatment condition. Finally, for 5 of the subjects, the high-preference condition demonstrated clear superiority. Figure 10–1 shows the data for these 5 subjects.

Why Use an Alternating Treatments With no Baseline Design?

The investigators were interested in determining (a) if this sample of individuals with PWS had a preference for one type of food over another and, if so, (b) whether high-preference food could be used to increase their activity levels. Because of the nature of the program, there was a limited number of days to conduct this study. The clinical importance of having the subjects increase their activity level was evident. Because collection of baseline data before intervention is not a prerequisite for an alternating treatments design, the investigators chose to begin their alternating treatments immediately. However, a no-treatment condition was included as one of the alternating treatments to help determine the relative efficacy of the two food reinforcement conditions. This was important because of the conflicting reports about the presence of food preferences in this population.

Limitations of the Study

As noted earlier, three of the subjects did not respond to any of the three treatment conditions. This could have been due to their inability to discriminate among the treatment conditions. The authors did note that

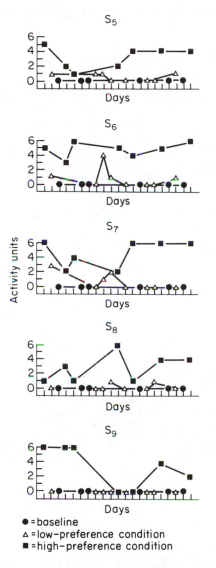

S_5

S_6

S_7

Activity units

S_8

S_9

● = baseline
△ = low-preference condition
■ = high-preference condition

Figure 10–1. Data for five of the subjects in the alternating treatments with no baseline study. *Note.* From "An Investigation of the Use of High- and Low-Preference Food as a Reinforcer for Increased Activity of Individuals With Prader-Willi Syndrome," by M. L. Caldwell, R. L. Taylor, and S. R. Bloom, 1986, *Journal of Mental Deficiency Research, 30,* p. 351. Copyright 1986 by Blackwell Science. Reprinted with permission.

Table 10–1. Summary of "An Investigation of the Use of High- and Low-Preference Food as a Reinforcer for Increased Activity of Individuals with Prader-Willi Syndrome."

Feature	Description
Type of design	Alternating treatments with no baseline
Goal of study	Determine effectiveness of using food reinforcers to increase activity level
Subjects	Eleven adolescents and young adults with Prader-Willi syndrome
Setting	Residential summer program on university campus
Dependent variable	Activity units (20 min of exercise = one activity unit)
Independent variables	High- and low-preference foods
Results and outcomes	High-preference foods were effective in increasing activity in 5 of the 11 subjects; no or unclear effects were found in 4 subjects; 2 subjects showed increases under high- and low-preference food conditions

these three subjects had lower IQs and mention other areas in which individuals with PWS with lower IQs differ from those with relatively higher IQs. In this study, using multiple subjects confounded the overall results because there was not a consistent pattern across all subjects. However, the demonstration of a functional relationship was strengthened for those subjects who did respond consistently.

Summary

A summary of the relevant dimensions of this study demonstrating an alternating treatments design with no baseline can be found in Table 10–1.

BASELINE FOLLOWED BY ALTERNATING TREATMENTS DESIGN

Weismer, S. E., Murray-Branch, J., & Miller, J. (1993). Comparison of two methods for promoting productive vocabulary in late talkers. *Journal of Speech and Hearing Research, 36,* 1037–1050.

Research Question

The investigators determined the effectiveness of two methods of promoting productive vocabulary in young children identified as being late talkers. The instructional methods were modeling and modeling plus evoked production.

Subjects

The subjects were two boys and one girl, ranging in age from 27–28 months at the beginning of the study. Each had been identified as having restricted productive vocabularies based on a variety of test scores. The actual vocabularies of the 3 subjects consisted of 51, 52, and 87 words.

Setting

The actual setting of the study was not described. The subjects received both individual and group training by three trained graduate students.

Dependent Variables

The investigators developed a different set of two control words, three target words for individual instruction, and four words for group instruction for each subject. These consisted of object and action words from the *Early Language Inventory*. In addition the sets of words for each treatment condition were also different. Thus for each subject there was one set of two control words, two sets of three words for individual instruction, and two sets of three words for group instruction. There were three dependent variables used to evaluate the effectiveness of the treatment programs:

1. The frequency of use of the targeted words per probe session.
2. The number of different words (lexical diversity) produced per probe session.
3. The number of targeted words acquired. This occurred when a subject used a target word in two or more probe sessions.

Independent Variables

As noted previously, there were two treatments being evaluated. The first, modeling, occurred when the target words were stated by the investigator but with no required response from the child. The second, modeling plus evoked production, was similar to the first in that the target words were stated by the investigator. Under this condition, however, the child was given the opportunity to repeat the word and receive feedback. A third condition, called approximation, was also used. This phase might be considered a no-condition phase in which the set of control words was used but without any modeling.

The Design

The three conditions (modeling, modeling plus evoked production, and approximation) were presented in semirandom order, making sure that no more than three sessions of any one type occurred consecutively. The initial order of treatments was also counterbalanced across subjects. Baseline data were collected over four sessions before the introduction of the treatment conditions for the individual instruction only; no baseline data were collected for the group instruction.

The Intervention

Three trained graduate students conducted the instructional sessions. Each subject was assigned a graduate student to implement all of the individual sessions. Group instruction was rotated among the three trainers. In both the modeling and modeling plus evoked production conditions, the trainer engaged in an activity in which the target words were introduced a specific number of times. In the modeling plus evoked production condition, the subject was given the opportunity to produce the target word and receive feedback. For example, for the word *pen*, the subject was shown a witch's kettle and was told that she or he was making a brew by adding several things while stirring. Eventually a pen (the target word) was put in the kettle and the trainer said that the magic word is *pen*. The subject then was told it was her or his turn to say the magic word and to put the object in the kettle. If the subject said *pen* she or he was told, "Right, that's a pen." If no response was given, she or he was told, "It's the pen, isn't it?"

Obtaining the Data and Plotting the Results

After each session production probes were conducted (e.g., "What is this? What am I doing?") as objects or actions were shown or demonstrated. Each target word was sampled twice. The same probes were used for the control words. There were 20 sessions for individual instruction (plus four baseline sessions) and 24 group instruction sessions. For each subject, two graphs were generated for each of two dependent variables—frequency of target word per probe session and lexical diversity per probe session for both individual and group instruction. As an example, Figures 10–2 and 10–3 present the frequency and lexical diver-

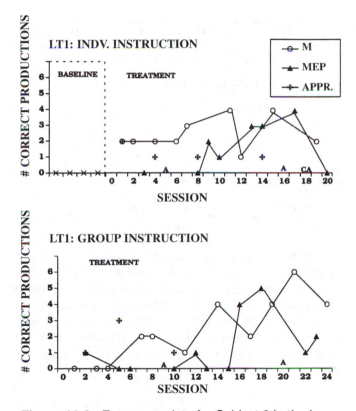

Figure 10-2. Frequency data for Subject 3 in the baseline followed by alternating treatments study. *Note.* From "Comparison of Two Methods for Promoting Productive Vocabulary in Late Talkers," by S. E. Weismer, J. Murray-Branch, and J. Miller, 1993, *Journal of Speech and Hearing Research, 36,* p. 1046. Copyright 1993 by the American Speech, Language, and Hearing Association. Reprinted with permission.

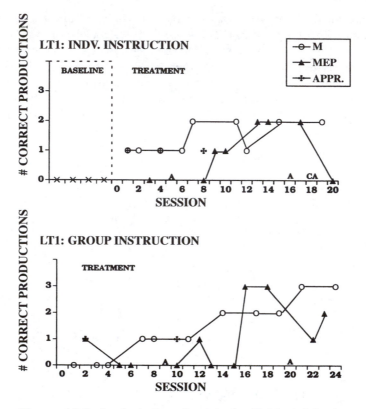

Figure 10-3. Lexical diversity data for Subject 3 in the baseline followed by alternating treatments study. *Note.* From "Comparison of Two Methods for Promoting Productive Vocabulary in Late Talkers," by S. E. Weismer, J. Murray-Branch, and J. Miller, 1993, *Journal of Speech and Hearing Research, 36,* p. 1046. Copyright 1993 by the American Speech, Language, and Hearing Association. Reprinted with permission.

sity data for Subject 3. For the third dependent variable, acquisition of the target words, the authors provided a table that summarized the data.

Results

The results indicated that each subject responded differently to the treatments. Subject 1 was more responsive to modeling, Subject 2 did not appear to respond consistently to either treatment, and Subject 3 responded to the modeling plus evoked production condition. Figures 10–2 and 10–3 visually demonstrate the superiority of the modeling plus evoked production condition for Subject 3, particularly during individual instruction. Taken as a whole, these results would have to be interpreted as inconclusive regarding treatment efficacy. The control (approximation) condition, however, did not result in noticeable gains, so the improvement when using either of the two treatments over a no-treatment condition is evident, primarily for Subjects 1 and 3.

Why Use a Baseline Followed by Alternating Treatments Design?

Clearly, the authors' goal was to determine which of the two treatment conditions would be most effective in increasing vocabulary. The condition that included prompting the subject to respond was sufficiently different from the modeling alone condition to allow for their discrimination by the subjects. The authors also state that, although baseline data are not required in an alternating treatments design, they collected them for the individual sessions to "further document the lack of target vocabulary in the child's repertoire before teaching" (p. 1040). It is unclear why baseline data were not collected for the group sessions as well. The nature of the dependent variable—vocabulary production—also precluded the use of a single subject design such as a withdrawal design. It is anticipated and educationally desirable that the subjects retain the vocabulary words once they learn them.

Limitations of the Study

The results of this study were somewhat inconsistent with those previously reported in the literature. The authors predicted that the modeling plus evoked production treatment would be superior. Although they do not make specific recommendations, the authors do provide cogent arguments for the presence of specific subject characteristics, such as learning style and personality factors, that might differentially affect response to treatments.

Summary

A summary of the relevant dimensions of this baseline with alternating treatments design can be found in Table 10–2.

Table 10–2. Summary of "Comparison of Two Methods for Promoting Productive Vocabulary in Late Talkers."

Feature	Description
Type of design	Baseline followed by alternating treatments
Goal of study	Determine effectiveness of modeling procedures to increase vocabulary in young children
Subjects	Two boys and one girl ranging in age from 27 to 28 months who had very limited expressive vocabularies
Setting	Unspecified
Dependent variables	(1) Frequency of targeted words; (2) number of different words produced; (3) number of targeted words acquired
Independent variables	Modeling alone and modeling plus evoked production[a]
Results and outcomes	Equivocal results, with each subject responding differently

[a] A no-treatment condition was also used.

BASELINE FOLLOWED BY ALTERNATING TREATMENTS AND A FINAL TREATMENT PHASE DESIGN

Singh, N., & Winton, A. (1985). Controlling pica by components of an overcorrection procedure. *American Journal of Mental Deficiency, 90,* 40–45.

Research Question

Multicomponent overcorrection procedures have been used effectively to control pica, or the ingestion of inedible objects, in individuals with mental retardation. The investigators were interested in assessing the effects of using the separate components of an overcorrection procedure in controlling pica. They argued that if a simple, single-component intervention was effective, it would be more efficient and accurately implemented than a multicomponent procedure.

Subjects

The subjects were two females with profound mental retardation living in an institution. Each displayed high levels of maladaptive behavior including a long history of pica. Several interventions had been used unsuccessfully in the past to control their pica.

Setting

Each subject received treatment sessions in three settings in the institution—a large, furnished day room; a smaller sun room; and the dining room.

Dependent Variable

For this study, pica was defined as "an inedible or nonnutritive substance either touching the subject's lips or being placed in the mouth" (Singh & Winton, 1985; p. 42). The investigators made every attempt to ensure that the subjects did not swallow any object. The rate of pica (total number of pica responses per 15-min session) was recorded for each subject.

Independent Variables

The independent variables were the three separate components of a multicomponent overcorrection procedure. For all three treatments, the first step was for the subject to remove the object from her mouth. In the first component, tidying, the subject then had to put the object in a trash can, and then empty the trash can. The second component was oral hygiene, in which the subject had to brush her teeth and gums with a soft toothbrush soaked in Listerine for 5 min. The third component consisted of personal hygiene. After the object was removed from the subject's mouth, she would be required to wash her hands and fingernails for 5 min.

The Design

Baseline data were collected for 5 consecutive days for 15 min in each of the three settings. In the alternating treatments phase each of the three treatments was randomly assigned to each setting on a daily basis. The next phase involved using only the most effective treatment in each of the three settings. The final phase involved using only the most effective treatment but with different therapists.

The Intervention

After baseline, each subject was given the designated treatment assigned to each setting each day. These treatments were all given by the same therapist. Observers noted the frequency of pica incidents in each 15-min session. Time spent in each treatment itself (approximately 5 min) was not included in the 15-min observation period. After 10 days, only the most effective treatment (oral hygiene for both subjects) was continued. This occurred in all three settings and was again initiated by the same therapist. To test for replication of effects, the oral hygiene treatment was then continued but with three new therapists providing the treatment in a predetermined order. The study was concluded when there were no instances of pica for a subject during any session for 5 consecutive days.

Obtaining the Data and Plotting the Results

The number of pica responses per minute was graphed for each subject in each of the three settings. This frequency was based on the 15-min observation period not counting the time that each subject spent engaged in the treatment itself. Figure 10–4 shows the graphed data for this study.

Results

The investigators found that the oral hygiene treatment was the most effective in reducing pica in each subject. For Subject 1, the average pica incidents per minute was .40 for baseline and was reduced to an average of .17 during the alternating treatments phase (.09 during the oral hygiene component). Subject 2 averaged .70 pica incidents per minute during baseline, which was reduced to an average of .28 during the alternating treatments phase (.09 for the oral hygiene component). The mean rates were .06 and .10 in the oral hygiene final treatment phase for Subjects 1 and 2, respectively. Finally, the pica rates were reduced to an average of .02 and .04 in a phase when multiple therapists were used.

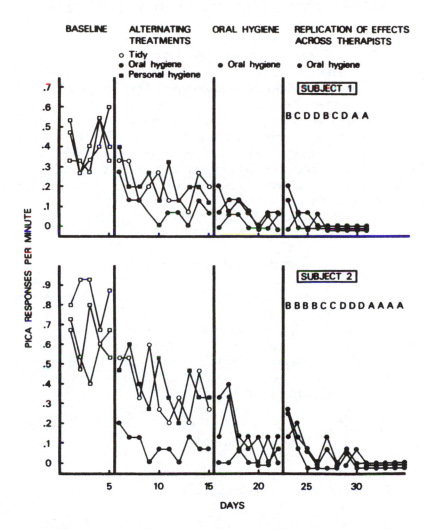

Figure 10–4. Data for the subjects in the baseline followed by alternating treatments with a final treatment phase study. *Note.* From "Controlling Pica by Components of an Overcorrection Procedure," by N. Singh and A. Winton, 1985, *American Journal of Mental Deficiency, 90,* p. 41. Copyright 1985 by the American Association on Mental Retardation. Reprinted with permission.

Why Use a Baseline Followed by Alternating Treatments and a Final Treatment Phase Design?

Although research had indicated that a multicomponent overcorrection procedure was effective in reducing pica, the investigators were interested in determining if the individual components alone could have powerful suppressive effects. If so, the treatment would be easier to implement. Baseline data were collected to strengthen the study by showing the rates before treatment sessions began. The use of alternating treatments, particularly across the three settings, allowed each component to be evaluated with a minimum of sequence effects. The last two phases were included both to test for maintenance and generalization and to leave the subjects with a reduced rate of pica. As noted in Chapter 9, the single-component/most effective treatment phase also helped demonstrate that the results were not affected by multiple treatment interference.

Limitations of the Study

The authors acknowledge that one limitation of the study was that their design did not allow for the demonstration that the subjects would return to baseline levels if the treatments were withdrawn. They suggested that a no-treatment condition in the alternating treatments phase would have addressed that concern. The long history of pica in the subjects, however, probably indicated that it was more clinically appropriate to focus on the actual treatment conditions.

Summary

The salient components of this study that demonstrated the addition of a final treatment phase can be found in Table 10–3.

Table 10–3. Summary of "Controlling Pica by Components of an Overcorrection Procedure."

Feature	Description
Type of design	Baseline followed by alternating treatments with a final treatment phase

continued

Table 10–3. *(continued)*

Feature	Description
Goal of study	Determine if individual components of a multicomponent intervention procedure would reduce the frequency of pica
Subjects	Two adults with profound mental retardation with a history of pica
Setting	Three separate rooms in an institution
Dependent variable	Frequency of pica (# of incidents per minute)
Independent variables	Three components of an overcorrection procedure—tidying, oral hygiene, personal hygiene
Results and outcomes	Oral hygiene was the most effective; its use was effective across settings and therapists

The alternating treatments design is sometimes rather complicated and can be difficult to manage and implement. In addition, there may be situations in which a researcher wants to change behavior in a more systematic, stepwise fashion. When this is the case, the changing criterion design discussed in the next chapter might be selected.

CHAPTER 11

Overview of Changing Criterion Designs

IMPORTANT CONCEPTS TO KNOW

THE BASIC CHANGING CRITERION DESIGN

ISSUES RELATED TO CHANGING CRITERION DESIGNS
    Length of Each Phase
    Magnitude of Criterion Changes
    Number of Criterion Changes

PREDICTION, VERIFICATION, AND REPLICATION

ADVANTAGES OF THE CHANGING CRITERION DESIGN

DISADVANTAGES OF THE CHANGING CRITERION DESIGN

ADAPTATIONS OF THE CHANGING CRITERION DESIGN
    Reversal to a Previous Criterion Level
    Reinstate Baseline Conditions

THE BASIC CHANGING CRITERION DESIGN

The changing criterion design was first named by Hall (1971) and later described in greater detail by Hartmann and Hall (1976). A similar, unnamed design was described a decade earlier by Sidman (1960). The changing criterion design involves the evaluation of the effects of a treatment on the gradual, systematic increase or decrease of a single target behavior. This is accomplished by carefully changing, in a stepwise fashion, the criterion levels necessary to meet contingencies to increase behavior (e.g., positive or negative reinforcement) or to decrease behavior (e.g., differential reinforcement procedures or punishment). In other words, the effect of the intervention is demonstrated when the target behavior changes to the predetermined criterion levels specified by the experimenter.

The changing criterion design was initially referred to by Hartmann and Hall as a unique type of multiple baseline design. It is also considered a variation of the A-B design discussed in Chapter 5. In the changing criterion design, after baseline data are collected (A), the treatment phase (B) is divided into subphases, with each subphase requiring changes in the target behavior that more closely approximate the terminal behavior or goal (Poling, Methot, & LeSage, 1995). The following steps outline the procedures to be taken when using a changing criterion design.

Step 1—Carefully define the target behavior. The behavior should be one that can be changed gradually and in a stepwise fashion.

Step 2—Collect baseline data. These data should be gathered until they are stable or moving in a counterproductive fashion (Hartmann & Hall, 1976).

Step 3—Determine level of performance (criterion levels) required for the contingent presentation of the reinforcement or punishment.

1. Determine terminal behavior or goal. For example, a teacher might want to increase a student's typing rate to 50 words per minute or decrease talking out behavior to zero.
2. Determine criterion level for the first subphase. To do this, Alberto and Troutman (1999) made the following suggestions:
   a. Set the criterion level at the mean of the stable portion of the baseline data, particularly if the initial rate of responding is low. For example, if a target behavior occurred 2, 0, 4, 0, 4, 2, and 2 times during baseline, the average would be 2. Therefore, 2 would be used as the initial criterion level. Alberto and Trout-

man also suggested that in this situation the criterion level for each subsequent phase would be increased by 2.

   b. Take 50% of the average of the baseline data and add to the average. In the above example, the initial criterion level would be 3 (50% of 2 = 1; 1 + 2 = 3).

   c. Choose the highest or lowest data point (depending on the goal) and use that as the criterion level. This is particularly useful with social behaviors.

   d. Use professional judgment. For example, if the baseline rate is zero, there are no objective data to use as guidelines. In this situation the experimenter must make the best estimate based on the available information about the subject.

3. Establish the criterion levels for the subsequent subphases. This usually involves a gradual increase or decrease in the criterion levels in the direction of the goal. There need to be at least two subphases, although three or more are generally used. The issues of the number of subphases to be used and the magnitude of the criterion changes are discussed later in this chapter.

Step 4—Begin the intervention. The criterion required to obtain the treatment (i.e., contingencies to increase or decrease behavior) is applied.

Step 5—Introduce the next subphase level after the initial criterion level is met. One important point relates to the length of each subphase. In other words, how long must the subject respond at the criterion level before moving to the next subphase? Alberto and Troutman suggested that, at a minimum, the behavior should occur for two consecutive sessions or two out of three consecutive sessions. It is important, however, to continue until a stable rate has been established because each subphase actually acts as a baseline for the subsequent subphase (Hartmann & Hall, 1976). This strengthens the functional relationship between the dependent and independent variables. The issue of the length of the subphases also will be discussed later in more depth.

Step 6—Continue through each subphase in a stepwise fashion until the terminal goal is reached.

The following is an example of the use of a changing criterion design.

Mr. Barkley was concerned that Danny, one of his third-grade students with a learning disability, was not completing his math worksheets during class. Typically, the students had about 15 minutes to complete a mixed review worksheet at the end of the math lesson. Danny could do the problems correctly but wasn't particularly interested in the task. He would frequently lose interest or attention, completed very few, and subsequently had to finish the worksheets for homework. Mr. Barkley first developed several worksheets that were similar to those used in class. They included 20 addition, subtraction, multiplication, and division problems (5 each in a random order). He gave Danny a worksheet each day and allowed him 15 min to complete it. The same contingencies were in effect as before. In other words, if he didn't finish the worksheet he had to take it home to complete. The 1st week he completed 6, 7, 5, 8, and 6 problems. On the basis of these baseline data, which average slightly over 6 problems per 15 min, Mr. Barkley established an initial criterion level of 8 correct problems. Danny was told that if he completed 8 problems correctly he would be given 10 min of free time at the end of the day to play video games. The contingency immediately had an effect. After stable responding was noted, the next subphase, requiring 11 problems completed, was introduced. This procedure was continued with the criterion levels set at 14 and 17 problems completed. The final subphase (the target goal of all 20 problems completed) was then put in effect. Figure 11–1 shows the data from this example.

ISSUES RELATED TO CHANGING CRITERION DESIGNS

Hartmann and Hall (1976) noted that there were three very important issues that must be considered when using changing criterion designs: the length of each phase, the magnitude of the criterion changes, and the number of phases or criterion changes. They pointed out that these three issues are highly interdependent.

Length of Each Phase

As noted previously, in the changing criterion design the level of responding of each phase (subphase) actually serves as a baseline for the subsequent phase. It is therefore important that each phase should continue until stable responding has occurred. The nature of the design, however, should generally allow this to occur quickly. In other words,

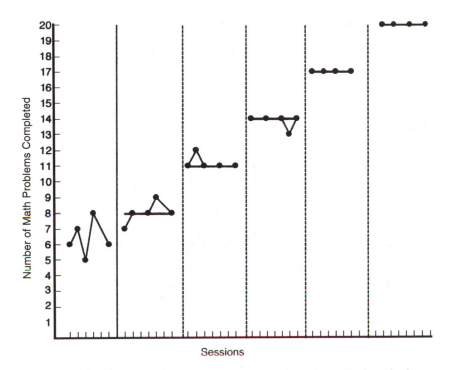

Figure 11–1. Example of data from a basic changing criterion design.

the presentation of a new criterion level should result in an almost immediate change in the target behavior to that new level. This is particularly true for behaviors that can change rapidly. In the first example shown in Figure 11–1, Danny already had the target behavior in his repertoire. The issue was one of compliance, not his ability to do math. Thus, when the new criterion levels were set, the behavior could change rapidly. For the most part, if the behavior can change rapidly, the phases can be shorter than if the behavior is slow to change. In that situation the phases may need to be longer to demonstrate experimental control (Cooper, Heron, & Heward, 1987).

The evidence for the functional relationship between the independent and dependent variables is strengthened when the behavior changes to exactly the criterion level and stays at that rate until the criterion level changes in the next phase. For this reason, the actual lengths of the phases should vary to demonstrate that control. In the previous example, more evidence for the effectiveness of the video game reinforcer on the number of math problems completed could have been made by varying the number of sessions within each phase. Figure 11–2 indicates

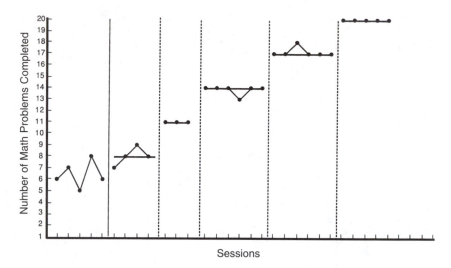

Figure 11–2. Example of data from a changing criterion design with different phase lengths.

that the level of responding changed to the criterion level and remained relatively stable within each phase, regardless of the length of the phase. This stability demonstrates greater internal validity. Another method that rules out threats to internal validity such as maturation and practice effects is to reverse the direction of the criterion level in one or more phases. The criterion levels for both Figures 11–1 and 11–2 were 8, 11, 14, 17, and 20. Suppose, however, that the criterion levels had been 8, 11, 14, 17, 14, 17, and 20. By showing that the level of behavior changed only to the specified level (i.e., increased to 17 in Phase 4 and then decreased back to 14 in Phase 5), an even stronger relationship can be demonstrated than when a linear trend is in effect (see Figure 11–3).

Magnitude of Criterion Changes

This issue focuses on the question "How much change in the target behavior is required before the subject receives the treatment?" This is a very important question—if the required change is small, the subject might progress, but it would be difficult to determine if the change was not due to other factors such as maturation or practice effects. If the required change is too large, however, there are at least two possible problems. First, because the target goal will be reached in fewer phases, there

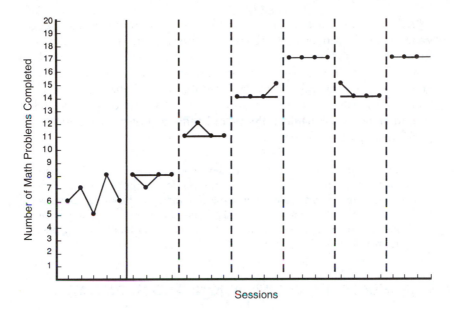

Figure 11–3. Example of data from a changing criterion design with a reversal to a previous criterion level.

might not be enough phases to demonstrate experimental control in the study. Second, requiring drastic changes might contradict good instructional practices (Cooper et al., 1987). In our example, if the criterion levels had been 10, 15, and 20 (and the behavior changed to those levels), the effects would look impressive because the behavior changed so dramatically. However, the fact that the behavior was controlled in only three phases compromises the validity of the study. One logical method of determining the criterion changes is to use the baseline data as an indicator. In general, smaller criterion changes should be used for more stable behaviors whereas larger changes would be necessary to demonstrate control for behaviors that are more variable (Hartmann & Hall, 1976).

Number of Criterion Changes

The number of criterion changes actually refers to the number of phases (subphases) that should be included in the study. The determination will depend on both the length of the phases and the magnitude of the criterion changes. This demonstrates the interrelationship of these issues noted by Hartmann and Hall (1976). For example, if there is a limited amount of time available for a study (e.g., only a month left in the school year), then the longer each phase is, the fewer the number of phases there can be. Also, as previously discussed, the greater the magnitude of the criterion changes, the fewer the number of phases before the target goal is met. In general, the more times the target behavior changes to meet a new criterion, the more control is demonstrated. The researcher should be aware of artificial floors and ceilings, however. Cooper et al. (1987) described this concern.

> An obvious mistake of this sort would be to give a student only five math problems to complete when the criterion for reinforcement is five. Although the student could complete fewer than five problems, the possibility of exceeding the criterion has been eliminated, resulting in an impressive-looking graph perhaps, but one that is badly affected by poor experimental procedure. (p. 221)

PREDICTION, VERIFICATION, AND REPLICATION

Although prediction and replication are easily addressed within a basic changing criterion design, verification is somewhat more difficult to demonstrate (Cooper et al., 1987). In general, **prediction** of the levels of future behaviors is made when stable responding is attained within each phase. **Verification** is possible when either of two of the previously discussed suggestions to increase internal validity are made. By varying the lengths of the phases, verification of the treatment effects is made. Similarly, and perhaps more convincingly, verification is demonstrated when the direction of the criterion levels is reversed and the behavior returns to a previously set criterion level. **Replication** occurs every time that the behavior changes in the predicted direction based on the predetermined criterion levels.

ADVANTAGES OF THE CHANGING CRITERION DESIGN

Used appropriately, the changing criterion design can be an effective tool for the single subject researcher. It is particularly helpful when working with target behaviors that can increase or decrease in a step-wise fashion. The behavior should already be in the subject's repertoire and be measurable using a number of recording procedures, including frequency, accuracy, duration, or latency. Examples of behaviors that are ideally suited for the changing criterion design were offered by Hartmann and Hall (1976). These include increases in writing or reading rate, improvements in peer relationships, as well as decreases in smoking, overeating, and latency of compliance behaviors. The changing criterion design is also helpful when determining the effects of contingency programs specifically designed to increase or decrease behaviors. One somewhat controversial use of the design is its evaluation of the effectiveness of shaping procedures. Its use for this purpose has been recommended by some (e.g., Alberto & Troutman, 1999; Hartmann & Hall, 1976) but questioned by others (e.g., Cooper et al., 1987). The argument against its use has to do with the nature of shaping procedures, in which a new behavior that is *not* in the subject's repertoire is developed by reinforcing successive approximations toward that behavior. In other words, a different form of behavior is required at each phase instead of different levels of the same behavior.

Two other advantages are worthy of note. First, it can be helpful to use when the terminal goal that is set takes a relatively long time to reach (Alberto & Troutman, 1999). Thus, the gradual movement toward the goal results in educationally or clinically desirable outcomes while at the same time demonstrating experimental control. A second, related advantage is that the treatment does not have to be withdrawn to show its requisite functional relationship with the target behavior. In fact, after baseline, treatment conditions can stay in effect so that the subject is always moving toward the goal. The only exception occurs if the researcher wants to demonstrate greater internal validity and reverses the direction of the criterion changes within the study.

The changing criterion design would be appropriate to use in the following instances:

- When the target behavior can change gradually in a stepwise fashion;
- When the behavior is already in the subject's repertoire and needs to be increased or decreased;
- When the effects of contingent reinforcement or punishment procedures need to be evaluated;
- When withdrawal of treatment is not appropriate;

DISADVANTAGES OF THE CHANGING CRITERION DESIGN

The same characteristics of the changing criterion design that make it particularly useful for some behaviors and treatments also limit its use with other behaviors and treatments. For instance, it is not appropriate unless the behavior can be changed in a gradual, stepwise fashion. Also, as noted earlier, many researchers argue that the target behavior should already be in the subject's repertoire. In other words the goal should be to increase or decrease a behavior, not develop a new one (Cooper et al., 1987).

A related disadvantage is that the behavior should change only to the specified criterion level in order to demonstrate the greatest experimental control. However, this might not always be educationally or clinically desirable. If the terminal goal can be met faster, then is it appropriate to "hold back" the subject for research purposes? A final disadvantage relates to the planning and implementation of the changing criterion design. As discussed, considerable thought must be given to determine the number and length of phases and the magnitude of the criterion changes. For example, if the criterion changes are set too high, the subject might be adversely affected because the contingency is applied infrequently or not at all. Conversely, if the levels are set too low, the subject's optimal responding may be slowed. Similarly, a problem might exist when phases are short and similar in length. This might result in a linear trend that could also be explained by factors such as maturation or practice effects.

It is not appropriate to use the changing criterion design in the following situations:

- When the target behavior cannot be changed in a gradual, stepwise fashion;

- When the target behavior is not in the subject's repertoire;

- When treatments other than the presentation of contingencies are being evaluated;

- When time and effort cannot be given to determine the important parameters of the design (number and length of phases, magnitude of criterion changes).

ADAPTATIONS OF THE CHANGING CRITERION DESIGN

The adaptations of the changing criterion design primarily involve (a) the addition of a phase or phases in which there is a reversal to a previous criterion level or (b) a return to baseline. Both of these adaptations are used to demonstrate greater experimental control of the independent variable on the dependent variable. Also, the previously discussed issues of number and length of phases, and so on, can result in basic changing criterion designs that look quite different when they are visually graphed.

Reversal to a Previous Criterion Level

As noted, one of the strengths of the changing criterion design is its ability to show that changes in the target behavior correspond to the changes in the specified criterion levels. However, if the direction of the criterion changes is always in the same direction it is more difficult to demonstrate that the changes "are not naturally occurring due to either historical, maturational or measurement factors" (Hartmann & Hall, 1976; p. 530). Therefore, a reversal to a previous criterion level, although not a requirement of the basic design, is sometimes used to help demonstrate that the treatment was responsible for changes in behavior. Figure 11–3 includes an illustration of a reversal phase. The following is another example, this time showing more than one reversal phase.

> Mr. Harris was interested in increasing the writing fluency of one of his middle school students with Attention Deficit Disorder in his third-period English class. When given a writing assignment, the student, Sam, would write a few sentences but rarely more than two or three. Mr. Harris wanted Sam to write at least an 80-word product when given 10 min. The topic for the writing products would be related to a unit on Shakespeare that he was currently teaching. During baseline conditions, Sam's written products were very limited and were headed in a downward direction (20, 10, 7, 7, 7, 5). Mr. Harris set the initial criterion level as 35 words to receive the chosen reinforcer of 15 min of basketball during his free period. He set the subsequent criterion levels at 40 and 50. Although Sam met these levels consistently, Mr. Harris was not convinced that the basketball reinforcer was responsible for the increased writing production. He felt that if this could be established, basketball could be used for several other of Sam's behaviors that needed changing. He subsequently specified the remaining criterion levels at 40, 60, 50, 65, and 80. The data from this study can be found in Figure 11–4.

Reinstate Baseline Conditions

Although used rarely, a changing criterion design with a return to baseline conditions is possible. This is a more radical reversal of conditions than just returning to a previous criterion level. In a sense it is similar to

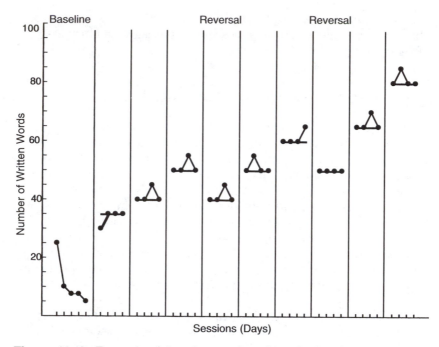

Figure 11–4. Example of data from a changing criterion design with multiple reversals to previous criterion levels.

the A-B-A or A-B-A-B design discussed in Chapter 5. In this case, the B phase is the stepwise criterion changes required for the presentation of the contingencies. This design does show a powerful functional relationship between the independent and dependent variables similar to a withdrawal design. However, it also has the ethical liabilities of the withdrawal design because the subject is placed in a nontreatment phase. This is particularly true if the study ends in the baseline condition.

The following is an example of a changing criterion design with a return to baseline.

Barbi, a fourth-grade student with Down syndrome, frequently uses inappropriate verbalizations during instructional time. This consists of calling out short phrases that are typically not related to the information presented. Even when her verbalizations are appropriate, they typically disrupt the class. Barbi has a number of communication problems, so the speech and language clinician was very familiar with her. She suggested developing a program that would ignore Barbi's inappropriate verbalizations and provide her with immediate reinforcement if she decreased them to specified levels. Barbi loves Disney characters, so the reinforcement chosen was three Disney stickers that she could place into her sticker book. The teacher collected baseline data during the 20-min period at the beginning of each day when announcements were made and the events of the day were planned. The baseline data were relatively consistent; she averaged 15 verbalizations per 20-min period (17, 13, 15, 14). Barbi was told that she must initially reduce her verbalizations to 12 and she would receive the three stickers at the end of the 20-min period. The teacher also gave her the following verbal prompt when she would lose the reinforcer if she made another verbalization. "Barbi, if you speak out of turn one more time, you will not get your stickers today." After the 2nd day she was meeting the criterion level. The next levels that were specified were 8, 4, and 0. Figure 11–5 shows the data indicating that Barbi was able to successfully decrease her inappropriate verbalizations. To determine the effectiveness of the reinforcement even more, Barbi was then told that there would be no stickers available. This return to baseline conditions resulted in a sharp increase in her verbalizations, although not quite to baseline level. For obvious reasons, the terminal goal and conditions were then reinstated. This reduced her verbalizations almost immediately.

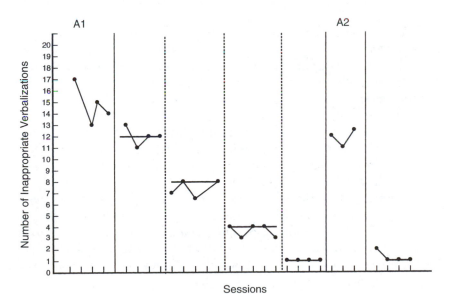

Figure 11–5. Example of data from a changing criterion design with a return to baseline phase.

Summary Checklist

Basic goal—Evaluate effects of a treatment on the gradual increase or decrease of a single target behavior; frequently used when reinforcement or punishment contingencies are in effect.

Basic changing criterion design—After baseline data are collected, phases are introduced in which the criterion levels required to meet the contingency in effect are changed in a stepwise fashion. Experimental control is demonstrated when the target behavior changes to each new criterion level.

Issues

Length of each phase—Phase should be long enough to allow stable responding; length of phase should be varied if possible.

Magnitude of the criterion changes—Should not be too large or too small; use baseline data to help make the determination.

Number of criterion changes—Related to the length of the phases and the magnitude of the criterion changes (e.g., the greater the magnitude of the criterion changes, the fewer the number of phases before the target goal is met).

Prediction—Occurs when stable responding within each phase predicts the behavioral levels of subsequent phases.

Verification—Accomplished by varying the lengths of the phases and/or by changing the direction of the criterion levels and showing changes in the direction of the target behavior.

Replication—Occurs when the behavior changes to the predetermined criterion levels.

Advantages of the changing criterion design—Withdrawal of treatment not necessary; good design to evaluate contingency programs to increase or decrease behavior; gradual change in target behavior results in educationally or clinically appropriate outcomes.

Disadvantages of the changing criterion design—Target behavior must be able to change in a gradual, stepwise fashion; requires time and effort to determine important parameters of the design (e.g., the number and lengths of phases); not appropriate for treatment approaches that do not use contingent procedures to increase or decrease behaviors.

Adaptations

Reversal to a previous criterion level—Instead of a steady, stepwise increase or decrease in the criterion levels, the direction is reversed one or more times; provides additional evidence of the functional relationship between treatment and the target behavior.

Reinstate baseline conditions—More radical reversal in which the stepwise progression is interrupted by returning to baseline conditions; a more powerful method of demonstrating experimental control.

References

Alberto, P., & Troutman, A. (1999). *Applied behavior analysis for teachers* (5th ed.). Columbus, OH: Merrill.

Cooper, J., Heron, T., & Heward, T. (1987). *Applied behavior analysis*. Columbus, OH: Merrill.

Hall, R. V. (1971). *Managing behavior: Behavior modification and the measurement of behavior*. Lawrence, KS: H & H Enterprises.

Hartmann, D., & Hall, R. V. (1976). The changing criterion design. *Journal of Applied Behavior Analysis, 9,* 527–532.

Poling, A., Methot, L., & LeSage, M. (1995). *Fundamentals of behavior analytic research*. New York: Plenum Press.

Sidman, M. (1960). *Tactics of scientific research*. New York: Basic Books.

CHAPTER 12

Application of Changing Criterion Designs

In the last chapter we described the basic changing criterion design and several of its adaptations. The changing criterion design can be used when evaluating the effects of an intervention on the gradual systematic increase or decrease of a target behavior. In this chapter we provide examples of a basic changing criterion design, a changing criterion design that incorporates different phase lengths, and a changing criterion design with a return to baseline phase.

BASIC CHANGING CRITERION DESIGN: INCREASING BEHAVIOR

Davis, P., Bates, P., & Cuvo, A. J. (1983). Training a mentally retarded woman to work competitively: Effect of graphic feedback and a changing criterion design. *Education and Training of the Mentally Retarded, 18*, 158–163.

Research Question

In this study, the authors demonstrated the effectiveness of a graphic feedback procedure to increase rate of breakfast tray stripping (i.e., cleaning) for a young woman with moderate mental retardation.

Subjects

The subject was a 20-year-old woman with moderate mental retardation (IQ of 42 on the Wechsler Intelligence Scale for Children) who had resided at home all her life.

Setting

The study took place in a hospital kitchen where dishes were washed in a production line format.

Dependent Variable

The dependent variable was the speed (rate per minute) of stripping trays. Stripping trays consisted of disposing of waste, stacking dishes, and soaking silverware. In addition, a corollary dependent measure (questionnaire) was used to determine how the subject's coworkers perceived the effects of the intervention. This was administered to the kitchen supervisor and coworkers and consisted of eight questions concerning the goals, procedures, and outcomes of the study.

Independent Variables

The independent variable was graphic feedback concerning rate of work for the first three intervention subphases. During the fourth subphase, verbal feedback for sloppiness was added to graphic feedback. In the fifth and final subphase, only graphic feedback was provided. Additionally, a changing criterion was used.

The Design

The subject's rate of tray stripping was evaluated using a changing criterion design to produce a stepwise increase in the target behavior. Criteria during the intervention phase were changed when met for at least 3 consecutive days, with one exception. If the subject's performance was increasing, the criterion was not changed until performance stabilized or a decreasing trend was evident.

The Intervention

The subject's primary task was breakfast tray stripping. Each training session lasted the duration of time required to strip 130 to 150 trays. Based on the subject's rate for 16 baseline observations and the competitive rate, criteria for the various subphases were determined. Initial criteria were set based on baseline performance. The trainer timed one regular tray stripper and determined a rate of 2.38 trays per minute was commensurate with a competitive employment rate. Therefore, 2.4 trays per minute became her criterion from the third intervention subphase to the end of the study. Graphic feedback (along with the changing criterion) was used as the independent variable until the fourth subphase, when verbal feedback was added as a reminder concerning the quality as well as quantity of her work. The final subphase included only the graphic feedback and criterion. The questionnaire was completed by all coworkers within 1 month of the study's termination.

Obtaining the Data and Plotting the Results

The rate of tray stripping was recorded daily. The mean rate was calculated by measuring the length of time it took the subject to strip 10 consecutive randomly selected trays. The total number of minutes to strip the trays was divided by 10 to determine the mean number of trays stripped per minute. Interobserver reliability mean was .999, with no measure below .997.

Results

Figure 12–1 depicts the results. This figure includes a number of phase change lines indicating when there was a change in the criterion for reinforcement. During Phase 1 (baseline), the subject stripped 1.33 trays per minute on average across all baseline observations. During the first intervention phase, when tray stripping Criterion 1 (1.8 trays per min-

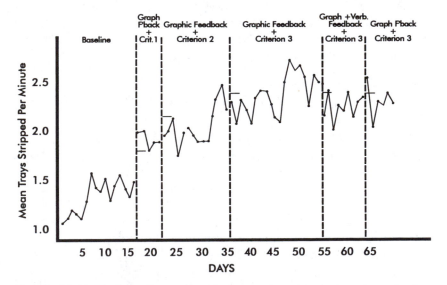

Figure 12–1. Data for the subject in the study using a changing criterion design for increasing behavior. *Note.* From "Training a Mentally Retarded Woman to Work Competitively: Effect of Graphic Feedback and a Changing Criterion Design," by P. Davis, P. Bates, and A. J. Cuvo, 1983, *Education and Training of the Mentally Retarded, 18,* p. 161. Copyright 1983 by the Council for Exceptional Children. Reprinted with permission.

ute) and graphic feedback were in effect, her production rate increased to an average of 1.9 trays per minute. During Criterion 2, the subject's tray stripping mean performance was 2.05 trays per minute. During Criterion 3, the subject's tray stripping speed increased but her coworkers did not accept the quality of her work. As a result, Criterion 3 was extended for another 9 days and the subject was provided with verbal feedback on the quality as well as the quantity of her work. The graph includes when verbal feedback was added to the intervention. Following this feedback, her quality of work improved and it was accepted by her coworkers. Verbal feedback was then dropped from the intervention. When graphic feedback and the changing criterion were provided for speed of tray stripping, the subject's speed increased to 97% of the competitive rate during this last phase of the study. From beginning to the end of the program, the subject's tray stripping rate increase represented a savings of 44 to 51 minutes per day over baseline levels. The results of the questionnaire indicated that the majority of coworkers believed the intervention was acceptable and was responsible for the subject's improved performance.

Why Use a Changing Criterion Design?

A changing criterion design was very appropriate because it allowed the trainer to change the criterion gradually and demonstrate that increases in tray stripping were due to the changing criterion design and the feedback given to the subject.

Limitations of the Study

There are two limitations in this study. First, the training program ended while the subject was performing at an acceptable level but the trainer was present. To ensure that the subject would maintain competitive work rates, the trainer should have gradually faded his or her presence and feedback in order to bring the subject's work performance under natural conditions. Second, the trainer did not allow the subject to strip lunch or dinner trays to generalize her skills.

Summary

A summary of the relevant dimensions of this changing criterion study can be found in Table 12–1.

Table 12–1. Summary of "Training a Mentally Retarded Woman to Work Competitively: Effect of Graphic Feedback and a Changing Criterion Design."

Feature	Description
Type of design	Basic changing criterion design
Goal of study	Determine the effectiveness of a graphic feedback procedure to increase speed of breakfast tray stripping of a young woman
Subjects	20-year-old woman with moderate mental retardation
Setting	A hospital kitchen
Dependent variable	Speed of tray stripping
Independent variable	Graphic feedback procedure and the changing criterion
Results and outcomes	Graphic feedback procedure and a changing criterion increased the subject's tray stripping rate

BASIC CHANGING CRITERION DESIGN: DECREASING BEHAVIOR

Foxx, R. M., & Rubinoff, A. (1979). Behavioral treatment of caffeinism: Reducing excessive coffee drinking. *Journal of Applied Behavior Analysis, 12*, 335–344.

Research Question

In this study, the researchers were interested in determining the effectiveness of a behavioral treatment program in reducing the ingestion of caffeine. The treatment program was modeled after one that had been successful in decreasing smoking.

Subjects

Three adult subjects volunteered for the study. They each met the following criteria: (a) drank eight or more cups of coffee daily (over 1,000 mg caffeine); (b) reported related physiological and behavioral symptoms (e.g., nervousness); and (c) wanted to decrease their caffeine intake.

Setting

The subjects self-monitored their coffee drinking throughout the day in any and all environments.

Dependent Variable

The dependent variable in this study was the total daily caffeine intake. This was determined by having the subjects record the number and type of beverages containing caffeine that they drank. The researchers had predetermined the amount of caffeine in the drinks that the subjects indicated they consumed (e.g., brewed coffee, instant coffee, tea, colas).

Independent Variable

A treatment program used effectively to reduce smoking was used as the independent variable. This involved the subjects' paying $20.00 at the onset of the program, which would be reimbursed if they met target goals. A contract was signed by each subject that explained the rules and procedures. A changing criterion was also used to produce gradual, stepwise reductions in caffeine intake.

The Design

The authors used a basic changing criterion design for decreasing behavior. This included a baseline, four treatment phases, and a follow-up phase that included probes up to 40 weeks after the program ended. Although three subjects allowed the researchers to produce replication across individuals within their study, this is not requisite.

The Intervention

As noted previously, each subject deposited $20.00 at the beginning of the study. They could earn $10.00 back in four payments of $2.50 if they met the four criterion levels specified by the researchers. If they did not exceed the criterion level on any day within a treatment phase, they would also receive a $1.00 bonus and be eligible to receive a $10.00 bonus at the end of the study. If they exceeded the criterion level within any treatment phase they would lose the $2.50, the bonus, and the eligibility.

Obtaining the Data and Plotting the Results

Subjects self-monitored their caffeine intake by recording the number and type of caffeine drinks they consumed. They used a provided conversion chart to keep a running record of their daily caffeine intake. At the end of the day, they recorded their total intake. Determined from baseline data, four criterion levels were specified that would gradually reduce the caffeine intake to 600 mg or less. After the treatment phases were completed, each subject was called every 2 weeks and asked to monitor his or her intake for the next 2 days.

Results

Subject 1 decreased her caffeine intake from an average of 1,008 mg per day during baseline to an average of 357 mg per day during the final treatment phase (see Figure 12–2). Her intake at the 40-week follow-up was further reduced to slightly under 300 mg. Subject 2 showed similar

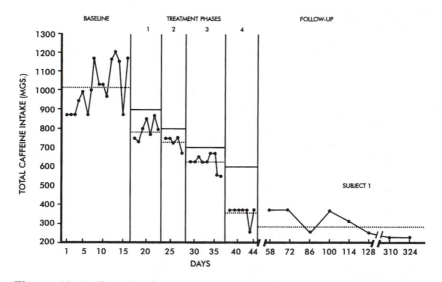

Figure 12–2. Data for Subject 1 in the study using a changing criterion design for decreasing behavior. *Note.* From "Behavioral Treatment of Caffeinism: Reducing Excessive Coffee Drinking," by R. M. Foxx and A. Rubinoff, 1979, *Journal of Applied Behavior Analysis, 12*, p. 339. Copyright 1979 by the Society for the Experimental Analysis of Behavior. Reprinted with permission.

decreases, going from an average of 1,147 mg at baseline to an average of 357 mg during the final treatment phase to an average of 250 mg during follow-up (see Figure 12–3). The results for Subject 3, although generally favorable, were not as convincing (see Figure 12–4). He decreased his consumption from an average of 1,175 mg during baseline to an average of 314 mg (final treatment phase). However, he exceeded the criterion level for 1 day in both the third and fourth treatment phases. His consumption during follow-up increased to an average of 537 mg. The authors did note that his level was still below the 600 mg average targeted for program success.

Why Use a Changing Criterion Design?

The nature of this study makes it ideal for a changing criterion design. The target behavior, consumption of caffeine beverages, can be decreased in a gradual, stepwise fashion. In addition, the visual nature of the graphs aided the self-monitoring procedure.

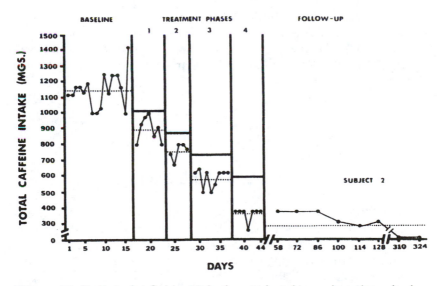

Figure 12–3. Data for Subject 2 in the study using a changing criterion design for decreasing behavior. *Note.* From "Behavioral Treatment of Caffeinism: Reducing Excessive Coffee Drinking," by R. M. Foxx and A. Rubinoff, 1979, *Journal of Applied Behavior Analysis, 12*, p. 339. Copyright 1979 by the Society for the Experimental Analysis of Behavior. Reprinted with permission.

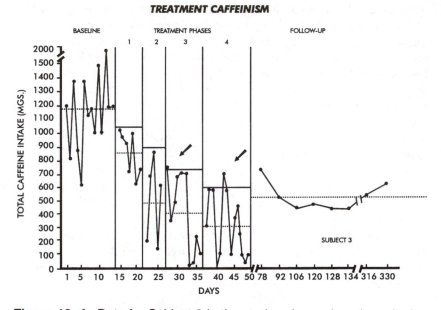

Figure 12–4. Data for Subject 3 in the study using a changing criterion design for decreasing behavior. *Note.* From "Behavioral Treatment of Caffeinism: Reducing Excessive Coffee Drinking," by R. M. Foxx and A. Rubinoff, 1979, *Journal of Applied Behavior Analysis, 12*, p. 339. Copyright 1979 by the Society for the Experimental Analysis of Behavior. Reprinted with permission.

Limitations of the Study

As noted previously, although positive results were found in this study, it is difficult to determine which aspect of the program was responsible. The authors also note that other factors, such as the subjects' desire to reduce their consumption and social pressure, could also have affected the results. The reliability of the self-monitoring procedure is also a concern.

Summary

A summary of the relevant dimensions of this basic changing criterion design can be found in Table 12–2.

Table 12–2. Summary of "Behavioral Treatment of Caffeinism: Reducing Excessive Coffee Drinking."

Feature	Description
Type of design	Basic changing criterion design: decreasing behavior
Goal of study	Determine effectiveness of a behavioral program designed to reduce consumption of caffeine beverages
Subjects	Three volunteers with a history of excessive coffee drinking
Setting	Natural environment
Dependent variable	Total daily caffeine intakes (mgs)
Independent variable	Behavioral program consisting of monetary reinforcement and a changing criterion for reinforcement
Results and outcomes	Treatment was effective for all three subjects in reducing their caffeine consumption from over 1,000 mg on average per day to under 600 mg

CHANGING CRITERION DESIGN WITH TREATMENT PHASES OF DIFFERENT LENGTHS

Smith, M. A,. Schloss, P. J., & Israelite, N. K. (1986). Evaluation of a simile recognition treatment program for hearing-impaired students. *Journal of Speech and Hearing Disorders, 51,* 134–139.

Research Question

In this study, the investigators demonstrated the efficacy of an intervention program to enhance recognition of commonly used similes by hearing-impaired students.

Subjects

The subjects were two 20-year-old college students. Subject 1 was a male who had a congenital bilateral severe to profound sensorineural hearing loss with etiology unknown. Subject 2 was a female full-time resident client with a bilateral severe sensorineural hearing loss due to maternal rubella. Both wore hearing aids during the investigation.

Setting

Subjects were enrolled in an adult therapy program at a university speech and hearing clinic. Therapy was conducted in a room equipped with a microphone and a two-way mirror leading to an adjoining observation booth.

Dependent Variable

The dependent variable was the subjects' correct application of eight similes (e.g., "As happy as a lark"). The authors developed 18 incomplete passages that would be relevant for each of the eight similes (e.g., "My mother won a trip to Hawaii. She was _____" for the above simile). Three incomplete passages were randomly chosen for each simile. Therefore, the total number of correct applications of the eight similes to the 24 incomplete passages was determined for each session.

Independent Variable

The independent variable in this study was an intervention program involving instruction, review, exemplars, and feedback along with a changing criterion for reinforcement.

The Design

The investigators used a changing criterion design with treatment phases of different lengths to evaluate the treatment effects. By having the subjects respond to criterion levels of different lengths, the possible confounding variables of practice and maturation are better controlled. More than one subject was not requisite, but if results were replicated across both subjects, this would strengthen the demonstration of a functional relationship.

The Intervention

At the first session of baseline observations, subjects (a) read the definition of the term simile, (b) were given examples of similies, and (c) were asked to match each of 144 passages to one of eight correct similes. During subsequent baseline observations, subjects were given 24 opportunities to respond to randomly selected passages by stating a correct simile. Nonspecific reinforcing statements were made but no feedback regarding the accuracy of responses was given. These two measures across baseline sessions indicated that each subject was in need of the intervention.

There were eight intervention subphases corresponding to the eight targeted similes. Similes were once again reviewed with the subjects. Then during intervention sessions, subjects were given specific reinforcement for correct responses and correction procedures for incorrect ones. Correction procedures continued until the correct simile was stated by the subject. Sessions were conducted three times a week for 30 min per session for a total of 35 sessions.

Criteria were set based on the following general guidelines. Subjects should recognize at least three additional novel passages of the 24 presented. Second, accuracy should be maintained for previously developed skills at 80% or higher. Subjects were informed of the criterion level before each session and informed that they must meet that criterion level for at least two sessions.

Obtaining the Data and Plotting the Results

Two independent observers recorded the number of correct and incorrect applications of the eight similes to the 24 incomplete passages selected from the original 144. Because the number of opportunities was held constant, the researchers needed only to report the total number for each session (up to a maximum of 24). Assessment data were graphed and shared with the subjects. Interobserver reliability was obtained at least once in each subphase by two independent observers.

Results

As can be seen in Figure 12–5, subjects 1 and 2 did not correctly identify any of the similes during baseline sessions.

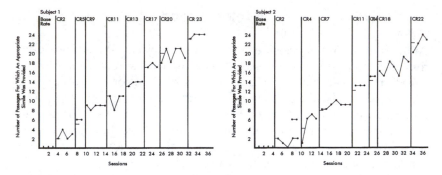

Figure 12–5. Data for Subjects 1 and 2 in the study using a changing criterion design with different phase lengths. *Note.* From "Evaluation of a Simile Recognition Treatment Program for Hearing-Impaired Students," by M. A. Smith, P. J. Schloss, and N. K. Israelite, 1986, *Journal of Speech and Hearing Disorders, 51*, p. 137. Copyright 1986 by the American Speech, Language, and Hearing Association. Reprinted with permission.

However, during treatment sessions, Subject 1's criterion levels for the first seven intervention subphases were 2, 5, 9, 11, 13, 17, and 20 (out of a possible 24). During Subphase 8, he obtained a correct response rate of 23 in each of the last three sessions. Subject 2 completed only seven subphases of the program due to time constraints. The criterion levels that were set were 2, 4, 7, 11, 14, 18, and 22. Figure 12–5 shows that her responses also generally increased to the criterion levels, although she did not meet the criterion level of 18 in four of the seven sessions. During Subphase 7, she obtained correct response rates of 20, 22, 24, and 23 in the last four sessions. Point-by-point interobserver reliability was no less than 95% for either subject during baseline or intervention phases.

Why Use a Changing Criterion Design With Treatment Phases of Different Lengths?

When the goal is a gradual increase in student performance, this design is ideal. The authors selected this design because it provides a logical, systematic, and positive evaluation of the intervention package designed to increase simile recognition skills of these subjects. This design allows for modest expectations for performance at the beginning and then increases as the students become more proficient. More experimental control was established by varying the lengths of the treatment phases.

Table 12–3. Summary of "Evaluation of a Simile Recognition Treatment Program for Hearing-impaired Students."

Feature	Description
Type of design	Changing criterion design with treatment phases of different lengths
Goal of study	Demonstrate the efficacy of an intervention program to enhance the hearing-impaired students' simile recognition skill
Subjects	Two 20-year-old college students with severe to profound hearing impairment
Setting	A speech and hearing clinic
Dependent variable	Subjects' correct application of similes
Independent variable	An intervention program involving instruction, review, exemplars, and feedback along with a changing criterion for reinforcement
Results and outcomes	Treatment program increased the subjects' ability to correctly match similes

Limitations of the Study

One limitation may be that this changing criterion design required high levels of involvement in collecting data and providing systematic instruction. Without support from others, a single therapist may have found it would be impossible to investigate a program of this nature.

Summary

A summary of the relevant dimensions of this changing criterion study can be found in Table 12–3.

CHANGING CRITERION DESIGN WITH A RETURN TO BASELINE PHASE

De Luca, R., & Holborn, S. W. (1992). Effects of a variable-ratio reinforcement schedule with changing criterion on exercise in obese and nonobese boys. *Journal of Applied Behavior Analysis, 25,* 671–679.

Research Question

The authors designed this study to determine if variable ratio (VR) schedules would increase and maintain high rates of exercise. This study was an extension of these authors' previous study where they used a fixed ratio (FR) schedule to increase students' exercise skills. They wished to compare the results of the two studies to determine if one type of schedule was preferable.

Subjects

The subjects were six boys, each 11 years old. Three of these subjects were obese and three of them were of normal weight. Again, multiple individuals may strengthen the design.

Setting

The study was conducted in an elementary school nurse's room. Each subject exercised on a stationary bicycle in the nurse's room.

Dependent Variables

The target behavior was pedaling on a stationary exercise bicycle. Pedaling was measured in (a) the subjects' overall responding rate per session and (b) the total time spent exercising per session.

Independent Variables

The independent variable was a token system in which subjects earned points by pedaling bicycle in exchange for reinforcers from a reinforcement menu (a handheld battery-operated game, kite, bicycle bell, flashlight, model car, model plane, puzzle, adventure and comic books). Different schedules and criteria for reinforcement were also used.

The Design

A changing criterion design with a return to baseline phase was used in this study. A VR schedule of reinforcement was implemented with a different criterion for performance for each subject.

The Intervention

Subjects were tested individually once a day, from Monday through Friday, for about 12 weeks. At the beginning of each session an identical instruction, "exercise as long as you like," was given to all subjects. Sessions were terminated when the subject dismounted from the bicycle or the assigned time of 30 min had elapsed. After stable baseline was established, the VR schedule of reinforcement (i.e., a rate of 70–85 revolutions per minute) was implemented for nine sessions. For each of the three VR subphases, a criterion of 15% increase over mean responding during the previous subphase was established. In other words, "a different criterion for performance was specified for each subject, based on his performance in the previous subphase" (p. 673). To further determine the effectiveness of the VR schedule, a return to baseline phase was implemented after the third intervention subphase. Finally, this same VR subphase was reinstated.

Obtaining the Data and Plotting the Results

The experimenter sat behind the equipment panels out of the subject's sight and started recording data when the subject began pedaling the bicycle. For accurate data collection the stationary bicycle was programmed to signal when the variable number of responses had occurred. Each time the bell rang and illuminated the light, the subject earned a point to be used in the token system.

Results

During baseline, the nonobese boys responded at a mean of 71.9 revolutions per minute and the obese boys responded at a mean of 59.2 revolutions per minute (see Figure 12–6). During the first subphase, the mean rates of responding for the nonobese and obese boys were 98.89 and 85.51 revolutions per minute, respectively. During the second subphase, the rates of responding per minute increased to 114.2 and 101.2. The mean response rates during the third subphase for the nonobese and obese boys were 130.0 and 117.0, respectively. Following this phase, a brief return to baseline produced a reduction in response rate to 95.3 for nonobese boys and 83.6 for obese boys. However, when the reinforcement was reintroduced, it produced the highest response rates in all boys (nonobese boys, 138.7, and obese boys, 123.6). The authors compared this VR schedule study with their previous FR schedule of rein-

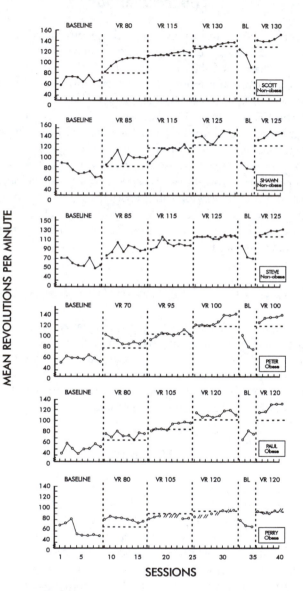

Figure 12–6. Data for the subjects in the study using a changing criterion design with return to baseline. *Note.* From "Effects of a Variable-Ratio Reinforcement Schedule With Changing Criterion on Exercise in Obese and Nonobese Boys," by R. DeLuca and S. Holborn, 1992, *Journal of Applied Behavior Analysis, 25,* p. 677. Copyright 1992 by the Society for the Experimental Analysis of Behavior. Reprinted with permission.

forcement study (De Luca & Holborn, 1990) and indicated that the VR subphases of the changing criterion design produced greater increases in the rate of exercise.

Why Use Changing Criterion Design With a Return to Baseline?

The investigators were interested in determining the effects of a variable ratio and changing criterion reinforcement procedure to increase the bicycle pedaling of nonobese and obese boys. This design provided the opportunity to set initial criterion based on the subjects' own baseline performance, and allowed each subject to increase his own rate through small successive increments. Through this manner, rates of exercise were increased gradually and systematically. By reinstating the baseline conditions and noting decreases in responding in all subjects, more convincing evidence of the functional relationship between the independent and dependent variable was provided.

Limitations of the Study

One limitation of the study was gender bias. It was noted in the study that there are more overweight girls than boys, yet the authors included only boys in the study. Therefore, the findings may not be generalizable to the general population.

Summary

A summary of the relevant dimensions of this changing criterion study can be found in Table 12–4.

Table 12–4. Summary of "Effects of a Variable-Ratio Reinforcement Schedule With Changing Criterion on Exercise in Obese and Nonobese Boys."

Feature	Description
Type of design	Changing criterion design with a return to baseline phase

(continued)

Table 12–4. *(continued)*

Feature	Description
Goal of study	Determine effectiveness of VR schedule to increase exercise rate of obese vs. nonobese children
Subjects	Three obese and three nonobese 11-year-old boys
Setting	Nurse's room in an elementary school
Dependent variable	Pedaling a stationary exercise bicycle
Independent variable	Token system to exchange for reinforcers from a reinforcer menu along with the changing VR schedule for reinforcement
Results and outcomes	VR schedule produced increased exercise rate

Note. VR = variable ratio.

The changing criterion design has been used in a variety of circumstances and is useful for producing stepwise changes in a target behavior. At this point, we have discussed each of the major designs and their adaptations. Regardless of which design is used, the researcher is collecting data that must be analyzed to determine if the functional relationship exists between the independent and dependent variables. The analysis of data may take visual, statistical, or qualitative methods. We explore each of these possibilities in the final chapter.

Reference

De Luca, R. V., & Holborn, S. W. (1990). Effects of fixed-interval and fixed-ratio schedules of token reinforcement on exercise with obese and non-obese boys. *Psychological Record, 40,* 67–82

PART 3

Analyzing Results
From
Single Subject Studies

CHAPTER 13

Methods for Analyzing Data

QUALITATIVE ANALYSIS
  When to Use Qualitative Analysis
  How to Use Qualitative Analysis
  Limitations of Qualitative Analysis
A FINAL WORD

In this chapter, we will discuss the analysis and interpretation of data through three possible avenues. First, we will discuss visual analysis of data, which is perhaps the most commonly used method for immediately examining results. Second, we will discuss statistical analysis of data. Because many experts have criticized the sole use of visual analysis, these methods are present in the literature more frequently. Third, we will examine the use of qualitative data analysis. Qualitative research methods have increased in popularity and their application to single subject studies may enhance the researcher's ability to analyze aspects of behavior change that are not always captured in numerical variables. The researcher should be prepared to use each and all of these methods in any given study. Each has its own particular advantages and limitations. Using these methods in combination, the researcher will likely enhance her or his ability to demonstrate a functional relationship, by increasing the amount and types of data collected. The significance of behavior change may be examined quantitatively and qualitatively. As stated many times in this text, the overall goal of the researcher is to demonstrate an experimental criterion has been met (i.e., a functional relationship exists between independent and dependent variable) and a therapeutic criterion is met (i.e., the change achieved is of significance; Alberto & Troutman, 1999). The reader should not feel compelled to select one method of analysis over another, but use all reasonably applicable methods in reporting and interpreting results.

VISUAL ANALYSIS

Richards, Taylor, and Ramasamy (1997) noted that professionals involved in applied research and practice frequently visually analyze data in making inferences about behavioral changes. However, these same authors stressed that visual analysis has its limitations because of the subjectivity that may be involved. What might appear to be subjective in this method of analysis is at least partially offset by common agreement among researchers about characteristics of graphed data that should be inspected and evaluated (Alberto & Troutman, 1999). We will first address when to use visual analysis, how visual analysis is applied, and what it offers the researcher. We will then address the limitations.

When to Use Visual Analysis

Visual analysis of data is used generally when continuous numerical data are gathered (i.e., using the methods described in Chapter 3), data are graphically depicted, and the researcher wishes to make formative as well as summative analyses of study outcomes. The researcher uses visual analysis to examine two overall aspects of the data. These are the level (i.e., performance on the dependent variable) and trend (i.e., changes or consistent patterns in the data path; Tawney & Gast, 1984). More specifically, the researcher should examine the number of data points, the variability of performance, the level of performance, and the direction and degree of trends that occur (Cooper, Heron, & Heward, 1987). Tawney and Gast also stressed that these aspects should be examined both within and between phases within the study (e.g., within and between baseline and intervention phases).

Cooper et al., (1987) offered several questions that the viewer of graphed data should answer before visual analysis. Although these questions are particularly relevant for a reader of research, it is worth noting that the researcher herself or himself should also consider the answers when determining how a graph should be constructed. We have modified the questions somewhat so that they appear in a manner more applicable to the researcher. These questions are

1. Are the legend, axes, and all phases labeled clearly?
2. Is the scaling of the y-axis (i.e., dependent variable) appropriate? That is, do changes in performance appear to be commensurate with their educational significance (e.g., a minuscule change does not appear as a huge change in behavior unless such a change would be significant). A relatively small change in the occurrence of a health- or life-threatening behavior might be depicted as a rather important one on the scale. Conversely, a change of a few percentage points in the accuracy of solving math problems might not represent such a significant change.
3. Do the data depict the performance of an individual or the performance of a group being treated as a single subject? In the latter case, is the range or variability of the individual performances within the group also included?

Cooper et al. stress that if the graph is not constructed correctly, then visual analysis of data should be withheld.

Applying Visual Analysis

As noted previously, visual analysis may be applied primarily in two ways: (a) to inspect changes within a phase or condition and (b) to inspect changes across phases or conditions. In the former, one should examine the number of data points, the variability of performance, the level of performance, and the direction and degree of any trends (Cooper et al., 1987).

Number of Data Points Within A Phase

The number of data points within a phase should be sufficient to make a reasonable determination of whether the data path accurately represents performance on the dependent variable. Clearly, the greater the number of data points, the more likely one may have confidence in such a determination. We have heard students remark that a baseline phase should contain at least 3 data points. One might just as well say 5, 10, or 15 data points. The number of data points may be limited if it is clear that the dependent variable is not likely to change unless there is also a change in phases. For example, if the target behavior was one that the individual could not exhibit (e.g., phoneme-grapheme matches) without instruction, then the number of data points in the baseline may be very limited. There may be a need to demonstrate only that the target behavior has not been acquired. When the target behavior is one that the individual exhibits, the need to collect more data to obtain an accurate portrayal of performance cannot be set at any fixed number. For example, if the target behavior is disrupting the class, the frequency may be quite variable and achieving a steady baseline cannot be guaranteed for a preset number of observations. Of importance is the variability present within the performance.

Variability in Performance

If an individual exhibits little variability in performance (i.e., a flat data path) or a steady data path with a clear trend (i.e., always increasing or decreasing), then the researcher may rely on fewer data points. When an individual's performance fluctuates, then a greater number of data points is needed. Cooper et al. (1987) noted that the number of times a phase has been repeated may also influence the number of data points needed. In a withdrawal design (see Chapter 5), one might encounter such a circumstance. For example, an individual is attempting to decrease her episodes of dysfluency. The intervention phase clearly depicts such a reduction to a predetermined criterion level. A second baseline phase is implemented (the withdrawal of intervention phase). Immediately the data path depicts an upward trend in episodes of dysfluency. Although one might argue a return to baseline levels of performance is desirable from a research perspective, one might argue more persuasively that such action could be detrimental to the individual and deemed highly undesirable by other concerned persons. Therefore, a sufficient number of data points to indicate a change in level (i.e., number of episodes of dysfluency immediately increases) and trend (across several data points the trend continues upward) is generally acceptable when there are such ethical considerations. One must also consider ethical treatment and social validity of procedures in other circumstances as well. Take, for example, an individual who is engaged in variable rates of self-abusive (but not health-threatening) behavior. Because, during baseline phase, possibly no new effort may be made to alter the target behavior (i.e., the status quo is maintained), the researcher may limit the number of data points as well (Cooper et al., 1987).

Level of Behavior

Level of behavior refers to the performance of the target behavior and possible changes that would be viewed vertically. That is, a significant and immediate change in behavior should be depicted as a jump in the data path either upward or downward (see Figure 13–1).

When there is variability within a phase, the level may be determined by calculating the mean performance and drawing a horizontal line across the phase. Other options are to determine the median point in the data to draw the horizontal line or to examine the range of performance (Cooper et al., 1987). See Figure 13–2 for depiction of a mean, median, and range of level performance lines. These lines may help the researcher better determine overall performance when variability in the data path is present. Also, they become important when data are examined across phases. Generally, the greater the variability the more preferable the median line or the range may be to a mean level line of performance. Tawney and Gast (1984) suggested that if at least 80% of data points fall within a 15% value range of the mean level line, then the data may be considered stable and the mean level line acceptable. This is a rule of thumb and not a standard, however. Familiarity with one's own dependent variable, the phase in effect, the nature of the desired outcomes, and the amount of data actually depicted with each point (e.g., an entire day or a single session of many in a day) all should be used in determining stability and the meaning of level as well as trend. One might also calculate the difference between the value of the first and last data points within a phase or the mean difference between the first few and last few data points in a phase (Cooper et al., 1987).

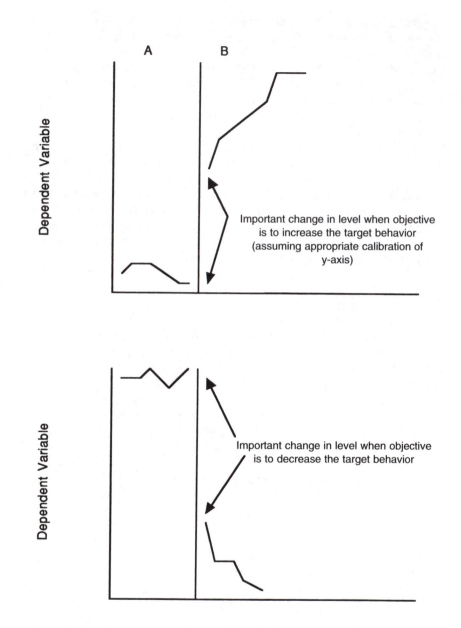

Figure 13–1. Example demonstrating change in level of behavior.

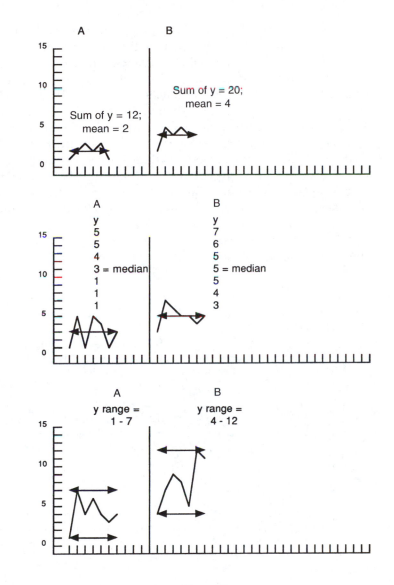

Figure 13–2. Example demonstrating mean, median, and range of level performance lines.

Trend

Trend is determined by examining the direction of the data path. The researcher is concerned with whether the trend is flat, increasing, or decreasing and whether it is variable or stable. Trend may be eyeballed to an extent. When the data path depicts a clear and steady direction the overall trend may be relatively obvious. Also, trend direction changes (e.g., from increasing to decreasing) may be reasonably clear. However, in most instances, data points are variable and the overall trend may not be apparent. Therefore, the researcher may need to construct a trend line. The split-middle line method is one method for constructing a trend line. Figure 13–3 includes procedures for producing the split-middle line (Figure 13–3 is adapted from Tawney & Gast, 1984). The split-middle line provides a better portrayal of the overall trend in the data. Although rates of acceleration and deceleration cannot be calculated accurately with equal-interval graphs as commonly used, one might use logarithmic charts to produce such rates if desirable (Tawney & Gast, 1984).

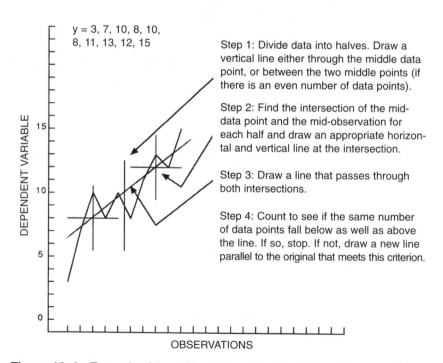

Figure 13–3. Example of the split-middle method for determining trend lines.

Assessing level and trend within phases is important to understand specifically what is occurring during baseline phase(s) and within intervention phase(s). Of equal importance is analyzing level and trend across adjacent phases. More specifically, evaluation of the data levels and trends as the study progresses from baseline to intervention phases or vice versa is at the heart of visual analysis.

Applying Visual Analysis Across Phases

The principles just discussed are equally applicable when one visually analyzes data as the study progresses from one phase to another. Of importance in this visual analysis is to determine if the level and trends in the data path changed in predictable fashion. If so, the researcher is more likely to have obtained verification. If those changes in level and trend are similar with other individuals, settings, and behaviors, and/or occur in response to changes in the intervention, then replication is more likely to have been achieved. We emphasize *more likely* because visual analysis is not always sufficient to determine these outcomes that demonstrate a functional relationship between independent and dependent variable. Nevertheless, it can be useful for understanding changes in the data path.

The researcher should examine the data for (a) an immediate change in level of performance on the dependent variable when there is a phase change, (b) the overall level of performance within a phase and how that compares to overall performance in other phases, and (c) changes in trend subsequent to phase changes.

Immediate Change in Level. An immediate change in level when a phase change occurs is generally a visual indicator that the intervention (or perhaps the withdrawal of the intervention) is having some effect (or perhaps no effect or even a detrimental effect). Suppose, for example, that the target behavior is consuming junk food (keep in mind we would need to define more precisely what we meant by "junk food"). A baseline reveals a high level of consumption that is stable (or possibly increasing). An intervention is introduced and the amount of junk food consumed decreases dramatically. The change in the data path would indicate that the intervention possibly had an effect on the target behavior (replication of this effect would be necessary to firmly establish the functional relationship). Conversely, assume that the target behavior is identified as playing appropriately. Baseline measures reveal a steady but very low rate of appropriate play. An intervention is introduced and appropriate play changes little. This would be an indicator that there was no or a small intervention effect. Tawney and Gast (1984) suggested that the level change between conditions may be analyzed by using the following steps.

1. Identify the last data point in the first phase and the first data point in the subsequent phase (i.e., the two data points separated by the phase change line on the graph).
2. Subtract the smaller value from the larger value.
3. Note whether the change indicates an improvement, no change, or deterioration in performance.

Of course, the number of data points collected over time would also be an important consideration. An immediately significant change might not occur, but a steady change may be evident over a number of data measurements, which would indicate verification of a prediction of behavior change in response to the intervention. Such an instance may exemplify an overall change in level of performance, although the change may or may not be dramatic.

Comparing Performance Across Phases. In general, when the range of performance in one phase does not overlap with the range of an adjacent phase, the researcher may assume a visual indicator that a change in behavior has occurred (Cooper et al., 1987; see Figure 13–4). When such an effect has not been achieved, a mean or median level line constructed for each phase may allow a better comparison. Tawney and Gast (1984) suggested calculating the percentage of overlap of data points between phases. This is determined by (a) determining the range of data point values in the first phase, (b) counting the number of data points in the subsequent phase which fall within that range, (c) counting the number of data points in the first phase, and (d) dividing the number from (b) by the number from (c) and multiplying by 100%.

Following is an example of this procedure.

> David is a student with a physical disability who is placed in Mr. Edwards' eighth-grade class. Mr. Edwards is working with David on reducing the target behavior of spending time in the bathroom. Duration recording (minutes per occurrence) is used. During the baseline phase, David spent 10, 12, 10, 11, 13, 11, 9, 13, 16, and 14 min per occurrence. Mr. Edwards implemented differential reinforcement for low rates of behavior within a withdrawal design (overall acceptable criterion level was set for 2 min per occurrence in three out of four consecutive observations). In the first intervention phase, David spent 9, 10, 8, 5, 3,

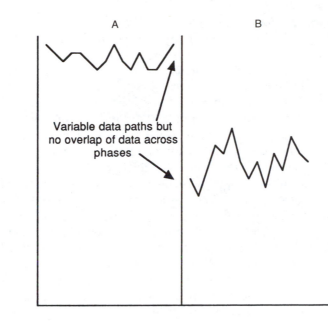

Variable data paths but
no overlap of data across
phases

Dependent Variable

Observations

Figure 13–4. Example of behavior change across phases.

3, 2, 2, and 2 min per occurrence. For (a) above, the range of data points in the baseline phase would be 10–16 min. For (b), only the 10-min observation would fall within that range. For (c), the number of data points in the baseline phase equals 10. For (d), we divide 1 by 10 and multiply by 100% to obtain a result of 10% overlap.

Generally, the smaller the percentage, the better the indication that the intervention has had an impact (assuming the phases compared are a baseline and intervention phase).

Trend Changes. Trend changes are evaluated in much the same way as they might be in within-phase procedures, although the researcher is typically predicting a shift in the trend (e.g., from a flat or accelerating baseline trend to a decelerating trend during the intervention phase). Similarly to level changes, an immediate shift in trend is generally an indicator that the intervention is having the desired effect (or the opposite of the effect expected). For example, an individual's target behavior is solving math problems. Both rate and accuracy are of importance. During baseline, the rate and accuracy are low although steady. When the intervention is introduced (a changing criterion for reinforcement), rate increases but accuracy decreases. The individual is attempting to solve more problems but is making more careless errors. Such an immediate shift in the accuracy would certainly clue the researcher that some other intervention must be implemented. Conversely, if the individual's rate and accuracy should both begin to accelerate, the researcher might reasonably assume that the intervention is having the desired effect, although replication of that effect would be desirable to demonstrate a functional relationship.

The split-middle line procedures discussed earlier are equally applicable when visual analysis is applied across phases. The overall trends may be less apparent than one might perceive at a casual glance at the data. These lines may assist the researcher in determining what the trends are and whether there are changes in trend that indicate desirable or undesirable changes in the dependent variable. The steepness of the trend line may also be examined for some indicator of the strength (or lack thereof) of the intervention. For example, a data path that indicates a number of consecutive accelerating level changes (when the overall goal is to increase the target behavior) may also serve to indicate intervention effects. One should, however, also keep in mind our earlier warning that graph construction on equal-interval graphs can be misleading if the intervals are either exceedingly large (steepness in the trend line appears more dramatic) or are exceedingly small (less steep trend line). Again, the use of logarithmic graphs may prevent this, although equal-interval graphs are still more commonly found in the literature.

Although visual analysis has been used for many years and is still commonly employed, there are serious drawbacks to its use. Several researchers have identified limitations to the use of visual analysis. First, we will discuss the possible advantages to the use of visual analysis versus statistical methods.

Advantages of Visual Analysis

Cooper et al. (1987) argued that visual analysis has four advantages. First, social significance is of primary importance. For example, a change in a target behavior may not be large enough to be statistically significant, yet may have considerable educational or clinical significance (e.g., a decrease in fire setting behavior). Second, visual analysis is more likely to identify independent variables that produce strong or socially significant results. Statistical significance may lead one to assume an independent variable is robust when the overall effects were weak in terms of social significance. Third, visual analysis encourages the researcher and reader to carefully examine every aspect of the data to determine sources of variability rather than just overall effects. Fourth, statistical methods require certain assumptions be met. Visual analysis allows for greater flexibility.

Limitations to Visual Analysis

There are limitations to visual analysis, however. DeProspero and Cohen (1979) noted that visual analysis may not be as reliable as statistical methods of analysis. These authors were concerned that two analysts may not reliably evaluate the same data because the guidelines are neither as stringent nor as precise as those employed in statistical formulas. Ottenbacher (1990) found that 30 individuals could not visually rate significant changes from baseline to intervention phases on 24 graphs when compared to an objective method of analysis. Similarly, Richards et al. (1997) reported that neither undergraduate nor graduate students studying applied behavior analysis could accurately rate behavior changes in those same 24 graphs compared to the objective method used. In fact, the actual performance of the visual raters in comparison to the objective method was less than chance. Richards et al. found that the raters were more likely to suggest a significant change had occurred when in fact one had not. Of course, in an applied research study, there are many variables to consider in determining what is a significant behavior change, and the Ottenbacher and Richards et al. studies have their own limitations. Still, these results provide useful caution. If visual analysis is used, then the raters must be well trained and versed in the procedures discussed. Also, it would be helpful if two or more analysts viewed the data independently and drew conclusions that could be compared for reliability. If two or more independent raters agree on the nature and degree of changes in level and trend, and the consequent significance of the behavior change, then readers may place greater confidence in the conclusions drawn from visual analysis. Richards et al. concluded, however, that visual analysis should perhaps not be the *only* method used to evaluate results. Because there are other options available to the researcher, these should be considered in addition to the use of visual analysis. The researcher may compare the statistical results to those yielded through visual analysis. Such a combination, when possible, may allow for an objective confirmation (or refutation) of a significant behavior change through statistical procedures, while providing the flexibility to examine changes in level and trend that may help explain more subtle aspects of the study.

STATISTICAL ANALYSIS

As with visual analysis, statistical analysis has its advantages and limitations. We will discuss when it should be used, how it might be conducted, and what cautions the researcher should consider.

When to Use Statistical Analysis

Kazdin (1978) suggested several situations in which statistical tests may be suitably applied in single subject research studies. First, when the researcher has failed to establish a stable baseline and a trend is evident, the use of statistical analyses may assist in determining any subsequent change is significant that occurs when the intervention is introduced. For example, an individual who emits self-stimulatory behavior may actually perform at a somewhat decreasing rate during baseline. No stability is present and the behavior may be changing due to variables already present in the individual or environment. Yet, the rate of change may be too slow so that intervention is still desirable. Statistical tests may allow the researcher to scrutinize continuous shifts across phases when a change in trend is neither visually evident nor rapidly changing in level (Kazdin, 1978). Second, the researcher may find that visual inspection does not allow a clear analysis of whether or not interventions were effective. This may be of particular importance when the interventions used have not been thoroughly researched previously and therefore their potential impacts are less predictable. Equivocal results may make visual inspection difficult if not impossible. Statistical analysis may lead the researcher to discover reliable although not obvious effects (Kazdin, 1978). Kazdin acknowledged the argument that large effects are generally associated with social significance, but researchers must not rule out smaller effects that are reliable as also being potentially useful for treatment. Third, Kazdin argued that single subject researchers increasingly conduct their studies in less well controlled settings with greater numbers of confounding variables. Consequently, variability in performance may be due less to the potential effects of the intervention, than to these extraneous factors. Statistical analysis may also be effective in determining a significant effect in such situations.

How to Use Statistical Analysis

There are two general types of statistical procedures typically used by researchers. Descriptive measures (e.g., mean, median, mode, frequency) are used to describe aspects of the data without inference to their statistical significance. Inferential statistics are used to test for statistical significance. Additionally, inferential statistics are used when the researcher wishes to generalize her or his findings to other individuals (or samples or populations). Descriptive statistics are typically not used with a specific aim toward generalization of results. Inferential statistics may be used to test the significance of relationships between or among variables (e.g., Pearson product-moment correlation, Spearman's rho) or to test the significance of differences between or among groups of participants (e.g., analysis of variance [ANOVA], *t* test). Assumptions to be met to use descriptive statistics are minimal. That is, the researcher may statistically describe her or his subjects without having to meet prescribed conditions. Therefore, we will not discuss the use of descriptive statistics. Their use is comparatively simple and easily understood.

The use of inferential statistics does demand that certain assumptions be met. These assumptions differ depending on which statistical procedures are used. Inferential statistics may be further subdivided into parametric and nonparametric, with each type having its own general assumptions. The reader should refer to a source that thoroughly examines the assumptions that must be met before employing any particular statistical test (e.g., see Kratchowill & Levin, 1992 and Kazdin, 1984 for very thorough discussions of assumptions and applications of many different statistical procedures in single subject designs). To do so here would require considerable devotion of words to procedures that would take us far afield of the issues most relevant to the novice single subject researcher. However, serial dependency or autocorrelation with single subject data must be addressed, as it serves as a violation of assumptions for the use of some inferential statistical tests (Kamil, 1995).

Particularly with parametric tests, there is an assumption that observations are independent of one another. This may not be the case with single subject research, as the researcher is working with the same individual for each observation of data rather than making observations of different individuals as in group studies. Also, the fact that the same observer often is collecting the data for each observation also introduces the likelihood of **serial dependency** in the data (Busk & Marascuilo, 1992). In fact, we have stated repeatedly that prediction, verification of predictions, and replication of those verifications are mandatory to demonstrating a functional relationship. Successive observations in a single subject design tend to be correlated, which means they are serially dependent (Kazdin, 1984). The correlation among data points tends to allow a prediction of future performance based on present performance (and hence the observations are not truly independent). The extent of this dependency among successive observations is assessed by examining autocorrelation (Kazdin, 1984). Kazdin states that **autocorrelation** refers to a correlation (*r*) between data points separated by time intervals or lags. When these violations occur, findings of significance may be more likely (Kamil, 1995). This presents the problem of committing a Type I error.

A **Type I error**, in everyday language, refers to the researcher concluding that a significant effect has been achieved from the independent variable when this is not actually the case (a false rejection of the null hypothesis). Autocorrelation increases the likelihood that a statistically significant result may be obtained, leading to a Type I error. Busk and Marascuilo (1992) reviewed the findings of several experts and concluded that the risk of Type I error may be doubled or higher when single subject data are autocorrelated. A lag 1 analysis is typically used to determine if this violation has occurred.

Autocorrelation of lag 1 refers to the pairing of data points from the same distribution. The first of the data points is paired with the second, the second with the third, the third with the fourth, and so on. A correlation coefficient is then calculated. Kamil (1995) recommends the use of Bartlett's Test (*r*). Kazdin (1978) noted that when there is no serial dependency or autocorrelation, the correlation coefficient should be zero or close to it (i.e., there is no significant relationship between the pairs of data points). However, if the coefficient significantly differs from zero (i.e., there is a statistically significant relationship between the distribution of pairs of data points), then autocorrelation has occurred. Lag autocorrelations can be extended to lag 2, lag 3, and so on, and procedures for such analyses are reviewed in Kamill (1995), although a lag 1 analysis is typically considered sufficient. When there is a significant autocorrelation of lag 1, use of conventional analyses is contraindicated. Following is a discussion of variations of tests that may be used when there is no autocorrelation.

t tests and ANOVAs

Experts have discussed the use of *t* tests and ANOVAs that may be used to compare data between phases (e.g., baseline and intervention phases or between more than two treatments) with the same individual. In essence, the measures within each phase are aggregated and compared (Busk & Marascuilo, 1992). The unit of analysis (what is actually compared) may be the means or medians for each phase and to an extent depends on whether changes in level of responding or changes in trend are of concern (Busk & Marascuilo, 1992). The *t* statistic or *F* ratio (in the case of ANOVA) is then computed; should a significant difference be obtained, the researcher may then determine which phase represented the higher mean (overall average across all data points within a phase). Subsequently, the researcher would consider whether the direction of difference was supportive of the prediction made. For example, a significantly higher mean might be obtained for the baseline phase. If the overall goal was to significantly reduce the target behavior, then one might well surmise the goal had been met. Similarly, if the mean were significantly higher for the treatment phase when the overall goal was to increase the target behavior, then the goal would be met. Kazdin (1978) noted that t tests might be used when one compares responding between two phases (e.g., baseline and intervention) and that ANOVA be used when three or more phases used. Kazdin (1984) stressed that with some designs (e.g., A-B-A-B), performances in the like phases (A1+ A2, B1 + B2) may be combined, which should reduce the influence of serial dependency. The greater the lag between observations (e.g., between A1 and B2), theoretically, autocorrelation should be reduced. Kazdin (1984) cautioned, however, that autocorrelation presents the possibility of a serious violation of the assumption that each observation is independent of the other, perhaps making the use of parametric tests problematic.

Kazdin (1984) also noted that t tests and ANOVAs are used to measure differences in means without respect to trends revealed by visual analysis. A baseline could be increasing and the trend could continue into the intervention phase. Although an analysis of trend might suggest that the individual was changing his or her target behavior before the intervention, a statistical test may suggest the difference between the mean performance between phases was significant. In other words, the target behavior may have already been changing and simply continued that change or perhaps accelerated under the influence of the independent variable. The statistical test could suggest that the change that occurred as a result of the intervention was a significant one. Busk and Marascuilo (1992) pointed out that these procedures are to be used when autocorrelation is insignificant, which may be seldom with single subject data. Other procedures may be used to help overcome this potential problem. One of these is time series analysis.

Time Series Analyses

Kazdin (1978) noted that with the use of time series analysis, a significant change in the mean across phases may be detected through a change in level (the change in data at the point when phases change), a change in slope (degree of angle present in data path) or trend, or both. With procedures that test for significance based on means, within-phase changes in trend, level, or slope of the data path may obfuscate the actual outcomes (Kazdin, 1978). See Figure 13–5 for examples of data paths across phases. In example A in Figure 13–5, the continuing trend from baseline to intervention makes visual inspection difficult and confounds the use of the *t* test or ANOVA. In example B, a change in trend occurs, but no significant change in level. In example B, both visual analysis and *t* tests or ANOVAs are confounded by the fact that overall performance across phases is not substantially different (i.e., the data points obtained

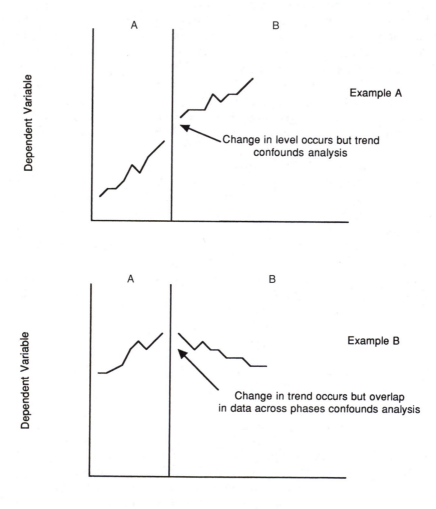

Figure 13–5. Example of data paths across phases.

in each phase are very similar to those obtained in the other phase). In example A, the lack of change in trend confounds the analysis. In example B, the lack of change in level confounds the analysis. Time series analysis is useful because it provides a *t* test appropriate for use when there is serial dependency in the data and it provides information about different characteristics of behavior changes across phases (Kazdin, 1984). The actual analyses are to be performed by computer programs and are rather complicated. We offer a brief overview summarized from Kazdin (1978) and Kamil (1995) to enlighten the reader.

The data are transformed so that serial dependency does not prohibit the use of *t* tests. This procedure takes into account the degree of dependency within the series of data points. There are several models that may be applied, each with its own assumptions (Kazdin, 1984). Subsequent to selection of a model, the data are transformed based on the degree of dependency (e.g., if there was no autocorrelation, the value used to transform the data would be zero). Separate *t* values that consider trend (slope) and level changes are generated for the data after the application of the transformation value. The *t* values are used to test the null hypothesis that the series of data points during the intervention phase are not statistically significant from the series within the baseline. There are instances when visual analysis may suggest a significant change in the dependent variable yet statistical significance is not achieved. Time series analysis is also better suited to multiple baseline designs, which are frequently used in single subject research (Kazdin, 1978).

Time series analysis also has its limitations. Kazdin (1978) noted that time series analysis requires a relatively large number of data points (Busk and Marascuilo [1992] suggested at least 35 per phase) to identify the model (transformation value) that best fits the series. Short phases will confound the reliability of results. That is, the researcher may not be able to identify the processes within the observation series itself to select a model that fits the data (Kazdin, 1984). This may lead to a **Type II error**. In simple terms, a Type II error occurs when a researcher concludes there is no significant effect from the independent variable when in fact one does exist (a false failure to reject the null hypothesis). Also, time series analysis is not widely studied and may be less understandable (at least initially) by the prospective researcher (Kazdin, 1978). McCleary and Welsh (1992), in an in-depth discussion of time series analyses, provide examples of how these analyses may result in erroneous or unsubstantiated conclusions when applied improperly. Kazdin (1984) stressed that the relatively short phases found in many single subject designs make the application of the time series analysis difficult and perhaps inappropriate. When neither variations of *t* tests, ANOVAs, nor time series analyses are suitable, the researcher may use randomization tests.

Randomization Tests

Because randomization tests are nonparametric, the assumptions for their use are less rigorous than those for the use of parametric statistics. Kamil (1995) stated that in a randomization test, a conventional statistic is calculated for repeated orderings of the data. The proportion of statistically significant results is then used as the test for how rarely the value obtained for the actual ordered pairs would be obtained due to a random effect (i.e., not due to a treatment effect). That is, the results indicate whether one can say with confidence whether the obtained result would be due to a chance effect. If the probability of this is small (e.g., $p < .05$), then one may conjecture the obtained result is due to the intervention effect. Computer analyses are necessary because the number of permutations of the data becomes quite large with even a small number of observations (Kamil, 1995). Randomization tests offer an alternative to *t* tests, ANOVAs, or time series analyses. Edgington (1992) also provided a discussion of the possible nonparametric procedures that may be used in randomization tests.

Randomization tests have their limitations. Kazdin (1984) noted that without consistently rapid reversals in performance (e.g., between baseline and intervention phases), when there are carryover (serial) effects from one phase to the next, or when a reversal in the target behavior is undesirable or it cannot be reversed, the use of the randomization test may be limited.

Statistical procedures should probably be used as a supplement to visual analysis (Busk & Marascuilo, 1992). These authors noted that randomization tests may be preferable procedures to the use of procedures that deal with group variation (i.e., *t* tests and ANOVAs). They also are simpler to understand than time series analyses. Whenever statistical procedures are to be used, the decision to use them should be specified a priori and before any data are collected for analysis (Busk & Marascuilo, 1992).

Limitations to Statistical Analysis

As previously discussed, there are assumptions that must be met to use many statistical procedures. These assumptions may be violated in single subject research, making use of those procedures tenuous. Statistically significant results may be quite useful, but they could conceivably mislead the researcher into assuming a significant educational effect had been achieved (i.e., the individual's personal functioning had been significantly improved) when in fact it had not. Statistical analyses generally require knowledge of computer statistical packages. Finally, statistical analyses are probably best used to supplement visual analysis.

In addition to visual and statistical analyses, qualitative analyses may prove useful to the researcher. These procedures, in simple terms, are more concerned with the telling of the story of the study and the people involved than analyzing quantitative data. For this reason, their use may become increasingly popular as yet another supplement to aid in analyzing and reporting the outcomes of research.

QUALITATIVE ANALYSIS

Much of the research in the educational and clinical literature is confined to quantitative research. With quantitative methods, the data collected are numerical and "objective" in nature. That is, the data themselves (e.g., test scores) require less interpretation. Single subject data are typically quantitative but often require further interpretation. Visual analyses are generally used and can be supplemented with statistical analyses as we have already discussed.

Qualitative research can be defined as research that has as its primary purpose the determination of relationships, effects, and causes that focus on individual variables (McWilliam, 1991). Denzin and Lincoln (1994) stated that qualitative researchers study events in their natural settings, and attempt to make sense of, or interpret, phenomena in terms of the meanings that people involved place on them. Qualitative analyses may involve case studies, personal experiences, introspection, life stories, interviews, and observational, historical, interactional, and/or visual texts (Denzin & Lincoln, 1994). In qualitative research the experiences and reactions of the individual researcher as well as other participants (potentially including the individual subject) are very important. This inevitably opens the door to judgments that are more subjective than the types we have previously discussed. However, the judgments made are outcomes of the research.

We will discuss when to use qualitative methods, what types of methods might be used, and what are the limitations of these methods. Although the use of qualitative procedures has become increasingly popular and is worthy of inclusion within single subject research, we would not suggest abandoning the designs and methods to which this text is primarily devoted. The use of qualitative methods may enhance the interpretation of the data, the social validity of the outcomes, and the telling of the story of the individuals involved. Single subject research is by its very nature personal and individualized, which in turn lends itself to qualitative research procedures.

When to Use Qualitative Analysis

Qualitative methods may be used in virtually any single subject study. In fact, the use of certain qualitative aspects are built into single subject methodology. For example, descriptions of the problems, the settings, the individuals involved, and people's perceptions of the ethics of the methods used and the validity of the outcomes may all be found in the literature. The story of the study is told in many journal articles as supplementary to the discussion of the visually or statistically obtained results. Ferguson, Ferguson, and Taylor (1992) argued that the goals of research are compatible with those of discovering good stories. These same authors also noted however, that the objectivist viewpoint (inherent in single subject research) restricts what may be included as qualitative research. Still, the telling of the story and personal interpretation are very important. That is, nonobjectivist world views or paradigms employ different standards for claims of discovering truth and knowledge (Ferguson et al., 1992). We do not wish to dispute the value of this second viewpoint nor discount its importance in research. We will, however, stress the complementary nature of qualitative research and single subject research. Readers wishing to employ exclusively or primarily qualitative methods should consult texts that are devoted to those methods.

McWilliam (1991) noted that the methods of both qualitative and quantitative research may be combined as follows. First, qualitative principles would be violated if the researcher spent too little time observing. A study comprising only 2–3 weeks may not allow the gathering of information that would allow the interpretation of qualitative data. Second, the researcher should maintain field notes. Personal interpretation of the events is important in qualitative research; numerical data collected via the methods discussed in Chapter 3 would not be sufficient for this type of analysis. Third, the researcher must be involved in the study and familiar with the individuals who are subjects, those who may be involved in collecting data and applying the treatment variable, and those whose lives may be affected by the outcomes (e.g., family members). If the researcher is distant, then she or he will be unable to access the information necessary to relate the interpretation of events by others. Fourth, the researcher must be prepared to collect data on variables that become important as the study evolves. Fifth, the researcher should interpret what is seen and heard. Finally, biases related to the study should be acknowledged (McWilliam, 1991). For the combination of qualitative and quantitative methods to be successful, quantitative principles should be adhered to simultaneously. First, interobserver reliability data must be available for formal quantitative observations. Second, operational definitions of variables must not be subjective. Third, a sufficient number of individuals (or in some designs a sufficient number of phases) must be involved. Fourth, phases must not be too long to accommodate collection of qualitative data. Fifth, confounding variables must be identified and controlled. Finally, the discussion of the formal observations must not stray too far afield of the objective data (McWilliam, 1991).

How to Use Qualitative Analysis

Denzin and Lincoln (1994) summarized a variety of techniques that may be useful in qualitative research. We have edited their summary to those we believe to be more relevant in complementing single subject research. Denzin and Lincoln delineated five phases in the research process, and we will include their suggestions (with some modification) as they outlined them by those phases.

Phase 1—The researcher examines his or her own multicultural nature and places himself or herself in historical context. Conceptions of self and others as well as the ethics and politics of the research may be included.

Phase 2—Theoretical paradigms and perspectives are discovered and applied as appropriate. These may include positivist or postpositivist (which would likely be included given the scientific nature of single subject research), constructivist, feminist, ethnic, Marxist, or cultural studies. These paradigms and theories are not mutually exclusive.

Phase 3—Research strategies are identified. These include the study design, case study methods, ethnography, participant observation, phenomenology, biographical method, historical method, applied methods, and clinical methods. Specific to single subject research, we have already discussed the research strategies that are typically used.

Phase 4—Methods of collection and analysis are identified. These may include interviewing; observing; examination of artifacts, documents, and records; visual methods; personal experience methods; data management; computer-assisted analysis; and textual analysis.

Phase 5—The researcher practices the art of interpretation and presentation. The researcher must identify criteria for judging the adequacy of the research, study the art and politics of interpretation, write interpretively, analyze policy as appropriate, evaluate traditions, and apply the results.

Denzin and Lincoln (1994) elaborated on Phase 5. They noted that the researcher creates a field text where observations, notes, and documents are gathered. Next, the researcher moves from this field text to a research text. Notes and interpretations are made based on the field text. Next, this text is used as a working interpretive text that includes initial attempts to make sense out of what has been learned. Finally, the researcher produces the public text to be read by others. This final tale may be confessional, realistic, impressionistic, critical, formal, literary, or analytic (Denzin & Lincoln, 1994).

Hepburn, Gerke, and Stile (1993) reconciled the positivist assumptions inherent in single subject research with the interpretive aspects in the following synthesis of paradigms.

1. There are multiple realities (ontology), although the reality of the individual participant is of primary concern.
2. Epistemologically, the interactions of individual participant, researcher, and others involved in the study are intertwined and require an understanding of differences in realities.
3. Generalization should be approached from a theoretical rather than statistical viewpoint.
4. Given multiple realities, causality should be viewed as mutual simultaneous shaping that does not preclude the demonstration of a functional relationship.
5. Axiologically, the values of all involved are delineated through the above processes in order to control bias.

The following serves as an example of how quantitative and qualitative approaches might be blended.

David was a student in fourth grade with attention-deficit/hyperactivity disorder. Three teachers worked with David, and his mother was very involved in his education. The teachers had noted that David, despite receiving medication for 1 month, still seemed to have attentional difficulties and subsequent problems in disrupting classes with inappropriate comments and movements. Dr. Katzen, the school psychologist, was consulted to assist with a program to improve the situation. Dr. Katzen interviewed (on several occasions) all three teachers, David's physician, his mother, and David himself. She discovered that each had differing opinions as to why David behaved the way he did, who actually had a problem, and what should be done (these opinions differed based on the relationship to David, how often the interviewee interacted with David, years of experience and training, and among the teachers their respective areas of certification). After observing David and consulting with each principal, an operational definition was devised for disrupting class. A differential reinforcement program, which was to be applied in a multiple baseline across settings design, was agreed to by all. After a steady baseline was obtained in each setting, Dr. Katzen spearheaded the implementation of the reinforcement intervention. Dr. Katzen conducted observations and took notes; she continued to interview the principals and David himself. She collected information about his academic gains as well. David's responding reached criterion levels in the first, second, and third classrooms. In the first and third classrooms, the change took some time. In the second classroom, the change occurred rapidly. Overall, the intervention was effective and a functional relationship (based on visual analysis) was achieved. Dr. Katzen concluded the study with additional interviews and observations of David, his teachers, and his mother. After long and careful analysis of her observations, field notes, and interviews, Dr. Katzen reached a number of conclusions about the study and wanted to include the perceptions and conclusions of those involved. When she reported the results of this study, Dr. Katzen found it important that David's mother felt that the primary cause of David's behavior change was that the teachers had learned some skills that were needed to provide structure and effectively communicate their expectations to David. The teacher in the second classroom concurred to some extent, as she perceived that her colleagues were initially ill-equipped to teach David and had actually exacerbated his problems through inappropriate reinforcement and punishment before the study's outset. David's physician was pleased with the results, but noted that individuals have different reactions and adjustment periods to medications and the effect of David's drug therapy may have been partly if not mostly responsible for the changes. She had seen many such cases. David himself was pleased that he no longer was getting in trouble, but he perceived that the real difference was the teachers were being nice to him now rather than mean. Finally, Dr. Katzen confessed that she was biased toward the idea that David had been inappropriately reinforced and punished for some time (her training was in applied behavior analysis) and that the program was as responsible for changing the behavior of his teachers as it was David himself. She noted that David's mother, the teacher in the second classroom, and, to an extent, David appeared to agree with this conclusion through their own perceptions and comments. She pondered to what degree the medication might have actually affected David. Ultimately, she theorized that mutual shaping had indeed occurred among the individuals. The teachers provided reinforcement to David, David was in turn more pleasant to the teachers, this in turn made David's mother happier, and her interactions with his teachers were more satisfactory, creating still more positive feelings toward David. All others involved concluded that Dr. Katzen's help had been invaluable, although she felt her role had largely been one of facilitation and documentation rather than true change agent. Finally, Dr. Katzen noted that despite improved behavioral changes, David's academic performance was not significantly improved at the study's conclusion. This affected her recommendations for generalization of the use of the intervention and her conclusions about whose behavior had changed. She also decided she would need to continue following David's case for an extended period of time to determine if academic improvement occurred and whether the behavior and/or perceptions of those involved changed over time.

In our example, we have suggested that objectively determined significance may not always tell the story of what actually happened. In fact, those involved may not agree as to why something happened or even exactly what did happen, even though they may agree the overall desired outcomes were achieved. By use of qualitative methods, the researcher is able to more fully develop and explain the data and the events (or realities), although our example by no means illustrates the breadth of qualitative research.

Limitations of Qualitative Methods

Hepburn et al. (1993) suggested that the major limitation of qualitative research is the time demand. Specifically, baseline and intervention phases may require extension in order to obtain qualitative data to understand such phenomena as mutual simultaneous shaping. The need for such may compromise the requirements for single subject methods; to not do so might compromise qualitative methods (McWilliam, 1991). Reid and Bunson (1993) noted that the resources and time needed to carry out labor-intensive approaches are scarce, that special educators have limited training in research methods, that the field tends toward conservatism (including journal editors, who appear to prefer more positivist approaches), and that quantitative methods fare better with funding agencies. Finally, McWilliam (1991) stressed that a little knowledge can be a dangerous thing in research. Some may confuse the inclusion of vignettes as qualitative research, and others may be untrained or unaware of all the methods available. Finally, the terminology may be unfamiliar and confusing (McWilliam, 1991).

In this chapter, we have discussed the use of visual, quantitative, and qualitative analysis in single subject design studies. Visual analysis continues to be the most popular method for analyzing the quantitative data. Statistical analyses may be used to supplement visual analysis. Statistical analyses must be used with caution, however, because the assumptions for their use may not be met. If they are met, the decision to use statistical analyses should be made a priori. Finally, the reader is encouraged to learn more about qualitative research from sources devoted to those methods. Over time, their use will likely increase as a supplement to quantitative methods.

A FINAL WORD

We sincerely hope this book has met and will continue to meet your needs. Although it would be difficult if not impossible to discuss every option available to the single subject researcher in reference to the designs and procedures discussed, it has been our intention to at least open your eyes. We have attempted to provide you with an understanding of the principles and the range of possibilities that exist for reading and conducting single subject studies. Many special educators and related services personnel do not consider these designs for teaching, clinical, or research purposes, although they are well suited for such applied research. Our hope is that you will consider and use these designs to improve the lives of individuals with special needs and their families.

Summary Checklist

Visual analysis of data—The researcher examines aspects of graphed data to determine if a significant change in the target behavior has occurred; visual analysis involves some subjectivity.

When to use visual analysis—When continuous numerical data are gathered, the data are graphically depicted, and the researcher wishes to make formative and summative analyses.

Applying visual analysis—The researcher typically inspects changes in the data within a phase or condition and changes in the data across phases and conditions.

Number of data points within a phase—There must be a sufficient number of data points to determine if the data path accurately represents the individual's performance.

Variability in performance—The degree to which the data path indicates variability affects whether the researcher's analysis may be accurate; the more variable the data within each phase, the more difficult the visual analysis.

Level of behavior—The performance of the target behavior and where along the y-axis the data points fall; when the level changes within phases, variability is created and mean, median, or range lines may be needed to assist in the visual analysis.

Trend—The direction of the data path (generally upward, downward, flat, or variable or stable); variability may necessitate the use of a split-middle line to determine trend.

Applying visual analysis across phases—The researcher is particularly interested in examining the changes in level and trend as the study moves from baseline to intervention phases.

Immediate changes in level—Assuming the change is in the desired direction, immediate changes may be indicative of (but not prove) a functional relationship.

Comparing performance across phases—Examining the range of performance across phases; the fewer data points in the intervention phase that overlap with the range of performance in baseline phase (and in the desired direction), the more likely the intervention is indicative of a functional relationship.

Trend changes—Changes in the direction of the data path across baseline and intervention phases; when the direction changes (e.g., from flat during baseline to increasing during intervention), the greater the indication of a functional relationship.

Limitations to visual analysis—May be less reliable than statistical analysis; two analysts may not arrive at same conclusions from visual analysis (subjectivity).

Statistical analysis—May be used primarily as a supplement to visual analysis.

When to use statistical analysis—May be used when there is variability in baseline data but a trend is evident; when changes in trend across phases are difficult to visually analyze; when visual analysis does not establish a clear intervention effect but one may be present; because applied research typically involves many extraneous variables that may affect variability of performance.

How to use statistical analysis—Descriptive and inferential statistics may be used; inferential statistics may be divided into parametric (e.g., *t* test, ANOVA) and nonparametric (e.g., randomization test) procedures; parametric procedures have more rigorous assumptions to be met for their use.

Autocorrelation—Occurs because the individual data collection observations in single subject research may not yield independent observations (*serial dependency is present*); because the same rater may be making each observation, this may also affect independence; autocorrelation may lead to violations of assumptions for the use of statistical procedures.

Type I error—The researcher infers there is a significant intervention effect when in fact there is not one.

***t* tests and ANOVAs**—Parametric procedures used to test for mean performance differences (typically across phases).

Time series analysis—A nonparametric procedure that may be more appropriate than parametric procedures but requires a large number of observations and is somewhat complicated for the novice.

Type II error—The researcher infers there is no significant intervention effect when in fact there is one.

Randomization test—A nonparametric procedure, with less rigorous assumptions than parametric procedures, that is recommended by several experts.

Limitations to statistical analysis—Assumptions for use may be violated; results may be misleading (Type I or Type II Error); generally require knowledge and use of statistical computer packages.

Qualitative analysis—Interpretivist approach in which the researcher typically attempts to tell the story of the study through the examination of variables that often are not quantitative.

When to use qualitative analysis—May be used in virtually any study so long as the researcher has identified some variables/methods a priori and is flexible enough to identify others as the study progresses; used as a supplement to either or both visual and statistical analyses.

How to use qualitative analysis—Typically, field notes and observations are made, compiled, analyzed, and presented by the researcher; a blending of research approaches and paradigms is required.

Limitations of qualitative analysis—Time demands may be greater; may require extensions of phases that are inappropriate; resources needed may be scarce; journal publishers and funding agencies may be less enthusiastic toward qualitative approaches than quantitative approaches; reader should study these procedures further.

References

Alberto, P. A., & Troutman, A. C. (1999). *Applied behavior analysis for teachers* (5th ed.). Englewood Cliffs, NJ: Merrill.

Busk, P. L., & Marascuilo, L. A. (1992). Statistical analysis in single-case research: Issues, procedures, and recommendations, with applications to multiple behaviors. In T.R. Kratchowill & J.R. Levin (Eds.), *Single-case research design and analysis: New directions for psychology and education* (pp. 159–185). Hillsdale, NJ: Erlbaum.

Cooper, J. O., Heron, T. E., & Heward, W. L. (1987). *Applied behavior analysis.* Columbus, OH: Merrill.

Denzin, N. K., & Lincoln, Y. S. (1994). Introduction: Entering the field of qualitative research. In *Handbook of qualitative research* (pp 1–17). Thousand Oaks, CA: Sage.

DeProspero, A., & Cohen, S. (1979). Inconsistent visual analysis of intrasubject data. *Journal of Applied Behavior Analysis, 12,* 273–279.

Edgington, E. S. (1992). Nonparametric tests for single-case experiments. In T. R. Kratchowill & J. R. Levin (Eds.), *Single-case research design and analysis: New directions for psychology and education* (pp. 133–157). Hillsdale, NJ: Erlbaum.

Ferguson, P. M., Ferguson, D. L., & Taylor, S. J. (1992). Introduction: Interpretivism and disability studies. In *Interpreting disability: A qualitative reader.* New York: Teachers College Press.

Hepburn, E., Gerke, R., & Stile, S. W. (1993). *Interpretive single-subject design: A research tool for practitiioner-guided applied inquiry in rural settings.* ERIC Document 358981.

Kamil, M. L. (1995). Statistical analysis procedures for single-subject designs. In S. B. Neuman & S. McCormick (Eds.), *Single-subject experimental research: Applications for literacy* (pp. 84–103). Newark, DE: International Reading Association.

Kazdin, A. E. (1978). Statistical analyses for single-case experimental designs. In M. Hersen & D. H. Barlow (Eds.), *Single case experimental designs: Strategies for studying behavior change* (pp. 265–316). New York: Pergamon Press.

Kazdin, A. E. (1984). Statistical analyses for single-case experimental designs . In D. H. Barlow & M. Hersen (Eds.), *Single case experimental designs: Strategies for studying behavior change* (2nd ed, pp. 285–324). New York: Pergamon Press.

Kratchowill, T. R., & Levin, J. R. (Eds.). (1992). *Single-case research design and analysis: New directions for psychology and education.* Hillsdale, NJ: Erlbaum.

McCleary, R., & Welsh, W. N. (1992). Philosophical and statistical foundations of time-series experiments. In T. R. Kratchowill & J. R. Levin (Eds.), *Single-case research design and analysis: New directions for psychology and education* (pp. 41–91). Hillsdale, NJ: Erlbaum.

McWilliam, R. A. (1991). *Mixed method research in special education.* ERIC Document 357554.

Ottenbacher, K. J. (1990). When is a picture worth a thousand p values? A comparison of visual and quantitative methods to analyze single subject data. *Journal of Special Education, 23,* 436–449.

Reid, D. K., & Bunson, T. D. (1993). *Pluralizing research options in special education: A roundtable discussion.* ERIC Document 364008.

Richards, S. B., Taylor, R. L., & Ramasamy, R. (1997). Effects of subject and rater characteristics on the accuracy of visual analysis of single subject data. *Psychology in the Schools, 34,* 355–362.

Tawney, J. W., & Gast, D. L. (1984). *Single subject research in special education.* Columbus, OH: Merrill.

Index